Praise

'Anyone who has got halfway thro̶u̶g̶h̶... ... 2060 adulthood isn't all they'd hoped will r̶... ... misspent youth howling with recognition and helpless laughter'

Elle

'Any book that sees the protagonist exclaim the line, "Beyoncé is an essence, not a human being" is literary gold as far as we're concerned'

Heat

'Heart-and-snot-on-sleeve honest, *The Wrong Knickers* is the real Bridget in all her hopeless glory'

Telegraph

'If you want a real page-turner that will have you laughing out loud, then this is the book for you'

Bella Magazine

'*The Wrong Knickers* is brilliantly funny, brilliantly honest, deliciously indiscreet and, at times, incredibly moving. It's the most truthful, evocative and hilarious account of what it is to be a twenty something girl in Britain that I've read in a very long time'

Polly Vernon

'Bryony Gordon is a very bad girl – and an even better writer'
Camilla Long

the wrong knick ers

A decade of chaos

BRYONY GORDON

headline

First published in 2014 by
HEADLINE PUBLISHING GROUP

First published in paperback in 2015 by
HEADLINE PUBLISHING GROUP

3

Cataloguing in Publication Data is available from the British Library

ISBN 978 1 4722 1014 2

Typeset in Berling by Palimpsest Book Production Ltd, Falkirk, Stirlingshire

Printed and bound in Great Britain by Clays Ltd, St Ives plc

Headline's policy is to use papers that are natural, renewable and recyclable
products and made from wood grown in sustainable forests. The logging and
manufacturing processes are expected to conform to the environmental
regulations of the country of origin.

HEADLINE PUBLISHING GROUP
An Hachette UK Company
338 Euston Road
London NW1 3BH

www.headline.co.uk
www.hachette.co.uk

For Mez, Jane and Naomi

Contents

Foreword

It started, as ever, with a kiss.
It always starts with a kiss.

It never starts with five pints of lager, three shots of tequila, and your bottom being groped in a dingy bar, does it? That just doesn't sound romantic enough. It isn't a good enough story to recount at your imaginary wedding, or to your theoretical grandchildren. 'Granny and Grandpa were off their faces in a Soho pub one Friday night, when they decided to go on to an illegal drinking den that is situated down a dark alleyway, behind a graffitied metal door, down some stairs, into a basement, where there was sawdust on the floor and God help us if anyone ever dropped a fag butt. Yes, Granny and Grandpa did used to smoke, quite a lot, actually – and they danced on the beer-sodden floor to the hits of Justin Timberlake and Beyoncé . . .'

The Wrong Knickers

I must pull myself together. I am getting carried away with myself again.

So it started with a kiss, in that illegal drinking den, as 'Crazy in Love' played over the speakers. This, I tell myself, is a sign. A sign that we are going to be together for ever. A sign that we are going to be the UK's answer to Beyoncé and Jay-Z, only perhaps without the amazing booty and the ability to twerk. I don't have an amazing booty – it is round, that's for sure, but round as in roly-poly rather than round as in ripe – and the only time I have tried to twerk – while alone in my flat after a night in the pub – I realised I looked like someone desperately trying to rid themselves of piles, or a hernia.

Still, right now, all of that is irrelevant. I am kissing Josh. Awesome, handsome Josh, with his dark brown hair and bright green eyes and his suit. A suit! He has stuffed his tie in his jacket pocket (I imagine that inside there is also an expensive pen and a selection of business cards) and has unbuttoned the top of his shirt to reveal a few strands of chest hair, a tantalising gesture carried out by a more sophisticated kind of man. But that's just Josh for you. He attended both Oxford and Princeton and now he is going into the Foreign Office. To do what, I couldn't tell you. It could just be admin, or research work, but I think we can all safely assume that he has probably been headhunted by some government honcho, who is going to fast track him into the diplomatic corps. I can just imagine the life we will have together, travelling the

2

globe, living in all the best ambassador's houses the UK Government has to offer, me taking high tea on the lawn and throwing cocktail parties for local dignitaries by the pool. We will start married life in Africa, our children running wild across savannahs, befriending elephants as they go, before moving to Singapore, or Bangkok, or Hong Kong – some hot and humid city, anyway – finally alighting in Washington, where we will be on first-name terms with the President and our children (by now trilingual) will become great friends with his or her children, vowing to be penpals when we eventually make our return to London society, living out the rest of our days in a white-stuccoed house in Notting Hill (during the week) and a cottage in the Cotswolds (at the weekend).

'Fancy a fuck?' breathes Josh into my ear, pricking the bubble that contains my fantasy world. Granted, it isn't the most romantic of proposals, but the fact that he is impossibly well spoken does serve to make this question sound rather alluring. And so it is that I find myself squealing 'YES!' over the dulcet tones of Jay-Z. The truth is, I don't fancy a fuck. I like to fancy that I am the kind of person who fancies a fuck – that I am wild and crazy and just the kind of girl who swings both ways from chandeliers. (Has anyone ever swung from a chandelier? I mean, reaching the height of the chandelier would require some sort of stepladder, and that requires a level of practicality that probably doesn't come naturally to chandelier-swingers.) But I am getting carried away again.

I don't fancy a fuck, but I do fancy a cuddle. I do fancy spending the rest of my life with this man. And I believe that fucking him will greatly improve my chances of spending the rest of my life with him, even if, actually, I have been brought up to think that the opposite is true. It will be different with Josh, I tell myself. Once he has one fuck, he will want more and more and more, endless fucks eventually leading to a hand in marriage or at the very least a relationship to help pass the time during the tricky years that are one's mid-twenties.

'Yes, I fancy a fuck!' I repeat.

Josh smiles at me and takes my hand in his. Then he rams his tongue down my throat and we are away. With hindsight I will realise that he isn't a great kisser. He is a bit toothy. He seems to lick the enamel of my mouth, as if he is trying to be some sort of human toothbrush, removing food and 52 per cent more plaque than ordinary, plastic toothbrushes, reaching parts that other oral cleaning instruments can't. It's not, in all honesty, amazing. But when I briefly open my eyes and make out the concentrated look on his face, I realise, with a sense of pity, that *he* thinks he is amazing, that he really believes his patented technique is a cut above those ones used by all the other human toothbrushes. So I resolve not to care. You can improve kissing, can't you? You can gently guide them with your tongue, and your lips. I decide to tell all my friends that he is the best kisser in the world, in the hope I might be able to fool everyone else into believing that I am a sex-mad seductress. If they believe it, perhaps I will start to believe it too.

'Let's go back to mine,' he says, urgently.

We get to his place with the help of an illegal mini cab (another great detail to share with the imaginary grandchildren), the type warned about in posters on buses and trains. Get in to the back of an illegal mini cab, warn the posters, and you may never get back out again – at least, not alive, or with your dignity intact. But the problem, I find, is that after a certain amount to drink, legal cabs refuse to take you, or pretend not to have seen you. They don't want you to throw up in the back of their vehicle, or to have to drive round for hours and hours while you sober up enough to remember where you live. Illegal mini cabs, however – well, they don't mind. You can vomit as much as you want in the back of their vehicle because it isn't actually theirs and, anyway, a bit of sick is the least of their worries when the car failed its last MOT and they don't actually have a licence to drive it. They will drive for hours around London until you remember where it is you live – in fact, they prefer it that way. It means they get more money. And if you can't afford to pay it, they will just threaten to kill your family. So here we are, sitting in the back of a people carrier that smells faintly of sick and has no functioning seatbelts, but one whose driver *does* allow us to drink and smoke in the back, something legal cabs never allow you to do, the spoilsports. And touch wood, or the slightly damp leatherette covering on the seat, nothing has gone wrong yet.

Josh lives in Fulham. Of course he does. All young men in suits live in Fulham – it's the law. Despite this distance being just over four miles, the illegal mini-cab driver charges us £50 for the journey. The problem is, we don't have £50. Between us, we have £20 and $40 US, left over from Josh's time at Princeton. 'That's for the beer you spill on the seats,' the cab driver explains, when Josh tries to protest at the cost. 'We need to go to a cashpoint,' says Josh. 'There's one a few streets away at the petrol station.'

'That will cost another £10,' says the cab driver with a confidence that suggests that in illegal mini-cab world, it is perfectly normal to charge a tenner for a 30-second journey. We are too drunk, too keen for what the rest of the night holds, to kick up a fuss. Sixty quid, done. Sixty quid is, I reason, a small price to pay for a life of globe-trotting with a handsome diplomat.

We head inside, upstairs to his top-floor flat. He rushes me through a kitchen, grabbing something from the fridge as he goes (champagne?) and then he pulls me up some more stairs into his attic bedroom. It's all cream and light browns, with a bookshelf that contains only four books – something by Tony Parsons, a biography of Bill Hicks, a travel guide to Mexico, his school copy of the English Oxford Dictionary. The other shelves are covered in certificates and awards gained while at school, telling of extraordinary sporting prowess on every surface imaginable: football pitch, rugby field, running track, swimming pool.

He is a twenty-six-year-old man who is still living off the glory of his sixth-form days. He is a twenty-six-year-old man who owns only four books. I should have left then.

He pulls me on to the bed and kisses me. I try and look for the champagne he has brought upstairs with him. I can't see it. Strange. We go through the motions, him unwrapping me from my clothes like I am a Quality Street. I feel nervous, inexperienced, like a fawn trying to stand up for the first time. I have had sex with precisely two people before: the first, a spotty seventeen-year-old who took my virginity on his living-room floor while his parents were out, an Olympics Opening Ceremony blaring in the background (I think it was Atlanta, 1996). The second was a long-term boyfriend I made wait until *I knew I really loved him*. And though I know that I really could love Josh, have imagined all the ways that our love might blossom, I am currently not that confident that he really loves me. Or if he simply admires my tits.

And where is the champagne? I want to take this slowly, sipping fizz from flutes as we go. He hasn't even offered me a glass of water. Who invites someone into their home and doesn't even offer them a glass of tap water? At the back of my head, I am slowly becoming unsure of Josh's intentions, though at the front I am still telling myself that this is it, the big one, the man who will father my children . . .

'I think we should use this,' says Josh, breath hot on my face. What does my expression say at this moment? I hope it says 'purrrrr', but I think it might actually say 'errrrrrrrrr'. Use what, exactly? An ice bucket to chill the champagne? A teacloth to mop up any spills should the bottle bubble over when opened? I am becoming desperate here. A CONDOM?

But Josh has other ideas, ones favoured by people who use fetish websites and like to wear latex. For Josh doesn't want to pour me champagne. He doesn't want to practise safe sex. What Josh wants to use is a packet of Lurpak butter.

You read that right. Butter. Salted, for her pleasure.

He holds it aloft, like a trophy, eyeing it lustily. He wants that packet of butter, I realise, possibly more than he wants me. 'It really helps smooth things,' he says, suddenly seeming less handsome suit-wearing Oxford grad, more sad former boarding-school boy. 'It makes it more . . .' I think he is going to orgasm right then and there, '... *pleasurable.*'

And the worst thing is that this doesn't put me off him. It doesn't make me gallop out of the door and into the Fulham night, searching for that sick-scented illegal mini cab to take me home. The worst thing is not that he wants to use a breakfast food as a lubricant, that he wants to butter up my vagina as if it's a piece of toast, thus possibly giving me thrush or cystitis or God-only-knows-what embarrassing condition that I will have to explain to a doctor. The worst thing is that, to allow my ridiculous fantasy of a life together to continue to flourish, I find myself making up an excuse instead of telling him to get lost. I find myself buttering *him* up, if you will.

'Oh,' I say, thinking on my feet. 'I'd love to, but I'm lactose intolerant.'

He looks at me blankly.

'I'm allergic to dairy. It makes me come out in hives. Puff up like a fish.' I blow out my cheeks for good measure. 'It means I've never really known the joy of a cream cake, or a chocolate bar. Can you imagine? It's terrible, really. I mean, if you had some margarine made from soya, we might be able to, but I'm afraid Lurpak is a no-no.'

Why don't I have the confidence to assert my right not to have my genitals covered in butter? Why am I blathering about milk substitutes instead? The truth is, I'm not intolerant of anything – men with strange sexual fetishes included, it would seem – even though I would dearly love to be. If I had allergies to bread and dairy I might not weigh eleven stone; I might not have people describe me as 'voluptuous' and – here's the worst one – 'Rubenesque', as if these were compliments, as if as well as being fat I am too stupid to realise they are barely concealed insults.

ARGGGHHHH! My life!

'That's a shame,' says Josh. He seems deflated of desire, suddenly sleepy. I panic. Instead of gathering up my clothes and leaving with my dignity vaguely intact, I try to initiate butterless sex. 'We could still, you know . . .' I try to wink at him. It comes off more as a squint. I crawl across the bed, start to kiss him. His body language says he is irritated by me, disappointed, let down. I realise, as it's happening, as he bears down on me, that he is having sex with me because he feels it would be rude not to, because he is so arrogant that he actually thinks he is doing me a favour.

And once he has done me this favour, he rolls over and falls immediately into a deep sleep without so much as a cuddle or a proposal of marriage.

I lie awake for another hour or so, still daydreaming of a cuddle or a proposal of marriage. Then I lie awake wondering what is wrong with me. Why don't I think, 'Yuk, this dude should be reported, possibly put on some kind of sex-offenders register'? Why do I actually continue to like him, despite the fact that I have an education, that I worked my non-amazing booty off to get good A-level results, that in every other way I am a reasonably intelligent human being? And yet. And yet and yet and yet . . . This butter-wielding hunk has rendered me as thick as several planks of wood.

I sleep fitfully that night, if indeed I actually sleep at all. Josh has a king-sized bed, but he positions himself across three-quarters of it, leaving me a measly slither of mattress and a corner of duvet to get comfortable under. It amazes me that even in sleep, a man could manage to express such arrogance in his body language – and then it amazes me that despite all of this, I still kind of want him. In fact, I might even want him more. I will later realise that this screwed-up behaviour on my part is not just some sort of one-off, that it's simply what I'm like. The moment someone goes cold on me, I don't, as I have always been told to do, think, 'Fuck you, I'm going to go cold on you, too.' Instead, I worry that I have done something terribly wrong to make the person go cold on me, and then go out of my way to stop them going cold on me. 'There must be some sort of psychological condition to explain this,' I tell my friend Chloe on one of many nights spent trying to work ourselves out. 'Yes there is,' she replied without hesitation. 'It's called being needy.'

Maybe I am. But right now, there is very little I can do about it. I lie there, trying to make my body smaller to fit the space, staring at the skylight above me. Even if I had half the bed, even if he had shared with me a meagre quarter of his duvet, I wouldn't be able to drift off. I am too uptight, too nervous about what might happen if I allowed myself to sleep properly. I might do a gigantic fart, waking him up in the process. And talking of farts, what if I want to do a number two in the morning? I can't do it here, in his flat. Although it's a simple biological fact that all humans must defecate, there is still a widely held belief among young men that women don't. What do they think we do? Do they think we remove it all via a designer colostomy bag when they're not looking? Do they think our colons are made of a delicate glittery substance that breaks down waste products into the bloodstream, meaning we don't have to shit? I mean, what on earth do they think we have bottoms for? Do they think God gave them to us just in case we decide to go into pornography, when they will come in handy if a director wants us to be taken roughly from behind? I mean, no! Just NO! Women shit, just as men do, and yet we have all agreed never to talk about it, meaning that in the morning I will have to hold it in all the way home – or, if he wakes up and wants to have sex with me again, thus making it impossible to get home without being late for work, until I can lock myself in the blissfully isolated disabled loo at the office.

Oh God, I really need the loo. And I don't even know where it is. If I'm not careful, I'm going to wee in the tiny corner of this bed, and then we're never going to Washington together. I also really need a glass of water. My mouth is drier than the Gobi desert. I bet you Josh has been to the Gobi desert, trekked across it. I bet there's a certificate somewhere in here, telling of his achievements. But where was I? Yes. I have to find the loo, because then I can both relieve my bladder and my thirst by sticking my mouth under the tap and drinking the equivalent of a pint of water from it.

And while I am there, I can touch up my make-up,

too, so I look half decent when he wakes up in the morning.

I try to creep out of the bed without waking him. I locate my handbag in the gloom, grab it and make for the door. I don't remember the stairs from the attic being this steep. I go slowly down, so I don't fall – Jesus, it would be embarrassing to break my leg at this point, especially when I need the loo so badly; especially when I am naked as the day I was born – and start opening doors in the hope that behind them there might be a bathroom.

I don't, immediately, find the bathroom. What I actually find is that Josh has a flatmate, who happens to be behind the first door I open. He is lit up by the glow of his laptop, which he slams shut as he sees me. 'FUCK!' I realise I have probably woken the whole street up, and then I realise I need to use the door and my handbag to protect what little modesty I have left. 'Fuck, fuck, fuck! I'm so sorry, I'm not a burglar, I promise!'

He starts to laugh. 'Funnily enough, most burglars tend to cover up entirely so nobody will be able to identify them. But you – well, let's just say I'd definitely be able to spot you in a line-up. I'm guessing you're with Josh.'

I try to smile. It's hard, when you're buck naked and the flatmate of the bloke you had hoped to marry has just reacted all too calmly to a naked woman walking into his room, as if this perhaps happens quite often. 'If you're looking for the loo,' he says, 'it's the first door on the right.'

In the bathroom, I admire Josh's collection of lotions and potions. It is, I note, larger than that belonging to most women. I go to the loo, use my finger as a human toothbrush, gulp down some water, borrow some of Josh's Clarins moisturiser. I apply another coat of foundation, mascara and lipstick. Ridiculous, I think. You are utterly freaking ridiculous. I look down at my phone. It informs me it is 3.21 a.m.

I get back into bed and try – and fail – to get comfortable. Alone with my thoughts, I begin to imagine what else could go wrong if I went to sleep. I might snore, for example. I might talk in my sleep, revealing to him that I REALLY like him. No, I can't go to sleep. Instead, I alternate between staring at the skylight and the back of his head as I wait for it to get light.

But even as the sun comes up, Josh continues in a state of deep slumber. How can a man who has just attempted to use butter as a sex aid sleep so soundly at night? I start to wonder what will happen when – and if – he wakes up. Will he drowsily put his arms around me, tell me what a great night he had. Will he kiss me on the forehead (I always imagine that after a night of shagging, couples kiss each other on the forehead) and run his hands through my sexy-just-woken-up hair?

I briefly consider extending a leg, brushing his calf sexily with a gracefully arched foot. Perhaps I could make the first morning move, start caressing his lower back with my hand. No, no, that's way too forward (the irony of worrying about being too forward with a man who hours earlier asked to cover you in butter is, for the moment, lost on me). But when he finally wakes up, he doesn't even put his arms around me. I have exposed myself to his flatmate, I have sacrificed a good night's sleep worrying if he will be affectionate to me when he wakes up, and he doesn't even extend the courtesy of a hug. I feel desolate. My stupidity is beginning to make me physically ache, though that could just be the hang-over.

I pretend that I am coming round from a great night's sleep, rubbing my eyes and stretching my arms above my head a little too theatrically. He springs out of bed and announces he is late for work, in a tone that suggests this is my fault, that the purpose of the human toothbrush bringing me back was to use me as a human alarm clock. If he'd just said, I could have had him up and out of the house hours ago. He dashes around his room letting out large huffs, as if taking me back to his flat and shagging me has actually turned out to be a bit of an inconven-ience. He starts throwing my clothes at me without managing a single glance in my direction. My Levi's, my bra, my vest top – clothes carefully selected a day ago to give off a nonchalantly sexy air, clothes that now just stink of stale fags and last night's beer.

And then he flings a pair of pink, silky knickers at me, which land on my lap, Agent Provocateur label side up, and he remarks to me, very casually, that those are pretty knickers. And it occurs to me that this is the only compliment he has paid to me since he woke up, and what's worse, it isn't even valid; it doesn't even belong to me. Because they are pretty, undoubtedly so, these silky size 8 knickers of sex. But while they are all of these things, they are most definitely not mine.

This is my first-ever one-night-stand. And these are the wrong knickers.

1

My so-called middle-class life

My name is Bryony and I am not quite having the life I imagined I would. In fact, I am having the complete opposite of the life I imagined I would. I am twenty-three years old but so far I do not own a flat, a car or a pair of Agent Provocateur knickers; I do own more than four books but I have nowhere to put them; I don't have a degree or any school certificates to prove that I was a really good goal attack in the netball B team. I can't cook, won't cook, and despite living off a diet of raw vegetables, houmous and cigarettes, I still don't look like Gisele. (Why even is that?)

At twenty-three, I had imagined that I might be a grown-up, or at least approaching one, my life a merry-go-round of cocktail parties and important meetings and dinner parties round my penthouse apartment. Ahahahahaha. Of all the stories my mum likes to tell me, her current favourite is the one about how when *she* was twenty-three, she had two kids, one of whom was at school. I'm not sure I quite believe her – she is cagey about her age, so much so that she thinks I should start lying about my own because 'I can't have a daughter who is almost in her mid-twenties', and looking at her passport, I'm not sure she had even met my dad at twenty-three, let alone had two children with him – but it still serves the purpose it is intended to, which is to make me feel like an ocean-going failure.

I have no boyfriend, and what is worse, I really care that I don't have a boyfriend. This is not supposed to happen. I have been brought up to be a strong, independent women, a f-e-m-i-n-i-s-t, to care only about my career, even though my career involves asking members of S Club 7 and Westlife what their favourite colour is. And don't get me wrong, because I love my job, working on the teen supplement of a newspaper, am lucky to have a job at all, actually, given that there has been a credit crunch, a double dip, an economic meltdown. It's just that despite having a job, a great job, despite the fact I should, in my spare time, be blogging about the gender pay gap and female genital mutilation and why there has never been a female James Bond or Doctor Who, all I can think about is a man. A man who doesn't care, who hasn't called, who doesn't respond to my texts. Who will, in all probability, never contact me again.

Which is really freaking dumb.

Like most people, the two decades that precede my twenties are unremarkable and comfortable and happy. There is absolutely nothing about them to suggest that the years to follow will be any different. I have a sister, Naomi, who is two years younger than I am, and a brother who came along when I was twelve – a little thing whom everyone but me thought was cute, and I didn't on account of the fact I had just learnt about the birds and the bees. Rufus, as he was named, as if after a dog. Rufus, Naomi and Bryony. How middle class is that?

Along with our mother and father – a journalist and a PR respectively — we all live in a terraced house on the outer reaches of west London with a dog and a couple of cats and, at one point, some stick insects. We go on holiday to Cornwall and occasionally Spain, and we really do have a Volvo that is covered in hair (the dog's), chewing-gum wrappers (Mum's) and squashed Ribena cartons (ours).

I go to an all-girl's school where I am average, never bullied and barely noticed. While the cool girls hitch their skirts up and get away with it, every time I try I am banished to detention for a week and given a conduct mark. Even from a young age, I am destined not to be a Cool Girl. My reports talk of my 'potential' and 'sunny smile'. One year I win something called the 'Progress Cup', which is a sort of booby prize for nobodies who never win anything.

When my friends and I start hanging out with boys I

never get the good ones. I end up with the off cuts, the leftovers, the last to be picked for the football team. My first snog is disgusting, with a boy called Derek who wears T-shirts covered in marijuana leaves and the colours of the Jamaican flag, despite the fact that the only thing he has ever blown smoke up is his teacher's arse, and the furthest he has ever been is Hanwell, which happens to be where he lives. I really don't want to snog him, but my friend Sally – who has deep dark eyes and dark hair and will always, throughout our lives, get the bloke – is snogging his friend Theo, his *handsome* friend, and I feel left out. Bored. 'Shall we?' says Derek, and now I think about it, almost every bloke I've snogged since has employed the same cocky, arrogant seduction technique.

I spend my adolescence longing for Theo, who only wants to be my friend. My best friend, but still, just my friend. I tell myself that this is because we have something special, something deep, and he doesn't want to sully it with something as base as SNOGGING, but I think we all know this is not true, that it's simply because he doesn't fancy me. Why would he? I have mousy hair, a mono-brow, and spend much of my time squinting because I don't want to wear the giant tortoiseshell glasses with milk bottle lenses forced on me by my mother after an unfortunate collision with an elderly man on a mobility scooter I failed to see because I was too short-sighted. (We were both fine; in the end, only my ego was bruised.)

But I still have my hopes and dreams. I want to be a

writer, like my mother, whose career seems perfect to me. She flies around the world to interview celebrities – I remember, when I was little, she was sent to Windsor Safari Park to do a story on feeding the lions. I like the idea of this, of fun being your job. I think that if I become a journalist, I could interview Take That and marry them all, or at the very least one of them. And if not Take That, I will settle for one of East 17, even though they are Take That's arch-enemies. It will be a way out of my humdrum existence. All the girls I went to school with, all the boys who ignored me, one day they will see me walking down the red carpet of a film premiere on the arm of say, Ronan Keating. (One of Boyzone will suffice, and if I'm really scraping the barrel, I will settle for a member of Westlife.) And they will think, 'God, I wish I'd paid more attention to her. I wish I'd seen her beauty, wisdom and humour, which now I come to think about it were there all along. Silly us!'

I write to *Smash Hits* most weeks asking for work experience. I never get it. I work harder and harder at school because nobody else is; they're all too wrapped up in Theo and Derek and Nick and Paul.

I know that I will come into my own when I go to university. Deep down in my bones – and I believe these bones to be very deep down, below my layers of puppy fat – I see university as a land of opportunity, somewhere I will thrive, a place I can reinvent myself and start again. I won't be mediocre, I won't be bound any more by my boring, middle-class existence. I will join political groups and go on protests, I will go to clubs every night and spend days discussing ideas and theories, and I will graduate and walk straight into a job at a newspaper or a magazine and I will look back on my teenage years as a necessary learning process, and young hopefuls will look to me for inspiration. I will be like those Hollywood starlets who preposterously claim to have been ugly ducklings who never got a date for the prom.

Except it doesn't quite happen like that. Of course it doesn't.

I decide I am going to read History of Art, because I am a creative, because I am different. The careers teacher tells me that this is a mistake and I should read English Literature instead. 'But I hate having to underline texts and write notes in margins,' I protest. 'I think that if I study English, it will ruin books for me FOR EVER.'

Look at me. I am such a prat.

I explain that I want to *learn* when I go to university, that I know little of the Italian Renaissance – I think I pronounce it re-NAH-ssaince, shudder – and Impressionism and Mannerism, and that if I study Art History I will spend three years discovering new things, as opposed to looking for meaning in books that I would rather just be reading in my free time. The careers teacher lets out a resigned sigh. She isn't seeing me for the learned lady I so clearly am.

'Miss Gordon,' she announces. 'I would advise that you

think very carefully about what kind of job a degree in Art History would be suited to. Would you like to become a curator? An art critic? An interior designer?'

It's hopeless, trying to reason with these elderly folk. (The careers teacher must have been about thirty-five, I realise now.)

I get a place at UCL and sign up to live in halls in central London. I get a room not in the beautiful ivy-covered building near Regent's Park, but on the eighth floor of a tower block off the Euston Road, a tower block with a broken lift. While my mum sheds a tear as we unpack my belongings – a hifi, an alarm clock (yeah, right) and a set of pink towels and matching bed linen that she has bought me from John Lewis (these will have to go) – I can't wait to be rid of her. 'Bye Mum,' I say, as she wipes her eyes. I think she is probably crying about the smell from the communal kitchen and the fact that the shared bathtub is covered in hair. She is probably crying because my room looks a bit like a prison cell, a problem I plan to remedy immediately with a bit of help from throws and posters I will buy at cool markets, ones on the Portobello Road and Brick Lane. 'See you at Christmas!' I beam. My plan to stay away for so long, it turns out, is highly optimistic.

University isn't quite the promised land I had thought it would be. In fact, as my twenties progress, nothing will turn out to be quite what I thought it would be. Perhaps my imagination is especially fertile, perhaps I read too many fairy tales as a child. But I don't think so. My expectations are no different from those of my peers. I want just the same things as every other twenty-year-old I meet at university: I want it all. We are the children of rich, globe-trotting baby boomers. We have been told by various authorities, including the Prime Minister no less, that education, education, education will be the answer to everything. University is only the start of it; it is merely the key to a glorious, prosperous life. And yet after a month there, I am not quite sure how that is going to work out for me.

We hardly do any studying – we are down for just eight hours a week. I suppose this isn't strictly a problem, as it leaves us to do lots of drinking and sleeping in until 4 p.m. But my body isn't used to it. It isn't just the alcohol; it's that I don't know what to do with myself if I'm not constantly in lessons, being hot-housed by teachers whose careers depend on league tables. I struggle with what lectures there are. I start to wonder if I should have taken the careers teacher's advice after all, and done English instead. One day, a professor sticks a slide up on the wall, not of some fantastical piece of sculpture, or a beautiful painting by Michaelangelo, but of a black square. A plain old run-of-the-mill black square. 'This black square,' announces the professor, 'represents all black squares and their freedom from political ideology.' I stare blankly at the projector screen. 'You may think this is just a black square . . .' yep '...

24

but this is actually a black square that is going to change your mind and your perceptions for ever.'

It sure does, though not in the way the professor intends. I stop going to lectures, and start writing to newspapers and magazines for work-experience slots. My mum refuses to help me out – she says that I need to get in to Fleet Street 'the proper way'. I don't join political groups, go on protests, attend nightclubs, or discuss ideas. There isn't really anyone to discuss ideas with, or anyone who wants to discuss ideas with me, more pertinently. There are only girls on my course – again, why didn't I take English? – and while they are all perfectly nice it just feels like being back at school again, only now my mum doesn't pay my travel expenses, and there isn't anyone to cook me meals after a long day doing nothing. I start going home a lot. One day, I accidentally leave my breakfast on the windowsill of my room at halls, and when I come back a week later, I have grown an entire new culture. Perhaps I should have done sciences instead.

When I receive word from a newspaper that I can have work experience, I decide to make my move. I go home and employ the 'Mum, I've got something important to tell you' tactic, the sentence delivered with a gravity that implies you are about to reveal something terrible. 'Are you pregnant, darling?' my mother says, colour draining from her face. 'Have you become a drug addict?'

'Worse,' my father says, looking up from his copy of the *FT*, 'have you become a Lib Dem?'

'Jack!' chastises my mother. 'Why can't you ever take anything seriously?' They start to argue. More correctly, my mum starts to argue, while my father bats her back with a series of jokes, which only serves to make her even more cross. I stand in the kitchen, tapping the table while this farce plays out.

'So as I was saying,' I interrupt.

'Yes, sorry darling,' says my mother.

'When are you due?' asks my father.

'I'm not pregnant!' I huff. 'I'm going to leave university.' Note the use of the word 'leave' rather than 'drop-out', which implies that you are useless, a no-hoper, destined to become a pregnant drug addict, though probably not a Lib Dem. I wait for them to stop bickering with one another and start arguing with me. It doesn't happen.

'OK, darling,' says my mother.

'I think that's a great idea,' chimes in my father.

I should have known then that something was very wrong.

I move back into my parents' house and inform the head of department in writing that I will not be returning for the second term. He replies with a stern letter that tells of his disappointment, of how it is a shame that the place I took did not go to someone who actually wanted it. I rip up the letter and have a little cry in my bedroom. It isn't just the letter that has upset me, although naturally, it doesn't much help. It's the fact that I have already failed, and proved that cocking careers teacher right. I don't graduate from university almost a grand in debt, fees for the mould-infested prison cell I hardly ever stayed in. Education, education, education. What of it, Mr Blair?

The rest of my life now hinges on a two-week work-experience placement. I mean, no pressure, Bryony. No biggie. 'What are you going to do after the two weeks?' my mother asks, not entirely unreasonably. 'I'll cross that bridge when I come to it,' is all I can reply.

My placement isn't at the *Telegraph* or *The Times* or even the *Sun*. It isn't at the *Guardian*, the *Independent* or the *Financial Times*. No, it's at – the *Express*.

The *Express* may have been a bastion of journalism in the fifties and sixties, but it's somewhat *different* now. Every day, it runs with a conspiracy theory about the death of Diana, Princess of Wales, or something about killer weather being on the way. Still, who am I to complain? It has saved me from a life of black squares, and for that I am eternally grateful.

I arrive at the office promptly for 10 a.m., wearing a grey suit my mother has bought me from Phase Eight, as if I'm eighty-four years old and not a spring chicken of twenty. I'm told someone will be down to collect me shortly. I sit in the lobby, watching in horror as journalists arrive for work dressed in jeans and trainers, the ones in suits letting un-ironed shirts hang out of their trousers, all looking as if they have got here not by public transport but by being dragged through a hedge backwards. I look like a nob, I realise. I am going to be laughed out of this newspaper as soon as I step inside it, sent packing and told to return to the job I have dressed for – as a librarian. I wait and I wait and I wait for my fate. But it doesn't seem to be getting any nearer.

At 10.35, I ask the receptionist if they know I'm here. 'Look, sweetheart,' she says, looking down her nose at me. 'This is a newspaper. Time is kind of fluid here. Let that be your first lesson. Once, a work experience sat here for a WHOLE DAY before anyone came down to get them, and even then it was only by chance as everyone left to go to the pub.' She smiles her fakest smile. 'But I'm sure that won't happen to you.'

I have read the paper cover to cover, sport section included, by the time I am fetched by a young man who appears not to have slept for three days. 'Hi,' he says, not bothering to extend a hand. 'I'm John, the features-desk lackey. Maybe, if you're really lucky, you can be a desk lackey, too, once you've completed your internship, or whatever posh word they're using nowadays, but I wouldn't count on it. Only the strong survive. Let that be your first lesson.'

'Actually, it's my second lesson,' I say, meekly. I notice he smells of stale beer and fags.

'What's that?' he says, clearly taken aback by the fact I am not mute.

'It's my second lesson,' I repeat, extending my hand to his. He shakes it limply. 'The woman on reception, she taught me my first lesson, which is that time is fluid in newspapers, and I didn't need to worry too much that you were an hour late to pick me up. Though that was probably my second lesson, and yours was actually my third. My *real* first lesson was that I shouldn't have turned up to a media organisation dressed like a dweeb.'

Why did I use the word dweeb? Why?

John pretends he hasn't heard and guides me into a lift.

'We've got a talker,' says John, introducing me to the journalists in the newsroom. There aren't many. I see now why I got an internship here relatively easily. They have almost no staff, and obviously need all the help they can get, even if it is from me. 'Right,' says John, sitting me down at one of the many empty desks. 'You'll be starting straight away. No lazing about as you "shadow" people. We'll be putting you to work immediately.' My heart starts thumping in my chest. Will I be assigned as a research assistant to an important investigative journalist? Will I be asked to take notes at an interview with a Hollywood film star? Will I just be making the teas? I'd be happy making the teas, honestly I would. Let me just go and make some teas now, and then we can get to work straight away.

John sees the panic on my face. 'Don't worry,' he says. 'You're going to have fun with this one, Britney.'

'Bryony,' I say meekly, immediately regretting my decision to correct him. 'It's Bryony. But, I mean, you can call me Britney if you like.'

'Whatever. Now look, you're going to like this, because

29

it means you are going to be able to change out of the librarian costume you showed up in.'

Am I being sexually harassed? Oh God, day one in the workplace, and I am being sexually harassed!

But John is pulling out a giant furry outfit that, from this angle, looks a little like a dead dog. 'Today, Britney, you are going to be CHEWBACCA.' My mouth drops open. I am powerless to close it. Chewbacca. My first assignment at a newspaper is to dress as Chewbacca. I am pretty sure I have just learned my fourth lesson, and possibly my fifth and sixth.

'We're doing a feature on *Star Wars* memorabilia,' explains John, 'and the model has pulled out. Actually, if I'm being honest with you, we never booked one in the first place. We thought we'd wait for a willing workie to take up the challenge instead. And we were worried we wouldn't have anything for you to do, otherwise, so we thought "dress her up as Chewbacca!" And I know that might seem humiliating, but honestly, last week's workie got Jabba the Hutt, so you know, every cloud and all that.'

I swallow my pride and get on with it. I quickly learn to do what I am told. I like to see dressing up as Chewbacca as some sort of initiation, and if I pass it, I will be accepted into the fold. Or the Force. I change out of my librarian clothes in the loos, and put on the musty, hot Chewbacca outfit. I walk down the corridor back to John, the costume at least hiding the embarrassment I feel as reporters snigger at me. 'Looking good, Britney,' says John, heavy breathing. He is wearing a Darth Vader outfit. 'It's nice to have someone to share the shame with.' Beads of sweat are dripping down my body under the furry suit, but I can't stop myself from laughing. 'You see,' says John, 'told you I was a lackey!' He links his arm through mine, and together we make our way to the paper's studio, where a photographer spends an hour taking pictures of us brandishing light sabres and Lego versions of the Death Star.

This is my first experience of journalism.

As the week progresses, I am dispatched to get teas, to do research on zorbing, to pull together some statistics and historical facts on Norwich City FC for a 'box'. I am told to transcribe an interview with a drunken cabinet minister, to take a cab to a restaurant so I can deliver the editor a copy of the *Evening Standard*. I go to Boots to pick up prescriptions and buy pairs of tights, but I don't mind. I love being in a newsroom, watching stories break and deadlines being met. John even decides to be friendly towards me, asking me to lunch and one evening even taking me to the pub with everyone. It is thrilling, it is wonderful. It is absolutely what I want to do.

The fortnight passes in a blur, and then they ask me if I want to stay on for another fortnight, and another and another, before John tells me that he has got a reporter's job and they are thinking of using me as his replacement. I get the job, and am over the moon. 'I'm going to be a lackey!' I tell my mother, who immediately starts to cry. 'I'm so, so proud of you,' she sniffles, and I still can't see that something is wrong.

I throw myself into life as a lackey. Before long, I am allowed to write the odd piece about 'yoof issues', as they are referred to. When I hear that a job is going on the teenage supplement run by the *Telegraph*, I take a deep breath and apply for it. I get the job, I meet someone, I fall in love. I cannot believe my luck. The first couple of years of my twenties are going exactly as I had planned them.

It won't stay that way for long.

2

We're just popping out
to get a divorce

In a pub in Soho, a girl is being embraced by a handsome boy wearing skater clothes and a beanie over his
dirty blond hair, despite the fact it is August. The girl is
twenty-three, the boy twenty-eight, and they are so in
love that, after three or four pints, the boy is minded to
tell the girl that, 'If we are still together in a year, I'm
going to marry you.'

That girl is me. That boy is Sam. We are introduced
by a mutual friend at a party and Sam twinkles at me.
That isn't a euphemism for him flashing me – what I
mean is, he seems to light up when I hone into view. He
is the coolest boy in the room. I say boy, because though
physically he is a man, he has otherwise yet to mature
past the age of fifteen. Naturally, I am incapable of seeing
that. I just think the fact he lives with seven blokes in a

flat carpeted with tobacco is kind of characterful. As is his room, containing only a single bed, which I view as *romantic*. A bit like living in a tiny garret in the artists' quarter of Paris, with no belongings and nothing to our names but our love for one another. That he smokes joints like cigarettes is obviously a sign that he is a creative, not a stoner. I adore evenings spent playing computer games with him – hey, I've always been a sucker for Mario Kart! – and what's not to love about the fact that he loves snowboarding? He is an athlete, too!

Man, I fall hard for Sam. We are like Romeo and Juliet without the sticky end; Scott and Charlene without the Australian accents; Posh and Becks without the millions. He is, depending on which way you are inclined to look at it, my first big love or my first big mistake. When I look back on it now, I laugh; at the time all I wanted to do was smile and gush in adoration.

Sam is from Huddersfield and thinks I am well posh. Of course, I love that he is from Huddersfield – it's so much more interesting than, say, Chiswick or Richmond or Hanwell or any of the other places the boys I meet usually come from. The fact that he is from Huddersfield says to me that he is down to earth, grounded, a boy done good. In fact, he is way posher than I am, having grown up on an estate – and by that, I mean a manor, not a tower block. But the fact he is from up north seems to excuse him from his poshness; he believes that geography has released him from the terrible tyranny of being almost upper class, in a way southern sissies will never manage. The only differences between the two of us are that he has an appealing Yorkshire accent – when I look back on it, I will think that this was probably faked, too – and a loathing of London matched only by his hatred of getting up before midday.

I'm sure you'll agree that he is quite a catch.

He listens to hip-hop, the Wu Tang Clan and Public Enemy. Isn't that cool? He's not like the boy I had a flirtation with before him, a PR boy I met early in my job at the *Telegraph* who was obsessed with the music of Bob Dylan and Jeff Buckley and played guitar in a band that wrote-their-own-songs (he was always keen to tell people that – 'Our band writes-our-own-songs,' he would say, puffing up like a peacock). The songs were awful, even I could hear that through my semi-smitten state, a load of bilge about soulmates seeping through their skin and into their bloodstreams, la-di-da-di-da, yada-yada-yada. He reminded me of the girls at my old school who insisted they liked Nirvana when you knew in reality they yearned to be mooning at posters of Take That. It was all for show, completely superficial, his musical pretensions the deepest thing about him. I remember, when we finally split up because he felt we were 'on different planes' (he had met someone even more naive than I am), he insisted that we lie on his sofa listening to Jeff Buckley's 'Last Goodbye', his crocodile tears matched in awfulness only by his caterwauling. I was relieved to be rid of him, frankly. When he told me that nobody would ever love me like he did (and it was news to me that he had ever loved me in the first place), I just thought, 'Thank the Lord and sweet baby Jesus for that.' And then, soon after, I met Sam, who could not have been more different. The night we met he told me I was wicked and we ended the night snogging against a lamppost – the physiological positions you can get into without doing your back in when you are young! – and the next day he texted me and asked to see me again, that evening, and it all felt so easy, so nice. The fact that there had not been any long text silences that were supposed to show how cool you are, showed me how cool he actually was. He just got in touch as soon as he could, and that was that. Likewise, I knew he was deep and thoughtful precisely because he didn't pretend to be. He was lightness itself, upbeat and jolly, though perhaps that was simply because he smoked so much dope.

It occurred to me much later that the only time I ever saw him laugh was when he was high. I had no interest in marijuana myself. I had tried it, of course I had, when I was fifteen, but it had made me throw up on my friend's parents' expensive cream carpet before sending me to sleep drooling on their expensive cream sofa, and I didn't think there was much point in embracing it after that. I loved a drink because it made me feel up and hyper; I didn't like marijuana because it seemed to do the opposite. I never actively smoked dope while I was going out with Sam, but that's not to say I wasn't high all the time. Given the amount of marijuana inhaled around me it is entirely possible that I too ingested a fair bit and was spangled without even knowing it. Perhaps that explains why I failed to see that Sam was not, actually, a fantastic creative with boyish good looks and charm. He was just a stoner who happened also to be quite fit.

For the first few months of our relationship, he called me 'Snookums', a term of endearment I totally dug, but which made all around us feel as nauseous as I had the first time I'd smoked a joint. Then, as time wore on, I became more and more aware of his digs at London. He hated the tube – hey, who didn't? – he couldn't stand the noise and he thought the people were wankers. It hurt me because I had grown up in London and so by extension those wankers were my friends and family.

I told everyone he was a writer because that is what he had come to the capital to do, but in reality he had ended up working as an admin assistant at a start-up website that dealt with cheap car insurance. That just about summed up my relationship with Sam: in the light I shone on him in my head he was a romantic, creative figure, about to pen a Booker Prize-winning novel or a poetic ode to me, his muse-like girlfriend, when in reality he was making tea for grey-skinned men in brown suits.

At the back of my head the idea that we would not be getting married, or indeed even be together in a year's time, was attempting to gain more and more traction. At the beginning of our relationship I had decided that Sam, being the cool guy he was, would wear a powder-blue suit to our nuptials, while I would wear a figure-hugging, hip-skimming dress that showed off my boobs, and when people saw the pictures they would think, 'Man, that couple are *cool*. Married, but *cool* . . .' because while I was traditional enough to want to get hitched, it was obviously still important to me to be seen as flouting convention. As a little bit different.

Given the picture I had painted in my head of our life together – in the back of my mind we were BOTH going to become really successful writers, and so within three years we could move to Cornwall where we could write books and surf, even though I had never surfed in my life – I was reluctant to allow thoughts to the contrary to become intrusive, or real. So I went out of my way to ignore them. I told myself that the reason for his lethargy, his crankiness about London, had nothing to do with me. It was because of his dead-end job. But I just had to convince him of that. I would do that by being supernice to him (it didn't occur to me at the time that I had never been anything but that), and we would do what he wanted, and I would never impose on him any of my worries or concerns and certainly not any *opinions* about what *I* wanted to do or where *I* wanted to go. I would be Cool Girl, malleable and relaxed and bright and breezy, and he would love Cool Girl, because what was not to love? And everything would get better and there would still be a powder-blue suit and a figure-hugging dress.

Except it didn't work that way. The more fun and relaxed I was, the more distant and cagey Sam became, possibly because he saw through my attempts to be Cool Girl as evidence of me being anything but (or, even more possibly, because he was being a dick). Our relationship was spiralling out of control into a non-relationship, and I didn't know what to do. A sensible girl would have told Sam to sling his hook, a play-hard-to-get technique that I had read about in magazines, one that would inevitably lead to him running back to me. But I was not a sensible girl. I just kept pushing him further and further away through kindness, and I didn't understand it at all. Why would you be so lofty to someone who was only ever nice to you?

How long did this go on for? Two months? Three? I analysed every little thing I did for evidence of it causing the demise in our relationship. Had I made a cutting remark about someone who happened to be from the north? Did he not like the fact I had cut my hair? Was he put off by the fact I still lived at home with my parents, spoilt little middle-class girl that I was? I was sending myself mad trying to work out what was going wrong, when deep down I knew exactly what had happened. He had got bored with me. He had been frightened off by me; alternatively, and more likely, he had told me he wanted to marry me and frightened himself. Sensible Girl would have fronted up to him and asked outright for confirmation. Not-So-Cool Girl was too scared to do that in case she got an honest answer.

And then, one day, out of nowhere, Sam suggested we go out for dinner. If this had been a happy relationship, a good relationship, I would have just seen this as par for the course, something normal, but as it was quite clearly an on-its-way-out-relationship, my initial response was one of total dismay. 'He wants to take me out for dinner,' I told Sally, in a state of utter panic. Sally, Sensible Sally, was in a proper relationship with Andy, a rugby-playing economics student she had met at university, and so far everything was going to plan for her. They had even moved in together, to a flat in Putney, where Andy, now a management consultant (whatever that was), had joined a rowing club (of course he had), and Sally had set about throwing dinner parties twice a week, spending her days as the assistant to a banker planning to cook ever-more complex trifles.

'What's wrong with that?' said Sally, her perfectly made-up face contorted in confusion. 'Isn't him wanting to take you out for a meal a nice thing?'

'No!' I squealed. 'Sam isn't the kind of man who goes out for dinner. I don't think he's ever gone out for dinner in his life, unless you count Subway. This is obviously BAD NEWS.'

He took me to Nando's.

The smell of the peri-peri chicken (or was it the fact

I was about to be dumped?) made me feel sick, so I didn't order anything to eat. 'I'll just have a beer,' I said, quietly. He didn't ask if I was sure, if I fancied at least a small portion of chips. He just went to the counter, got me the beer and himself a water, and plonked himself back down.

He wasn't even drinking. My God, this was a bad sign. He had come here to deliver his crushing blow, that was that, and he couldn't even be bothered to get drunk with me so I could cry on him in public and ask where it all went wrong. He hadn't even splashed out on a mineral water, opting instead for tap. Any moment now, a waiter (did they even have waiters in Nando's?) was going to come over and ask us to leave because we weren't ordering any food. This was terrible. This was worse than terrible. I would rather he'd just texted me 'IT'S OVER, SOZ :-)' than this. Sensible Girl would have pre-empted the inevitable and ended it then and there, but . . . well, but.

'I'm moving to Edinburgh,' he announced, as if he was just off to Sainsbury's to buy some fags.

'Oh,' I replied, peeling off the label on the beer bottle.

'I think it would be best,' he started to say, 'I mean, I think it's only fair on you if we, you know . . .'

I stared at the beer bottle. Alcohol: 4.7 per cent, it said. Do not drink if you are pregnant, I learnt.

'Well, if we, like, end things.'

Even though I had known this was going to happen for some time now, I still felt as if I had been punched in the stomach. Anxiety surged up my chest and my windpipe. I thought I was going to be sick, right there in Nando's near Victoria Station.

Not even a high street Nando's, you see. A *station* Nando's.

'OK,' I said.

'OK?' he replied, confused.

I started to cry.

'This is so embarrassing,' I started to say over and over again. 'I can't believe I'm getting so cut up about things.' I was trying to be Cool Girl again. Sam took my hand and put his arm around me. NOW he decides to be nice to me, after months of cool indifference. 'You're a great girl,' he soothed. 'An absolute gem. Stunning, funny, so much going for you, kind . . .'

At this point, Sensible Girl would have cut him off to thunder 'OH REALLY?' at him. She would have said, 'Well, Sam, if I'm so stunning, funny, clever (did he even say clever?) and kind, why are you dumping me? Why the fuck are you not dropping to one knee, whipping a diamond ring out of your baggy fucking trousers and asking me to fucking marry you? Is it because you're a total ASS-HAT? Is it because you are twenty-eight going on thirteen, and the only thing you'll ever have a lasting relationship with is your lame-arse SNOWBOARD?'

But as we are learning, I am not Sensible Girl. I am Not-So-Cool Girl.

'Why don't I move to Edinburgh with you?' I actually heard myself say.

Sam is stumped. He has no answer to that question. Actually, he does, its just that 'I don't want you to move to Edinburgh, I am moving to Edinburgh to get AWAY from you and your wanky London friends' would be too crushing to an already insecure girl whose hopes and dreams you have just drenched with a cold glass of tap water in a branch of Nando's. Nando's! 'You can't move to Edinburgh,' he eventually managed, 'when you have so much going for you *here*.' And it's true. I can't move to Edinburgh any more than I can move to the moon, or the planet Mordor. It's not just that everything I have is here – friends, family, the job I've just got on a magazine. It's also that moving to be with Sam would be so grossly stupid that it can't even be considered.

I never ask why he's moving to Scotland. I'm not sure I want to know. It could be for a girl. It's probably for a girl. I will torture myself with this for months to come, waste valuable energy imagining the person he has left me for, the colour of her hair (brunette, the opposite of mine, obviously), the cut of her jib (cool as opposed to not-so-cool). I am twenty-three years old. I DO have a lot going for me. But I am completely and utterly blinded to it by my amazing ability to concentrate on what I DON'T have going for me. Namely, Sam.

When did it all go so *wrong*? How come a simple break-up would lead me to years of wilful self-destruction, and one-night stands with tossers like Josh? When did life veer so drastically from the path set out for me and my peers by parents and teachers and feminists? I'm sorry, Emmeline. I'm sorry, Germaine. I'm sorry Anais. I'm sorry Sylvia and Gloria and Simone. I'm sorry that you set out to change the world, and still there are girls who will waste their energy over a stoner who wears woollen hats in August.

Two months after Sam and I break up (or, more accurately, he breaks up with me), my father tells me that he and Mum are planning on getting a divorce. 'A what?' I say, in disbelief. I am heating up some chips in the kitchen when he delivers this news to me in a relaxed style that suggests he has actually told me to take the rubbish out. 'A what?' I repeat, in case I have misheard him.

'A divorce,' he repeats, matter-of-factly.

'OK,' I say, as the tray of oven chips clatters to the floor beneath me. 'A divorce,' I say, trying to process the information. 'A divorce.' My mind goes blank. I run out of the house and don't return for the rest of the day.

When my mother finally locates me, pretending to watch an Arsenal match in the pub with friends, I burst into tears and ask her what the hell is going on. She bundles me into the Volvo. 'He shouldn't have told you like that,' she says, anger in her voice. 'Let's get you home and we can talk about this properly.'

'Fuck home,' I spit.

She takes me there anyway.

'I know this is not the news you want to hear,' my

mum starts, as we all sit at the kitchen table. 'But we've tried to shield you from it while you've been doing so well. We didn't want to ruin things for you.'

'You mean, you've known you were getting a divorce for some time?' I squeal.

'Only about ten years,' wisecracks my father.

'Jack!' snaps my mother. 'We told your sister and your brother a while ago because we thought they should know . . .'

'You thought my ELEVEN-YEAR-OLD BROTHER SHOULD KNOW BEFORE ME?'

'Actually, he's OK with it,' says my dad. 'He says that he was a freak at school for having parents who were still together, so that's something, at least.'

I stare at the table unsure what else to do. In the pattern of the wood I am sure I can see an eye, and a deer.

'You know, he has a point,' I say. 'Why didn't you do this ages ago, like NORMAL PEOPLE? Why didn't you get divorced when I was like, thirteen, like everyone else in my class? Then we would have at least got sympathy from our teachers, and an extra set of presents at Christmas and for birthdays. Jesus, you're fucking our lives up by getting a divorce, and YOU CAN'T EVEN FUCK THEM UP PROPERLY.'

It is their turn to make out woodland creatures in the pattern of the table.

'Why are you even getting a divorce? Which one of

45

you is running off with someone else? Is it both of you? Are we going to get step-siblings? Oh God, I really hope they're cooler than my real ones.'

'Bryony,' says my mother, employing her soothing voice. 'Neither of us is running off with anyone. We just feel we would both be happier apart. That's all it is.'

'That's all it is? Jesus, can't you at least get divorced for a GOOD REASON? How am I going to tell people that you're getting a divorce "just because", as if it's something to do on a wet weekend? Can't you just stay together miserably like everyone else does?'

'Bryony,' says my father, but I have run out of the room again.

He moves out soon after, into a flat around the corner. Within months, he has met someone else, a blonde woman twenty-five years his junior whom my sister and I dub Heather Mills – despite the fact we have never met her, Dad has no money, and has never bought a record that was made post-1955, let alone released one. 'She's very nice,' my dad explains. 'She's divorced herself, so she knows what it's like. She's helping me get back on my feet again.'

'Dad, that is so gross,' says my sister. 'We really don't want to know.'

It amazes me how quickly men move on. Twenty-five years my mum and dad spent together, and within four months it's as if Mum never even happened. I can't work out if I admire it or find it totally heinous. It's been ages since Sam disappeared from my life, and we were together for under a year, and yet I can't imagine getting over him before the age of forty. 'Are you hurt?' I ask my mum, one evening. She shakes her head. 'To be honest, Bryony, I'm relieved. It's so nice being by myself for the first time in decades. I know you'll find it hard to believe now, but being in a relationship isn't always what it's cracked up to be. Sometimes, you just want to be alone.'

I feel sad. I don't want to be alone. I think about Sam. If my dad has moved on that quickly, I imagine Sam has already been through another three girlfriends since breaking up with me, and barely even remembers my name. Life seems a little bleak, suddenly – even when you think you have found the one, even when you have been married for twenty-five years, it can still all go tits up quite magnificently.

I don't ever blame my parents' divorce on what happens to me over the next decade. That would be silly, immature. But I can blame them for handing their genes down to me, mixing them together in a single act of selfishness that can only result in giving life to a complete fuckwit. Yeah, I can do that. As I used to say, when I was about thirteen: I hate my life.

3

My flatmates, the silverfish

'Do you think we should live together?'

I'd always longed to hear these words. Just not from my sister. I don't want to live with my sister. We've lived together our whole bloody lives, stealing each other's Sylvanians and latterly Topshop clothes. 'I don't want to live with you,' I say disparagingly. 'You're annoying and you always smoke all my cigarettes. Plus, you don't have a job. You've been graduated from uni for three months and you've not bothered to get out of bed before midday, let alone look for work. It's bad enough living with you under Mum and Dad's roof. Or just Mum's roof. Or whatever our fucked-up family setting is nowadays. I dread to think what you'd be like set free.'

When you think about leaving home for the first time, it's to go to university or move in with a boyfriend or at the very least a stranger you met through a flatshare website (I don't count my brief spell in halls, given that it was more like going to borstal than moving out). Anyway, it's not with a member of your *family*, is it? I mean, you may as well just stay at home if you want to live with your sister. That way you get your meals cooked and your laundry done and there are enough rooms to hide in if she starts to drive you up the wall. I'm not living with my little sister. Not one moment longer. Now I am in my twenties, it is my human right NEVER TO HAVE TO LIVE WITH HER EVER AGAIN.

Plus, I don't like my sister. I mean, I do like my sister, obviously – I love her very much – but I don't like that she is everything I'm not. She has neat handwriting – even I can't read mine – and is sporty. At school, she excelled at gymnastics and was a champion diver, while I would pretend I had my period every time they tried to make me go swimming, until it got to the point that the PE teacher got in touch with my mum to ask if there was something wrong with me and suggest I take a trip to the doctor. 'It's just not normal for a young girl to be menstruating so often,' she not-so-delicately told my mother, who immediately booked for me to see a gynae-cologist. 'But Mum, I only menstruate once a month!' was the conversation my father overheard one day. 'I just say I've got my period to get out of having to do the butterfly. If you saw me doing the butterfly, you'd under-stand. I look like a whale having an epileptic fit!'

Things like that just never happen to my sister. She is slender with a cute button nose, while I have inherited the schnozz of my Jewish ancestors, a fact I could just about bear if I actually got to be properly Jewish, too. But no – Judaism ran down my father's side, meaning I have been denied even that exotic flavouring to my heritage. My sister – well, the only Jewish thing about her is her name. Physically, she is about as Aryan as they come. She has big blue eyes (mine are bland grey) and naturally blonde hair, while I have to spend £100 I don't have getting it dyed every three months. She isn't neurotic like me, she doesn't fret all the time. She is emotionally restrained and doesn't fart out every noxious thought that comes into her mind. That is the thing I hate and admire most about her.

'No,' I say, bluntly. 'I would rather gouge my eyes out with a rusty spoon than live with you.'

Once I've said that, I have to move out. It's like a challenge. If I don't go, she's won. Without doing anything at all, she's proved that I am destined to live with her for ever and ever. It's like a genius plan to get me out of the house. My God, I hate her.

I set about looking for a place to live. Without a doubt, this is the single most crushing experience of my life, more so even than breaking up with Sam (or Sam breaking up with me). Having grown up in a four-bedroomed terraced house that my parents bought for fifty pence when they got married, I am used to a certain level of comfort and space. I am dimly aware of news reports about house prices, but I feel too young and carefree to pay any attention to them. Instead, I watch *Friends*, and absorb the Manhattan loft apartment they live in as if this is the norm. I soon discover that it isn't.

It's hopeless speaking to estate agents. It's worse than hopeless; it's utterly dispiriting. I tell them my budget – £500 a month – and they pretend they haven't heard me. I think it's easier for them to pretend they haven't heard me, so pathetic is the idea of actually finding a place on the market for £500 a month. They sign me up to look at properties for £1,200, £1,400, flats with mezzanines and spiral staircases and minimalist, clean white surfaces, with underground parking, and I can't even drive. It's the very definition of rubbing someone's nose in it.

'You know that buying may be a better investment of your money,' says one estate agent, as we drive from one flat I will never live in to another. 'Have you thought about buying?'

I stare at him. Have I thought about buying? Have I? Yes, it once crossed my mind but I decided *never to think about it again*, because it sent me into such a state of lethargic despondency I didn't get out of bed for two days. Since then, I have thought about learning Mandarin more than I have about buying a flat.

I look in *Loot*. All the ads state 'NO JOB SEEKERS', which makes me feel as if I am one myself. I feel soiled, ashamed, like a scummy vagabond looking to squat somewhere. I go on Gumtree and arrange to see some houseshares. It will be like *This Life*, I tell myself. I will live with young, hip people, perhaps even a potential boyfriend (there is a potential boyfriend in *everything*). When we all get home from work we will cook chilli con carnes and spag bols together while we drink red wine (I don't drink red wine, I'm not sophisticated enough to deal with its richness, and it always stains my teeth dark red, but never mind). We will lounge around having fun, there definitely won't be queues for the bathroom in the morning, and nobody will make more mess than anyone else or eat a housemate's cereal.

No siree.

I go for an 'interview' at a house in Hammersmith. All the paint is peeling off the front of it and there's a mattress in the garden (if you could call it that), but hey, what's a yellowing mattress between friends? I climb the crumbling front steps and ring the door bell. I wait. I ring it again. I wait some more. I'm not sure the door bell, which I obviously ring once more, even works. I wonder what to do. Is calling too forward? Is knocking too aggressive? 'You here about the room?' says a gruff voice from behind me. I spin round. At the bottom of the steps is a man of about forty, unshaven, wearing dirty khaki trousers and a dark green top splattered with paint. He is holding a blue plastic bag full of beer cans. It's 11.30 a.m.

'Erm,' I say, 'yes'.

'Cool,' he says, barging past me. 'Come in.'

The door isn't even locked. It has been on the latch all along. I follow the man into the hall and step over a sea of pizza leaflets and flyers for local cleaners – I can already see that this house really needs the latter. There are three bicycles in the hall, two recycling bags full of more leaflets, and overhead an exposed lightbulb that flickers ominously. I could turn around and leave now, pretend that I am a Jehovah's Witness, but the middle-class girl in me tells me that this would be rude, and I should give these people a chance. So I stand in the hall and await instruction, while the man rummages in his plastic bag and pulls out two cans. 'Want one?' he smiles, revealing a mouth of half-teeth.

'I'm fine thanks,' I smile back.

He shakes his head and leads me into the sitting room.

A large coffee table dominates. I get the impression that it has never seen a cup of coffee in its life. It is littered with empty beer bottles, a three-quarters empty bottle of cheap vodka, and an empty two-litre bottle of Sprite. Two ashtrays overflow onto the surface, which is speckled with tobacco and Rizla papers. Old copies of *Loaded* lie below with takeaway leaflets that have had corners torn out of them (I was with Sam for long enough to know why anyone would do *that*).

There are pot plants that haven't been alive since Margaret Thatcher was in power. A fireplace that is never used other than for the candles that have long since melted away. The TV displays the end of someone's quest to drive fast cars around a made-up city, probably shooting down hos as they go. 'RESET? START?' It says. The Xbox is the main feature of this living room, if that is what you could call it. The forty-something has settled himself on a settee – it is absolutely that and not a sofa – that is covered in manky throws to disguise even mankier cushions. He snaps open his beer, swigs from it, and lets out a satisfied sigh.

It's not even 11.40 a.m.

He tells me to sit down, but I am too scared to take up that offer. I might get fleas or lice or walk out with chewing gum stuck to my bum. I am not averse to a bit of a house party, to having a good time, but if this is them making an effort for prospective housemates, then I dread to think what it's like on a bad day. This is the kind of flat that Jesse from *Breaking Bad* would turn his nose up at. It's the kind of flat that squatters would baulk at, squatters nowadays preferring to enter properties on Park Lane left empty by Russian oligarchs. (Maybe I *should* think about squatting?) This is the kind of flat that wouldn't even make it on to the cheap brown section of a Monopoly board.

'Is Kate here?' I ask the forty-something politely. Kate is the girl who placed the advert, the person I have been speaking to on email. 'Large, friendly houseshare seeks new housemate. Double room, own bathroom, internet and bills included. 5 minute walk from tube. £500pcm.' It seemed so reasonable, possibly too good to be true. Now I know that it is.

'Kate moved out last week,' grunts the forty-something. 'She's had to leave London because she got into a bit of trouble with the old,' he starts sniffing manically, 'you know . . .'

I don't know.

'You know . . .' More sniffing. Did Kate leave because she had a cold? Surely not. 'Anyway, she's gone back home to her parents, so now we have two rooms that need filling, if you know anyone who needs a place.'

I can't think of anyone who needs a place like this. It's like one of those houses you see on fly-on-the-wall documentaries about the council's pest inspector unit – all flies, hardly any walls.

'You can move in as soon as you want,' continues the forty-something. 'The room is on the first floor if you want to look at it. We ask for a deposit, but only so we can blow it on a big party to celebrate you moving in.'

I look startled. I've barely said a word, I've not even seen the room, and suddenly I am *moving in*?

'Actually, I've got some other places to look at.' I smile as sweetly as possible. 'Is it OK if I call you once I've finished doing the rounds? The place is FAB . . .' Why am I trying to impress this oaf without teeth? WHY? 'But I just want to keep my options open at the moment, if you know what I mean.'

He looks at me, baffled. He doesn't know what I mean.

'Yeah, well whatever,' he says, swigging from his can.

'You won't mind if I don't see you out. You know where the door is.'

I do, and I make a run for it. And while I am making a run for it, I also want to run back to my middle-class life and tell my sister that yes, I would LOVE to move in with her. But then she would have won, and I can't have that. So, instead, I return to the estate agents, to the least financially viable option.

'I'm going to live by myself,' I announce to my sister, rather loftily. 'I just really need my own place, you know.'

'You mean nobody will live with you?'

'No!' I grizzle. 'I mean that after all these years of having to live with YOU, I want to be by myself. I want my own *space*.'

But if I wanted my own space, I'd stay at home, where my bedroom, though not cavernous, is significantly bigger than any of the 'studio' flats I am shown around. When I think of a studio flat, I think of some sort of warehouse space in the centre of town. Perhaps Soho. But these are a forty-five-minute tube ride from anywhere in the least bit central, in Zones 4, 5 and even 6. 'Maybe it would be cheaper if I moved to Hull and commuted in,' I huff to my colleague, Chloe, over lunch in the *Telegraph* canteen one day. Chloe lives in a one-bed flat in east London with her boyfriend, a television 'executive' whose executive role seems to involve using the company expenses account to take gargantuan amounts of drugs. But that is another matter entirely.

'You should come and live over east,' she says. 'It's where all the cool people are. I know you'd have just loved a palatial one-bedroomed flat overlooking Hyde Park, but you may as well start looking for properties in Beverly Hills for all the likelihood there is of that. You're going to have to get *real*, Bryony.'

I hate that where you live in a city somehow informs who you are as a person. So if you live in south-west London, say Fulham or Chelsea, you are rich and a toff and as dull as the corduroy trousers and expensive loafers you wear, but if you live in west London, you are rich and a bit trendy, just because there happens to be an illegal all-night disco under Tesco on Portobello Road and a carnival for two days of the year.

But east London . . . now that's another story entirely. You move there and it doesn't matter if you grew up in a mansion, were in a secret society at Oxbridge or were forced by your parents to wear Hackett jumpers during your early adolescence. Now you live in east London – Dalston, Hackney, Stoke Newington, or 'Stokie' as the truly cool refer to it – you have a whole new persona. You can get yourself a 'directional' haircut (pay someone loads of money to butcher your tresses and make you look like a Lego brick) and never wash your skinny jeans because the distressed look is so in. You can wear really ugly clothes bought from a 'vintage' store (translation: a trumped-up second-hand shop where you pay double the price of something new for the privilege of being able to appear kooky and cool for not shopping in Topshop). You can start smoking roll-ups even though you are rubbish at it and all the tobacco falls out and gets stuck to your lip because you haven't sealed the Rizla paper tightly enough.

Obviously, I am going to have to move to east London.

But when I go there to look at places, it makes no sense to me. Why, to be socially mobile, do I have to move somewhere so downwardly mobile? As I visit flats on top of curry houses or hidden in cavernous estates in Hackney, something dawns on me about east London. And it is this: it is a shithole. A complete and utter shithole. There is no arguing about it. Not even an estate agent could disguise it, though goodness they try. 'On the up' means it's currently in the doldrums; 'cool' means nobody with any money would ever move there; 'vibrant' means that if you have any regard for your safety, you would think of somewhere else to live. My paternal grandparents lived in east London for most of their lives and couldn't wait to leave. I wonder what they would make of me now, banging down the door of a tiny bedsit on the Bethnal Green Road in a desperate attempt to escape my embarrassingly middle-class life.

The flat – sorry, room – that I decide is the place for me is above a chicken shop and a place that sells smoking paraphernalia. It is called the Ashtray. I actually live above an ashtray. I find the flat – sorry, room – through an advert on Facebook, and it is, if not perfect, then perfectly fine. It is not quite like something out of an Ikea catalogue – more a dog-eared Ikea catalogue from ten years ago with coffee-cup stains on it. The landlord is nice, an Irish guy with a wife and small child, and he wants *only* £600 a month for it, this room with a sofa that folds out to a bed, a small table, a tiny kitchen area, and a 'wet room' next to the front door (not quite a bathroom, given that the loo and the sink are perilously close to the shower, possibly even under it).

But I don't care. It's mine. Or at least it's sort of mine, for the time being, until I meet some dishy man who I will move in with elsewhere, when the room will promptly become someone else's. I buy a pot plant to put in the corner, but then I realise that there are no corners – no available ones, anyway – so, instead, I place it in the hall outside and hope the neighbours won't mind. I attempt to place all of my books on the shelves above the sofa/bed, but I realise the shelves aren't big enough for them, which leads me to spend three hours selecting the titles that make me look good – Chaucer's *Canterbury Tales*; *The Blind Assassin* by Margaret Atwood; Jonathan Franzen's *Corrections* – while repacking the ones that don't: *Bridget Jones*, a diet book, a Take That annual that's still hanging around from the early nineties.

I don't have a TV as I can't afford one and I know I will never get round to buying a licence, but I don't care as I plan never to be in, and anyway, not having one will only help my quest to be taken seriously as a human being. I buy a bright pink colander, which I fall in love with while I'm browsing in Selfridges. This is the kind of person I am, spending £25 on a colander I will never use because I like the colour of it, then moaning to my parents that I can't afford to eat. I get some cheap cutlery and two plates, just in case I ever eat anything that doesn't come out of a carton. There is no need to buy any more plates. It is unlikely you could fit more than two and a half people in here anyway.

But I try. I invite Chloe and her boyfriend and some of their friends around for a house-warming, or a bedsit-warming. I think about inviting Sally and Andy but I'm not sure I could stand the disapproval, or the look of pity that would surely be etched on their faces. No, this guest list is better, cooler.

We listen to Justin Timberlake through a tinny iPod speaker and all stand like sardines drinking cans of warm beer and smoking ourselves silly. It's a wonder we don't burn the place down. All Chloe's friends are gay – everyone in east London is gay, I am gradually realising – and they tell me that my place is 'darling, so bijoux' and everyone constantly disappears into my 'wet room', in pairs and trios. At first I think they're having sex but then when I note that they're sniffing a lot and their noses are running (it is June), I realise that they're probably doing cocaine.

I don't do cocaine, I am too cowardly to do cocaine, I have read that just one line can send your mental health into a downward spiral and put you in a home for ever (or is that ecstasy?) but I feel wonderfully grown-up and cool that *other* people are here in my flat doing cocaine. It's like being in a film, a fabulous eighties film. It's like Michael Douglas has turned up at my party with his mate Rob Lowe, and I feel high as a kite off that alone. I am cool! I have finally arrived, even if it's only in a tiny room that by now is doubling up for an ashtray!

'I think we should go to the Joiners,' says Chloe, when the neighbours start to bang on the paper-thin walls some time after midnight.

'Oh man, we *have* to go Joiners,' says her friend James.

'I think we should go Joiners!' I beam, even though I have no idea what Joiners is or where it is or if it is even a place as opposed to, say, a drugged-up concept.

'To the Joiners!' everyone says.

The Joiners, it turns out, is a place, though it's also very much a concept, and not a terribly high-end one. It's a large pub on the Hackney Road that thinks it's a disco. It's rammed with men who love men but also seem to be fond of me, telling me I am 'FABULOUS' and 'HAWT' and 'TOTALLY AWESOME'. Naturally, I love it. I don't care that if I want to go to the loo, I have to queue for half an hour for the one cubicle next to the fifteen urinals, that this cubicle is filthy, that there is barely any toilet paper left, that while waiting for it I have to watch men emptying their bladders. I don't care that it's 180 degrees in here, that the DJ has played Dolly

Parton four times now, or that there is zero chance of me pulling in this place. I get such a warm and fuzzy feeling off the compliments these men pay me while they are off their face, wearing their Gay Goggles, that I decide then and there to become a Fag Hag.

Later, much later, probably in about ten years' time, I will realise that falling in love with gay men is no different from pining for Sam, or a man who hands you back someone else's knickers, in that they are all unobtainable. Boy, I love an unobtainable man.

The next morning I wake up on my sofa having not bothered to pull it out into the bed. I still have my contact lenses in. Still having your contacts in is, I find, a sign of a good night out. Or, at the very least, an excessive night out. You come round, open your eyes, think that eight pints of lager, half a bottle of wine and two vodka and tonics has magically given you the power of sight, and then you feel that uniquely sticky feeling around your cornea, the feeling that tells you, you were simply too pissed to take your lenses out. You will have to wear the tortoiseshell spectacles you have had since you were fifteen all day.

Still, the fact I still have my contacts in allows me to see immediately the mess that my little bedsit-warming has left. Far from 'warming' the place, my party leaves a distinctly cold feeling in my bloodstream. Or the alcohol stream that currently masquerades as my bloodstream. The cheap faux wood floor is black with fag ends trodden into it. Half empty cans of lager – if last night they were half full, this morning they are definitely half empty – are littered everywhere. A wine bottle stands forlornly in the sink, its contents replaced with yet more fag butts. I tentatively put a leg off the sofa, and my foot sticks to the floor.

I run to the loo and vomit. I realise with a start that last night, somebody beat me to it.

The clean-up operation feels as if it should be carried out by professionals in biohazard suits. It's like sifting through the wreckage of my life so far. I think of Sam, far away in Scotland, probably waking up in his new double bed – of course he's got a double bed, now he's no longer with me; he's probably got a superkingsized bed, the bastard – with the fifth or sixth girlfriend he has moved on to since bidding me farewell. Oh God, I wish he was here now. If he was here now, none of this would matter. The clean-up would be done within half an hour, leaving us to go for a fry-up, followed by a walk around Columbia Flower Market, followed by an afternoon shagging our hangovers away before settling down in front of the TV to slag off *The X Factor*.

But I can't watch *The X Factor*, because I don't even have a TV.

Instead, I spend three hours scrubbing and vomiting, scrubbing and vomiting, the windows wide open to clear out the smell of stale fags and booze, so that I am scrubbing and vomiting and the whole street outside can hear.

'Great night!' texts Chloe. 'Just walking off the super-hangover with a trip round Flower Market!' I want to cry. I do cry, as a matter of fact, last night's mascara trickling down a face dried out from drinking too much booze.

When the operation is completed, my sister arrives to see the wonderful independent life that I have carved out for myself. She takes one look at my new abode, and starts to laugh. 'I know it's been bad at home with Mum and Dad,' she says, 'but it's not THIS bad. There's not even room to swing a cat in here. And you know it's only a matter of time before you get a cat, because it's not like you can get a boyfriend.'

If I wasn't so broken, I would punch her.

'I've bought you some post,' she says, sitting down on the clapped-out sofa and almost falling through it. She hands me a note. As I read it, my stomach churns. 'Just to let you know, you kept us up ALL NIGHT.' All night is underlined several times. 'It is simply NOT ACCEPTABLE to play music at the level you were last night. If this happens again, we will have to inform your LANDLORD.' Again, landlord underlined several times. 'Please desist from this kind of behaviour. In the twenty years we have lived in this building, we have NEVER' – never underlined, of course – 'experienced disruption like you caused with your little party. Yours, number 7. PS please can you move the pot plant. It is blocking the hall.'

'You've met the neighbours then,' smirks my sister.

I go and get the pot plant and stick it under the shower in the 'wet room', which is the only space for it at the moment.

'I have to say,' continues my sister, 'that I am very impressed. You live above an ashtray and a chicken shop that's open until 3 a.m. You are on one of the noisiest roads in London. And still, you manage to piss off the neighbours within a week of moving in. Nice one, sis!'

Perhaps, I muse, the contents of the pot plant would look good on her pretty head.

I hate my home so much that I spend as little time in it as I can. It's my own fault. I have soiled it by throwing a party, by pissing off the neighbours. When I leave in the morning, I run out the door and down the stairs, terrified of bumping into them. When I come home at night, usually after pub closing time, I skidaddle back up the stairs like a cockroach. I may as well be renting a bunk bed in a hostel for all the time I spend in my dank, dark bedsit.

I have been there for three months when I reach the end of my tether. My mum calls as I'm doing my usual run out of the building, late for work as ever. She just wants to know how I am, and if I want to come home for Sunday lunch this weekend. I do, I do, I DO, but I can't let her see how desperate I am for the middle-class comforts of home. It would be tragic if I was to turn up there with an Ikea bag full of laundry, looking grey-skinned from my diet of houmous and Kettle Chips. 'I'm busy,' I lie, because like most sad single people, I have no plans for the weekend other than lying in my own sweat and self-loathing until 4 p.m., when it has already started to get dark again. 'I'm going to an art exhibition with some friends, and then for lunch.' Hey, Bryony, don't get too carried away.

'An art exhibition!' she beams. 'What kind of art exhibition?'

'An art kind.' I am profoundly irritated. 'An exhibition kind.'

'Well, it sounds as if you're really thriving in your new place.'

'I am. It's great . . .'

I don't finish the sentence, because I receive a blow to the head. I automatically release my grip on the mobile, only to see a young boy make off with it down the street. It's 9.30 a.m. It's broad daylight. To my left, there is a bus stop full of people waiting for the 388. As I rub the back of my head and blink in the direction of the boy who has just stolen my phone, I dimly start to realise that I have been mugged. And that not a single person at the bus stop seems to have noticed.

'I, I . . .' I can't speak. Has this just happened? Am I hallucinating it? Why is nobody helping me? 'I think I've just been the victim of a CRIME,' I finally wail, sounding like an elderly lady from the 1920s.

'You OK?' says a bloke on some scaffolding above me. The number 388 arrives. Every other witness to the mugging gets on it, as if what they have just seen is perfectly normal – which, when I think about it later, it probably is. 'I thought he was your mate!' laughs the bloke from the scaffolding, as he climbs down a ladder to street level.

Even in my shocked, just-been-whacked-around-the-head state, I am able to see that friends don't hit each other and steal each other's possessions. 'You thought he was my MATE?' I parrot back at him. 'He was a fifteen-year-old boy in a hoodie and Reebok Classics! Do I LOOK like the kind of person who is friends with fifteen-year-old boys in hoodies and Reebok Classics?'

Oh God, if I'm not careful, I'm going to be assaulted again for being dangerously middle class.

'All right, lady,' says the man from the scaffolding. Lady? Lady? I'm no lady! Ladies are OLD! I'm a GIRL! This is the worst day ever, and it's not even a quarter to ten! 'Let's call the police and get this sorted out.'

'I need to call my mother,' I start to cry. 'My mother needs to know I'm OK!' Oh crap. What am I? A professional woman in her twenties who has just been mugged or a Girl Guide who has just been separated from her Brownie group on a day out playing Pooh sticks over the River Avon?

'There, there,' says the nice man from the scaffolding. 'Let's call the police and then we can call your mum.'

The police give me a crime number and thank me for

my call in a tone that suggests they are not altogether sure why I have bothered to make it.

'Did you go into a tunnel on the tube?' my mum asks. I explain what has happened. 'I'm calling your boss to tell them you're not coming in,' she says, frantically. 'You need a nice day spent with your MUMMY.'

So now I'm the girl whose mummy calls up to excuse her from work, as if she's a poorly eight year old who can't go to school because her tummy doesn't feel right.

But it feels nice to be with my mum. Even my sister is nice to me, which is something. There is a bath with candles around it, and big fluffy towels on warm radiators, and the fridge is full of delicious food that can be made into actual *meals*.

'Can I stay the night?' I plead.

'Of course, darling.'

And that night, as we eat roast chicken with potatoes and broccoli, it is decided that my sister and I will find a place together. She has won, I have been defeated, but I don't even care. I just want to be safe and cosy and not have to worry about being mugged outside my door in broad daylight in front of people who couldn't give a toss. Is that too much to ask? Really?

I give my notice to the nice Irishman who tells me it's a relief I'm moving out, given the complaints he got from the people next door. 'The noisiest neighbour they've had in thirty years!'

'It was twenty years the last time they complained,' I snap back.

The dispiriting search for somewhere to live starts again, although this time I am at least sharing it with my sister, who for the first time in both of our lives develops a modicum of respect for me for having ever found a place in the first place, even if that place happened to be the size of a postage stamp and the shower was a bucket under a hose right next to a loo.

The nice Irishman calls me a week after I move back home, just when I am beginning to believe I have escaped to safety relatively unscathed . . . 'I'm afraid I won't be able to refund you your deposit,' he announces. 'The cutlery was not in the drawer that I left it in when you moved in.'

'But it's in the drawer below,' I point out.

'I know that, but if the items on the inventory are not left in the places they were put when the inventory was made, then that means I cannot refund your deposit. I don't have the time to spend looking around the flat for where you have placed items, so as far as the contract you signed stands, if they are not where they were originally left, they are lost or damaged.'

'It's not as if the flat has a west wing and an east wing,' I say, stating the obvious. 'It would probably take you about 30 seconds to do a full recce of it. And for that you are actually going to take £600 off me?'

'Actually,' says the increasingly-not-so-nice Irishman, 'it's not just the missing cutlery.'

'The cutlery isn't missing. It's simply in another drawer.'

'If you will let me continue, Miss Gordon.'

Miss Gordon!

'I have also found a leak in a pipe in the bathroom. This leak has inflicted serious water damage on the bathroom. Had you informed me of it when it happened, which judging by the water damage is some time ago, I could have fixed it for a small cost. Now the bill I am faced with is not unsubstantial.'

'You are taking £600 off me because of a leak in a pipe hidden behind a wall, in a room where the shower is basically a bucket under a hose perilously close to a loo. Give you a massive clue, that room would have major water damage even WITHOUT a leak in a pipe.'

Is what I wish I had said.

But instead, I say this: 'Oh. OK then.'

I am too young, too naive, too clueless about the management of a property to fight back. I just assume that whatever someone older says is right. I just want him to go away, and leave me to my pathetic life as a boomeranger. I want to crawl into my bed and stay there until I am about fifty-five. So I don't argue with him, and I don't get my deposit back.

'Furthermore, there is a pot plant you left that I will now have to waste valuable time disposing of. I can't say I'm not disappointed, Miss Gordon.'

So I don't even get the pot plant back.

That chuffing pot plant.

My sister and I continue our search for a place that is affordable, nice (it doesn't even have to be pleasant, just nice) and within the M25 – a place that doesn't pose major health and safety risks, where the boiler has been serviced within the last fifteen years, and a place that doesn't look as if it was previously inhabited by Charlie Bucket and his family before he found one of Willy Wonka's golden tickets.

'It's like searching for a needle in a haystack,' says my sister.

'Perhaps we should just make a home out of a haystack,' I suggest.

My friend Steve saves the day. Steve is someone I work with, someone I go to the pub with, an older brother figure who seems almost as hopeless with the opposite sex as I am. He is pleasantly handsome, Home Counties handsome, with a nice line in edgy glasses and sleek suits. The first time we met, at last year's Christmas party, we ended up snogging in a corner, because *obviously* I am that person, the one who gets so drunk they jump on the nearest available male and embarrass themselves in front of the whole office. I spent the whole weekend in a state of terror about what Monday morning would bring. Did I say anything awful to my boss? Did I try and snog my boss, even though my boss was a woman? (Perhaps, ESPECIALLY because my boss was a woman, and I wanted to appear *de rigueur*.) Did I vomit, take my clothes off, try to simulate sex with a chair while dancing to Madonna? When I don't have any actual memory, my brain is quite happy to make up some replacements.

When I saw Steve on Monday I blurted out the usual post-drink platitudes. 'OhmigawdIwassodrunkIamsosorry-Isnoggedyou.' It was obvious even when I was kissing Steve that we would never become a couple, that my smooching him was merely my job as a dutiful snog nurse.

'A snog nurse?' says Steve, confused.

'A snog nurse,' I nod along.

'What's a snog nurse?'

'If I have to explain, we'd better go for a coffee.'

So we do, and as we sit outside Starbucks in the freezing cold drinking our lattes and chain smoking Marlboro Lights, I tell him what a snog nurse is. 'It's when you can see a bloke is clearly in need of an ego boost. You know, when he's just been dumped or something, as you so clearly have. And you feel sorry for him. And you are drunk, and to be honest, if you snog him it's going to give YOU a bit of an ego boost, too, because the bloke is all right looking and because as you snog him you see that he is so very grateful you have deigned to stick your tongue down his throat. Once you have finished your kiss, you have administered your medicine. Thus, you are a snog nurse.'

'You mean you took pity on me,' says Steve, incredulous. 'You mean to say that by snogging me you were performing some sort of altruistic service to SOCIETY?'

I nod. We have an argument.

But we also have the basis of a great friendship. I am Steve's wayward little sister, he is my screw-up older brother. We spend all our time together. My mum says, 'Why don't you and Steve get together?' and Steve's mum says, 'Why don't you and Bryony give it a go?' But as we already act like an old married couple, bickering constantly but always side by side, there is little chance of us actually becoming one. This isn't the movies. It's not a novel. It's real life, and in real life you never end up with the person who is right in front of you all along, even though everyone tells you that is what will happen. It would just be too easy. Nobody ever really wakes up one morning and thinks, 'Good Lord, the man I have been friends with all of this time is actually eminently shaggable and I have missed a trick! I MUST GET TO HIM IMMEDIATELY!' Your best male friend is not Harry, and you are not Sally. End of.

So Steve and I are great friends, and nothing more, and one day he tells me that the flat under his is to let. It's on Ladbroke Grove, and even though it's on the wrong end of Ladbroke Grove, in the Kensal Rise bit as opposed to the Notting Hill bit, it is still Ladbroke Grove, which is better than, say, Morden, or Woodford Green, or any of the other places currently within our price range.

We go and view the place. The building is covered in graffiti. 'Very Banksy,' I nod. When we go inside, the atmosphere is undeniably gloomy, but then it is in a basement. 'It has a proper bathroom,' I squeal in delight. 'With a tub and everything! And two bedrooms, which are separate from the kitchen and living room! This is a PALACE!'

My sister is standing in the doorway, looking pale. 'The ceiling,' she says. 'The ceiling.' I look up. It is a murky brown with cracks in it. It looks like it is about to fall down. 'Oh that.' The estate agent waves it away. 'The people upstairs left the bath running and had a bit of a flood. Don't worry, the landlady will deal with it before you move in.'

'We're moving in?' queries my sister.

'Yes, we're moving in!' I say, forgetting that the 'people' above are actually one man called Steve, and that the only time he has used the bath was to fill it with ice and beer when he had a party.

I am so excited about the fact that we are going to be living in an actual flat, and not a box above a chicken shop, that I ignore the fact I find a snail in the bathroom in the first week (how did a snail get all the way in from outside? Outside is a good thirty metres away when you factor in the hall), and the dog turd on the communal front step that I almost tread in during our third week. My sister thinks that we might be sharing the property – for it is a property, not a poxy little bedsit! – with some creatures known as silverfish, which look a bit like a cross between a woodlouse and a centipede, and are known to gravitate towards damp. I see them, too – hey, they aren't pretty – but I think she simply needs to get used to living away from home. 'You're not in Kansas now, Toto,' I say to her, when she moans one morning that there is no hot water and by the way, shouldn't we turn the heating on, given that it is December. 'The heating IS on,' I storm. 'I put it on half an hour ago!' We inspect the boiler, hidden behind Hoovers and brooms in a dingy cupboard, and note that it looks like it's a hundred and fifty years old. It's an old tank one, covered in that weird sticky, fluffy material that looks like it could be poisonous asbestos. I touch the material that looks like poisonous asbestos. It is freezing cold.

'I think the boiler's broken,' I announce.

'Wow,' says my sister, sarcastically. 'It's like living with my very own Super Mario.'

The landlady says she will get it fixed within the week. 'A WEEK?' my sister bellows, before promptly moving back home until the problem is sorted out. Me, I am made of stronger stuff. I decide to stay and tough it out. 'The silverfish will get lonely otherwise,' I sneer, secretly pleased that I will be able to raid her wardrobe of Topshop frocks without having to hide my outfits under a massive coat in the vain hope she won't see what I am wearing. But the problem is her Topshop frocks are just too cold to be worn under anything other than THREE winter coats. At night, I put on two jumpers and three pairs of socks to go to bed. I can see my breath in the air. I take to drinking whisky in an effort to create my own central

75

heating. I fall asleep thinking of Sam, wishing he was here to keep me warm. In the morning, I trudge up one flight of stairs to Steve's, where he lets me have a shower in his avocado bathroom suite.

'Can I bring some washing round tonight?' I ask.

'What am I?' he replies. 'Your DAD?'

'No,' I snap. 'More like my MUM.'

A week passes without so much as a boiler repair man knocking at the door. The landlady, who it turns out lives abroad, says there is a problem with her 'home insurance'. But it will definitely be done within the month. 'THE MONTH?! You mean I have to spend CHRISTMAS in a freezing cold flat with no hot water? Bah humbug to you, too!'

I imagine her lounging on a Spanish beach, cocktail in hand.

I decide to move home briefly, too.

Back in the comforting bosom of my broken family, I regress to a foetal state. I sleep all day and night, waking only to eat and go to the loo. I communicate mostly in grunts, and the often repeated words 'I hate my life'. I am a grown woman in my twenties, and yet you wouldn't know it to look at me.

'But it's Christmas, Bryony, a time of joy and happiness!' I can tell by the rictus grin on her face that my mum is forcing herself to be cheerful during this, her first festive season as a divorcee. We will spend Christmas Day with her, then Boxing Day with Dad and his new girlfriend. If I was less of a fuckwit, not-so-much of a flibbertigibbet, I would have my shit together and be spending my Christmas with a boyfriend, possibly on a beach somewhere hot, but instead I am forced to bend to the will of my parents. I feel like a small child, a fact only reinforced by the gifts Mum gives my sister and me. Matching Hello Kitty pyjamas, pink fluffy jumpers, slippers with rabbit faces on them. I push over-cooked turkey around my plate and play with my phone as we all pretend to watch the Queen's speech. I spend most of my day staring at my mobile, trying to magic some sort of Happy Christmas text from Sam. I decide to send him one myself, one that looks as if I have just casually sent it to everyone in my phone book. 'Happy Christmas! Hope you're having a great one! Bxxx'.

'Yeah, you too,' he replies, on Boxing Day.

'We've got engaged!!! :-)' comes a text immediately after from an old school friend. 'So, so happy, best Christmas ever!'

I want to poke myself in the eye with a turkey baster.

My dad's girlfriend is nice enough, for a woman roughly my own age who has decided to shack up with an old dude. She is really desperate to impress us, trilling in a high-pitched voice about 'the charts' and 'the time she went to Topshop', but I am too busy analysing this three-word text (no kisses, not even one; I mean, it would have been better if he hadn't replied at all) to pay any attention to what she is saying. I realise I am being hopelessly rude, but I also think that as the child of divorced parents, it is totally my prerogative to be hopelessly rude. She's lucky I'm even here at all, and not refusing to meet her on the grounds that my parents would have probably got back together had she not turned up on the scene, the gold-digging strumpet. That's not true, not for one moment, but old Heather Mills over there doesn't have to know that.

'Do you like clubbing?' she says, apropos of nothing as we wait for our second meal of overcooked turkey in as many days.

'Not really,' I muster.

'I used to go clubbing all the time when I was your age,' she perseveres.

'You almost *are* my age,' is all I can think to say.

'Ministry of Sound. The Fridge.' Oh my God. In a moment she is going to start pretending that she was in Manchester for the days of the Hacienda. 'Those were crazy days! Up until three in the morning.' Oooh, mad. 'Dancing to, well, dance music. Such fun!'

I feel sorry for Heather Mills. She is really quite nice. She has use of both of her legs, she is not a gold-digger, and nor is she a mad woman, unless you see the fact she likes my dad as proof of insanity. She's only trying to be kind to the ungrateful, odious offspring of the man she loves.

'Did you take loads of drugs?' says my sister.

'What?' says my dad's new girlfriend.

'You know, drugs.' My sister is flicking through a copy of the Christmas TV guide, not even looking at our potential new stepmother. 'E. Acid. Whatever.'

'Darling!' interjects my father. 'There's no need to ask rude questions.'

'I'm not being rude. I'm trying to have a CON-VER-SAT-ION.'

'Why are you with my dad?' asks my little brother, looking up from the Xbox he has plugged into Dad's TV. 'You're really young and pretty, and he's all old and wrinkly.'

It's only what everyone is thinking.

Back at home that night, my sister and I hatch a plan. We are desperate to see our friends, be with normal people, so we decide that we will throw a New Year's Eve do in our new flat. The memory of the hangover from the last party I had has been erased from my mind, in a process that I imagine is similar to your brain eradicating all recollection of childbirth (given the way I am going, this is the closest I am ever going to get to having a baby). We send out texts, we buy balloons and streamers and Kettle Chips and plastic cups. It's going to be awesome.

At the back of my mind, I'm sure I'm going to be the kind of person who spends New Year's Eve in a cottage in Suffolk, booked far in advance with friends, marshmallows toasting on open fires and glasses of red wine in our hands. It's just I don't like marshmallows and I'm still not sophisticated enough to drink a colour darker than rosé, and the only friends I have who possess the necessary skills to organise such a thing are in couples, and who wants to start the new year with a load of loved-up buffoons who will inevitably go to bed at 12.02 a.m. so that they can get up early and hold hands as they go for a long country walk?

Not me.

So our party guest list is made up entirely of the dregs of society, the people who are too wasted or unmotivated to plan a night that has been in the calendar all year. 'Yeah, I'll come, got nothing else to do,' is the not entirely enthusiastic RSVP we receive from most people. 'Want us to bring anything?' That, I now know, after years of throwing parties, is an entirely rhetorical question. You can't say, 'Yes, actually, could you bring all the booze you're planning to drink on the night so that I don't have to spend a fortune down at Asda stocking up on nasty wine and manky vodka and cans of beer I'm too weak to carry home?' That's not the kind of party I'd want to go to. You wouldn't be a good host if you did that.

And so it is that in an effort to win friends and influence people, we find ourselves spending a fortune down at Asda, stocking up on nasty wine and manky vodka and cans of beer we are too weak to carry home, meaning we have to get a cab, which adds another ten quid to the bill. And let us not forget fags, which, though we were going to give up when they got to £6 a pack, turn out to be really quite addictive, so now they are £8 for 20 and for a good party you need at least two of those, adding another £16 . . .

And you know what happens next, because it has happened before, with my bedsit-warming. If the definition of madness is doing the same thing again and again and hoping for a different result, then, hey, welcome to our twenties. Most of the fags end up tipped on the floor from the makeshift ashtrays we fashion from bowls. The carpet is soaked through from booze. We spend January the first scrubbing up after people we don't even really like, who have gleefully trashed our flat and left us to deal with the mess.

And so starts another chaotic year of my twenties.

4

All aboard the cocaine express

I never meant to do cocaine. I don't really need to. I am naturally verbose, the kind of girl who feels the need to fill every silence because silences make her uncomfortable and nervous and bring her out in a rash and make her face appear all puffy and God, it's not like my face could get any puffier in the first place anyway, what with all the chins my cripplingly low self-esteem has hallucinated on to my face. But where was I? Ahah! Cocaine! Whitish powder that you stick up your nose or rub on your gums if, like someone I once met at a party, you do so much that there is a constant stream of chalky snot running down your face.

So yes, cocaine. I never meant to do it. I didn't need to do it. I'm the first to admit that I was always a bit scared of doing it. Shortly after the bedsit-warming, Chloe took me to another house party. Cool Chloe, as she was becoming known in my head, as compared to Sensible Sally, who would never have approved of a party like this, where guests openly snorted coke off kitchen surfaces and scratched Stone Roses CD cases, and I sat meekly in a corner keeping my hand over my can of Fosters at all times, lest a tiny speck fell in my beer and poisoned me for ever. I couldn't believe what I was witnessing, this flagrant, open taking of a Class A drug, by almost everyone but me. This was way too edgy, way too out there. This was like being transported into some cool New York underground club that I had accidentally been allowed entry to when the woman with the clipboard turned her head for a moment.

Except it wasn't New York. It was Archway. And these people weren't underground – they were totally normal. They were graphic designers and journalists and trainee lawyers and accountants. They were teachers and nurses and there was even a tree surgeon. 'That was wild,' I remarked the next day to Chloe, who laughed at me on account of my innocence. It clearly was about as wild as a cat pissing in its litter tray.

The more I went out, the more it became clear that, to many people, taking a line of cocaine was just what a Friday night entailed, as normal an accompaniment to a pub drink as a bowl of salted peanuts. Why else did every drinking joint in central London have signs up in their loos warning of a ZERO TOLERANCE policy to drug taking, if not because all of their customers had the very opposite of one? Why else were all of the cisterns hidden behind walls, all the lids taken off the toilets, all the remaining available surfaces covered in a greasy substance, cocaine's Kryptonite. 'When you see how much more people can drink on it, how much longer they can stay out for, you realise that it can only ever increase their profits,' explains Chloe to me one evening. 'I mean, it's a sensible business decision actively to encourage people to do cocaine in your pub.'

'Until the police shut you down,' I sniffed.

I'm not trying to excuse my drug-taking. I'm not making out that it was the result of peer-pressure, though I have never been anything other than hopelessly weak-willed when it comes to trying to resist the lure of following the crowd, lemming-like. I'm just trying to explain – to my mum, mostly – that it is normal, everywhere, and that if you have the patience to wait an unknown quantity of time for an unreliable drug dealer unregulated by a body such as, say, Ofcom or Ofsted (what would they call it? Ofcoke? Ofgak?) then it is very easy to get hold of, too.

It was a Sunday night when I finally popped my Class A cherry. Sunday! Who even does drugs on a Sunday? Why wasn't I on the sofa, reading the supplements and waiting for *Downton Abbey*, or whatever the equivalent was at the time? I was twenty-five, and this in itself seems dunderheaded to me. Waiting until you are twenty-five to take Class As is like suddenly taking up smoking in your mid-thirties, having never touched a fag in your life. What is the point, honestly? Why get that far only to cave in when all of your peers have long since moved on to something much more enjoyable, like, say, marriage and a good box set? How typical of me, not to have got my cocaine phase out of the way during my brief time at university, that I have my cool, crazy, out-there phase six years after everybody else.

I was with Chloe at the time. She had just broken up with her boyfriend, whose 'executive' position in television had come to an end when it was found that he had been using the company car account to pick up narcotics, most of which he kept in his desk drawer. It was ironic that Chloe had always been coolly uninterested in drugs until her drug-addict boyfriend had bitten the dust, and that this should have been the event that caused her to go on a four-month bender, taking me with her for much of the way, but I suppose that having watched him get out of his tree for three years, she felt it was time she did the same. It was her turn.

I had gone round to hers for what she called a Sunday roast. This Sunday roast actually turned out to be some pizza and several bottles of wine with some of her gay friends. My sister had just started going out with someone, my wingwoman had become wrapped up in her very own wingman, and so it was that I had spent the weekend mostly alone, sitting in the flat watching trash television and having a takeaway with Steve. When Chloe's text arrived in the early hours of Sunday morning (6 a.m., actually, but I didn't get it until I woke up some hours later, just before midday), I was so thrilled that I actually let out a whoop, and even called my mum to let her know that this really cool girl I worked with had invited me round for lunch. Finally, I was going to be the cool girl, too.

I craved Chloe's company. I was desperate to be her friend. She looked like she had walked off the cover of a Roxy Music album, all cheekbones and slicked back hair and sequinned clothing (even at work, sometimes!). She was almost precisely ten years older than I am, and the idea of actually being friends with someone in their thirties seemed to me incredibly glamorous. She DJed at club nights thrown by her transvestite friends. Rumour had it that she had once been best friends with Kate Moss, but that they'd had a falling out when Kate borrowed one of Chloe's vintage dresses and managed to burn several holes in it, smoking fags. I didn't know if this was true. I was too scared to ask, too frightened of being seen as some wet-behind-the-ear whippersnapper who was desperate for some glamour by proxy.

She was ice cool, Chloe. I looked at her and knew that she would never have let Sam treat her like that, that she would never have been stupid enough to go out with Sam in the first place. Little was known about her background, other than that she left her home in Belfast when she was seventeen and moved to London to seek her fortune, losing any hint of an accent on the way. She was that mysterious that she could wipe all evidence of you from her life in an instant.

She never said please or thank you. She had no time for pathetic niceties. Her wit and wisdom alone were enough to draw people in, to make them fall in love with her. That she wanted me in her life for even two hours on a Sunday afternoon, rather than just as a lunch buddy at work, made me so jubilant that I sat on the Circle Line all the way east to her place with a big fat smile on my face.

Stuff Sam. I had awesome friends like Chloe!

Her flat was a loft apartment – a proper loft apartment, like something out of *Friends* – with exposed stone walls and a mezzanine level up to the bedroom and ensuite bathroom. I had no idea how she afforded it – it was a mystery, like everything else in Chloe's life. I just knew there had to be a walk-in wardrobe, and her extensive collection of heels would be lined up in shoe boxes with their Polaroid picture stuck to them. The walls were lined with limited-edition prints from artist friends, and a signed picture of Gilbert and George. It was like *Dazed* magazine come to life. The open-plan 'living space' had a kitchen with a breakfast bar and all mod cons, looking as if they had never been used. I flushed with shame and embarrassment about the bedsit I had invited her to.

In the middle of it all was a giant coffee table, glass,

expensive looking, lit from beneath. I later discovered it had been designed by Daft Punk – of course it had! – and that Chloe had managed to blag this limited-edition item from the PR of Habitat. On the table rested a collection of back copies of *Jane*, a cool New York magazine for women, which had been closed down for being too niche, too edgy. It was exactly the kind of magazine that Chloe would have worked for if she lived in the States, and now I came to think about it, she probably had (but nowhere as obvious as New York or LA. Chloe would have done somewhere offbeat, like Nashville or New Orleans.) And then there was a 12-inch vinyl copy of an album by Chic, upon which sat several perfectly chopped lines of cocaine.

Chloe's gay friend James sat hunched over it, snorting a line through a straw. I felt a surge of anxiety. I wasn't meant to be here, I didn't belong, I would soon be exposed as a fraud, the kind of loser who had never done a line of cocaine in her life and who had thrown up one of the few times she had smoked dope. 'Darling!' exclaimed James, throwing his head up into the air and sniffing hard. 'Let's get this girl a drink!' He sashayed over to the breakfast bar, where he promptly made me a cocktail in a martini glass that seemed to consist of 99 per cent vodka, 1 per cent crushed ice.

I sat on one of the duck-egg-grey sofas, patted down a shocking pink cushion, and tried to drink the concoction without visibly retching. Chloe was putting on some music I didn't recognise, eighties-sounding disco that she probably listens to all the time out on 'the scene' (oh man, I will never be part of 'the scene') and came tottering across the expensive wood floor in a pair of vintage Louboutins. 'James and I have been having a weekend of decadence to celebrate the fact I'm rid of that loser,' exclaimed Chloe, putting herself down next to me. 'No more finding him collapsed in the wet room' – I bet hers was a proper wet room and everything, not a bucket under a shower like something you would find on a campsite – 'no more evenings spent wondering if he's been killed by a drug dealer. I'm FREEEE BABY!' She threw a head of tousled hair over the album, snorted a line of coke, flicked her fringe out of the way as she sat back up. 'And I am so glad that you can be part of my celebrations. James, Bryony just broke up with her boyfriend, too. He left her to move to SCOTLAND.'

'Poor baby,' says James, reaching across to pat my hand. 'That's got to be worse than being left for another woman. Or another man!'

We all laugh, Chloe and James perhaps a little more than me.

'You need a line darling,' says James, pushing the album cover towards me. My stomach tightens. My cheeks flush red, though that might be from the glass of vodka I have downed for Dutch courage. He throws a straw that has been cut in half to me, and I wonder how I'm going to wipe the dregs of snot from it while still appearing polite.

'I, I . . .' I don't know what to say. I really want to be friends with Chloe and James. I think I might like the sensation of cocaine, and though I probably shouldn't do it on account of my mental history of insecurity, this is probably precisely the reason I will end up taking shed-loads of the stuff. I'm worried I will do it all wrong, that I will blow it out instead of inhaling it, and it will send me mad in an instant, make me strip off all my clothes and run down the street naked. I take a deep breath. 'I've never done cocaine before.' As I hear the words tumble out of my mouth, I wish there is a way to shovel them back in.

'That's OK,' says Chloe, calm, almost motherly, if your mother was sat next to you high on coke, that is. 'I suspected as much from your reaction when we went to that party the other week. You don't have to do anything you don't want to.'

'No, no, I've always meant to try it,' I lie, wiping the straw on the underside of the pillow. I'm worried that Chloe is disappointed she has invited around a total partypooper. I need to impress her, *now*. 'I've just never quite got round to it. Always been waiting for the right opportunity, which is now I guess. *Carpe diem!*'

They look at me as if Harry Potter has just gatecrashed their party.

'Seize the day,' I mutter. 'But just one thing . . .'

'Ahah,' says James, looking at his phone.

'Will it give me a heart attack?'

They laugh.

'No seriously. Will it send me mental? I wouldn't want you having to deal with a mental me . . .'

'Relax,' says Chloe, taking the album away from me and using her credit card to carve one big line into two smaller ones. 'Take one of these. It just takes the edge off drinking. It only lasts, like, twenty minutes. It's not like E.' I nod along, as if I have a clue what it's like to be on E.

'You have done E, right?' asks James.

My pained silence tells them all they need to know.

'Just give it a go,' says James, as if it's an oyster or an olive. (I never had either until I was twenty-four, now *there's* proof of how utterly unprepared for life I am.) 'If you don't like it, you don't ever have to do it again.'

Chloe passes the album back to me. I put it on the Daft Punk table in front of me, hover the straw over one of the tiny lines, and I snort. I snort and the sensation is so shocking and new to my system that I immediately start to cough, sending the remaining lines flying across the album. My eyes begin to water, my nose begins to run, my cheeks burn even redder.

I feel great.

'Woah,' I smile, as Chloe and James laugh at my inept first attempt to do Class A drugs. 'That's pretty awesome.' I look at the white powder, blown all over the album. 'Ohmigodimsosorryimsuchanidiottrustmetofuckevery-thinguplikethat!'

'Don't worry,' says Chloe, simultaneously patting me

on the back and rearranging the scattered cocaine back into lines, before snorting another one. 'You'll get better at it.' And I do. I really do.

That day, afternoon turns into night and then night turns into morning. One small line turns into another big one, which turns into more and more and more. At 10 p.m., James disappears for, what? Ten minutes? Fifteen? An hour? I don't know. But when he returns he has another load of cocaine, wrapped up neatly in a lottery ticket.

It doesn't matter that we all have work tomorrow. I discover, quickly, that I am not the kind of girl to get put off a late night by an early morning. 'If we go to bed at, like, three a.m.,' says Chloe, 'that means we will get five hours sleep, and five hours sleep is totally fine for a day in the office. Plus, it just means we get PAID to have a hangover!' Put like this, it sounds like a great idea. But 3 a.m. rolls around without us even noticing, so caught up are we in talking about Chloe's ex and my ex and James's numerous currents. 'The thing is, one minute he's saying he wants to marry me, the next he's moving to Edinburgh! I mean, what's that all about? I know he's going to regret it one day.'

'I bet he's sitting there now, wondering what the fuck he has done, missing you like crazy,' burbles James, even though Sam is probably fast asleep, like every other normal human being in the world. 'He's given up, like, the best tits in London.'

'Hahaha! Ha! The best tits in London!' I jiggle them up and down in my top. 'Do you know they're like a thirty-two F. I went to this shop and they, like, measured me by looking at me and they said you're a thirty-two F and I said nofuckingway I thought I was a thirty-six D and then they put me in this new bra which cost, like, almost the price of a boob job and then suddenly I was like WOW THAT IS SO AMAZING THEY LOOK SO PERKY but the bra is like MEGA LAME and looks like something a GRANDMA would wear.'

'How did we get onto talking about your boobs?' asks Chloe, who is mixing yet more drinks at the breakfast bar, now covered in the detritus of a good twelve hours abusing drugs and alcohol. 'Did you know, I always had to take my ex to task for staring at other women's tits. Yet ANOTHER reason to be rid of him.'

'I'd hate to have tits,' chimes in James. 'Two lumps of fat strapped to your chest. I mean, how UNWIELDY. I'm surprised you're not all wobbling around the place like Weebles.'

'WEEBLES!' screams Chloe. 'Do you remember them?'

And so starts an hour-long conversation about the toys we had as children.

So we don't make it to bed at 3 a.m. Nor do we manage it at 4 a.m. or 5 a.m. or 6 a.m. At 7 a.m., Chloe suggests we switch to coffee, and think about getting showers. I can borrow some of her clothes, she says. I'm so excited about this I tell her I don't need coffee, and instead pour myself another glass of wine. We finish the cocaine at 7.45 a.m., an hour and a quarter before we are due in the office.

James decides to call in sick, but there is no way that Chloe and I can do that, as we remember that at about 9 p.m. the night before, we both posted on Facebook about the wild time we were having together drinking martinis. I have a shower in Chloe's wet room – a proper wet room, just as I suspected – and wipe my make-up away with her expensive lotions and potions. I brush my teeth with my finger, and gargle with Listerine. I feel empty inside, but strangely, satisfyingly, not hungry. I think it is entirely possible that I might never eat again.

Chloe lends me a pair of leggings and a jumper with sequins on the shoulders, and I look ridiculous, because she is five foot ten and a size 8 while I am five foot five and verging on a size 14. As we leave her flat and walk outside into the sunlight I am suddenly filled with pure panic. There are birds tweeting in the trees, families on the school run and commuters on their way to work, as if nothing has happened. And yet, the world has just changed all around me. I become convinced that everyone knows I have been up all night taking drugs. They must know, from the wild look in my eyes to the stench of martinis now seeping through my skin, from the fact that it's Monday morning and I look as if I'm attending a fancy-dress party as a disco ball. And all the while there is this, hanging in the air around me – I am going to have to wait another twelve hours before I can go to sleep, and it is twenty-four hours since I was last in my bed.

This is going to be the worst day ever.

'Relax,' says Chloe, not for the first time. 'I've got your back!'

Despite deciding on that Monday that I am never, ever doing drugs again, I am doing them again within a fortnight. In fact, I take to casual cocaine use like a duck to water. I assimilate myself into Chloe's group of achingly hip friends, who all work in TV or run club nights or manage comedy acts, and every Friday night there is a massive drinking session, usually somewhere in Soho, followed by another twelve hours spent at someone-or-other's flat, where music TV blares in the background and people take mountains of cocaine while playing Boggle and Scrabble and Trivial Pursuit. These games go on so long that on more than one occasion we find ourselves going through a box of Trivial Pursuit questions several times, so out of our trees that we never remember who the Shah of Iran was during the 1953 coup, despite having been asked the question twice.

When I am high on cocaine, I don't think of Sam. No, that's a lie. I do think of Sam, and I do talk about Sam – a lot – but when I'm thinking and talking about Sam on cocaine, I at least feel I'm in some way getting to the bottom of why it all went so wrong. Cocaine gives me all the answers. It's just a shame that it then brings up more questions the next day, when I'm miserable and sleep-deprived and my seratonin levels are so depleted that I think the sky is about to fall down.

And while I am talking about Sam – a lot – that's not to say that I'm eschewing all men. Quite the opposite. After the wrong-knickers debacle, the margarine incident, as Chloe refers to it, I decide to get back in the saddle and snog men as if it's going out of fashion. When I'm on cocaine, snogging people seems really easy. It loosens my tongue in more ways than one. Whereas before I was a pathetic concoction of insecure and naive, now I am brave, brazen, out there, funny (if I say so myself).

I notch up an impressive tally of lovers in a short space of time. I have liaisons with a banker, a scientist, someone who claims to be a ventriloquist (no jokes at the back), a butcher, a baker, a candle-stick maker. The more lovers I have, I reason, the more attractive I must be. Although I see no future with any of them, each conquest convinces me I am moving myself further and further on from Sam. I'm kidding myself, of course, mixing up emotional detachment with emotional fulfilment, but it's an easy mistake to make when you're in your twenties, and it works for me at the time.

On coke I can do anything, from solving the problems in the Middle East in one hour-long conversation with a stranger, to having a threesome with a couple I have just met at a party. To be fair to me, they are a handsome couple, him all rugged and unshaven, her a bouncy blonde with almost as much dark eye make-up on as I have. At first, I think their interest in me is down to a genuine fascination with journalism, but even in my coked-up state, I can see that they can't hear me over the loudness of the party, and their eyes are glazing over as their pupils dilate and they sniff incessantly. 'This party is lame,' says the girl. 'I tell you what, why don't we go back to our flat where we have loads of champagne and way more drugs and carry on the party there?'

Her boyfriend punches the air in celebration. 'Great idea! Come on Bryony!'

Back at their flat, as I do one of the communal lines of coke off their coffee table, I become aware of a hand on my breast. A female hand. I don't feel nervous or weird – I feel high as a kite. Like anything goes. Coke makes me so all-powerful, so super-on-top-of-the-world, that while I'm on it, it always seems such a shame to restrict my super-snogging skills to the male of the species. So while I have never before had an inkling of an interest for women, on coke it seems totally normal, totally *right*. Snog, snog, snog. Anyone who stands near me on a night out is in danger of ending up with my tongue down their throat.

'Do you think you might decide to become a lesbian?' asks Chloe, when I tell her about the threesome night, about the weirdness of it, of how I had ended up being left out, gathering up my clothes, and sneaking out of their flat into the breaking daylight as they carried on shagging, oblivious to me (how do I even manage to get rejected at a threesome?).

'Why do you say that?' My body contains the dregs of toxins, filling my head with paranoia. 'Do you think everyone will think I'm a lesbian because I had a threesome? Oh God, everyone is going to call me a nymphomaniac lesbian! Everybody!'

'I don't think there's anything wrong with being a nymphomaniac lesbian,' says Chloe. 'Ironically, you might find it actually makes you more attractive to men.'

'It's a good point, but I'm not sure it's the way to go. I think it would be pretty insulting to real gay people if I became gay out of desperation. Plus, I think I could only go out with a girl if she was blonde and had big tits and was just like me, and I don't think that's lesbianism – I think that's actually known as narcissism. So I think I'll leave lesbianism to proper lesbians.'

Nobody calls me a nymphomaniac lesbian, but Chloe's gang do begin to refer to me – affectionately, I think – as the Harlot, their 'little slut'. Bizarrely, and totally against all of the feminist principles fostered within me as I was growing up, I am not affronted by these nicknames. I take them as a compliment. In my mind, people who have lots of luck with members of the opposite sex (and the same sex) must be really attractive. I have read somewhere that promiscuous people are also deeply insecure, and feel that having multiple partners validates them, but I brush that to one side as dreary kitchen-sink-psychology.

Clap-trap. Everyone is insecure. Only psychopaths aren't insecure. What matters is that I am fun, I am out there, and I will almost always be the last woman standing at a party. If I'm bubbly and up all the time, nobody will ever know that deep down I am actually a bubbling cauldron of neuroses. Nobody will cotton on. Right? They'll just think I'm fab and great to be around, right?

Right?

Out of the chaos of my life, a pattern emerges. On Wednesday, Thursday and Friday I go out at night and stay up drinking until the early hours of the morning. On Saturday and Sunday I tell myself that I'm giving up booze, going on a detox, only drinking wheatgrass juice, that kind of thing. On Monday and Tuesday I spend my evenings in the gym, pounding on the tread-mill where I can run away without actually having to go anywhere, swimming up and down a crowded pool, not quite believing that although I haven't touched a drop since Saturday, I still feel terrible, paranoid, morti-fied by behaviour I can't actually remember because I was too out of it.

On Wednesday, as I allow myself an organic fairtrade decaf soya latte – because this, obviously, will make up for all the misery of the drugs trade I have, in my own small way, helped to perpetuate – I start to feel better. I develop a spring in my step, get my perkiness back. One drink won't hurt anyone, I tell myself.

That night, I start the whole goddamn-awful cycle all over again.

I am frequently late for work. I tell myself that it's OK given the first rule of journalism I learnt – in newspapers, time is fluid. Except it isn't really. Deadlines still have to be met, meetings still need to be attended, a paper still has to be produced. If time really was fluid, newspapers wouldn't exist. I become sneaky with my lateness. After a night out, I never wash my hair – washing your hair is a surefire sign that you have been out the night before and have spent the morning scrubbing your excesses away. I invest heavily in dry shampoo, slather my skin in sweet-smelling moisturiser. I bulk buy Smints, so that my breath is always minty fresh. 'Steve,' I whisper, exhaling on him.

'Jesus! Why are you breathing on me?' he doesn't whisper.

'Shh, I want to check I don't stink of booze.'

'Urggh. You don't. You stink of coffee that you've tried to mask heavily with chewing gum or something.'

In my desk drawer I keep: a spare pair of tights, in case I have to come straight into work from a night out; a toothbrush, toothpaste and Listerine for similar reasons; a clean top; a fresh pair of knickers. It never occurs to me to store notebooks or files in there, as everyone else does. Instead, they teeter precariously on my desk, ready to collapse on the man I sit next to. A bit like my life.

I get good with excuses. They become ever-more

fantastical. I even start to believe them myself. Should you ever want to use them, they include:

Pretending that you got halfway to the tube station before realising you had left your wallet at home. 'I just can't believe how utterly stupid I have been!' you say when you finally arrive in the office, flapping your arms about, red-faced and out of breath (you need to run the last few hundred metres to work to give this an air of authenticity). 'I mean, durrrrrrr, only I could be so ditzy!' Colleagues enjoy this one, because it enables them to laugh at you.

Pretending that you had a doctor's appointment for a woman's issue. 'I know I should have told you in advance,' you tell your boss, 'but I have just been too embarrassed about it. I've been hoping it would just go away, right up until I woke up this morning, but it hasn't and so I thought it best to just bite the bullet and take the appointment. I'm really sorry.' Your boss will be too horrified to question this excuse.

Your bus broke down. I mean, what are they going to do? Call up the transport company and check? I hardly think so.

You scraped your eye on the branch of your Christmas tree. I've actually never used this one, but Chloe did. It amused me, not least because Chloe is too stylish ever to consider ruining her loft apartment with a brightly lit, bauble-covered Christmas tree. Furthermore, I'm not sure that Chloe even celebrates Christmas. She told me once that she found it vulgar and that she didn't need presents – if she wanted something, she'd just buy it herself. 'I don't need novelty tat cluttering up my life,' she once said to me. 'I get enough of it with you year round.' But I applaud this excuse, because it's so utterly random you sort of have to believe it, on account of the fact that *surely* nobody would make it up. Chloe even wore an eye-patch that day, a dark purple one made of silk. I think she probably saw it in one of her vintage shops, fell in love with it and decided to make up the excuse purely so she could wear it. She was probably only late because she spent two hours trying to choose exactly the right outfit to go with the eye-patch. I wouldn't try this excuse unless you have exhausted all the rest. And definitely not if it's, say, midsummer.

With my excuses and lateness, I create a role for myself within the organisation, and the role is that of the ditzy flibbertigibbet. Because of that, I seem to get away with things, mostly. In fact, my boss decides to embrace it fully. 'We want to give you a column in the magazine,' she tells me when she calls me into her office. 'A column about being a single girl about town.' I am well chuffed with this, I'm not going to lie. I thought she was going to tell me off for being late, but instead she is congratulating me for it. I am twenty-five years old, and I am being paid to go out and get pissed and write about it. My life could not get any better even if I was to shag Jake Gyllenhaal on a kingsized bed in a six-star hotel and have him feed me fish fingers and chips afterwards.

'This is terrible news,' says Chloe, when I tell her what has happened.

'How could you possibly say that?'

'Because, if we continue in this way, we're going to look like Courtney Love within a year. And that's if we're lucky. If we're unlucky, we're going to look like Kurt Cobain after he's been dug up. We'll look at pictures of us before we went mental, and pictures after, and we'll wonder if we're not looking at those mug shots of addicts that anti-drugs campaigners release to warn of the dangers of crystal meth.'

'I'd never take crystal meth,' I say, my self-restraint almost a matter of pride.

'Oh my God, you're actually joking about this. Don't you get it? Work is what stops people from turning into complete and utter car crashes. Knowing that if you continue to get in late, you'll be sacked and won't be able to pay the bills – well, that's what stops a person from going completely off the rails. But you've just been given permission to go mental. I mean, if we're being honest here, they're going to want you to go utterly loopy, because it makes for better copy. They'll want you to make a total hash out of things – relationships, friendships, everything – so they can publish spicier columns.'

'You mean to say that the more of a mess I make of

my life, the more of a success I will make of my career?'
I smile.

'Exactly,' frowns Chloe.

'My God, I am the luckiest girl in the world.'

All the casual drug abuse, all the binge drinking, it starts to take a toll on me. I find it difficult to sleep, and when I do wake up, I have palpitations. My lower back constantly aches, something to do with the kidneys, I think. I seem to be worried the whole time for no particular reason. I sit at my desk trying to grab hold of the anxiety that floats freely past me. I never manage to.

The best thing to do would be to go on a proper health kick. Maybe a juice diet. It would be just to stop taking drugs and drinking so much. But I can't. I'm not addicted to it, but I am *used* to it. The idea of going out for a few innocent glasses of wine simply does not compute – that's something other people do, people with stable lives. 'What if it takes an OVERDOSE to stop us?' I wail dramatically at Chloe. She lets out an exasperated sigh. 'The only thing you're in danger of overdosing on is too much drama, Bryony.'

So we carry on going out. I think the nadir, a point so low I can never actually bring myself to write about it in one of my columns, is when Chloe introduces me to a reasonably successful author. 'You can talk bookzzzzzzz all night,' is Chloe's opening gambit. The man is a bit older than I am, and not much taller, but he has a rugged arrogance to him that naturally reels me in hook, line and sinker. He tells me about the library he has just had installed in his house, and that he has taken to collecting old copies of a book called *Donkey-Oatey*. 'It's such a wonderful novel,' he says, placing a tiny hand on my knee. I nod along, unaware of what he is talking about, bemused that this self-confessed Man of Letters would be so into a book about a Donkey called Oatey. Perhaps, I tell myself, it was his favourite book as a child. I mean, it hardly sounds grown-up, does it? It hardly sounds *literary*.

'Who wrote this *Donkey Oatey* book?' I finally say, emboldened by a line of coke snorted with him in the disabled loos of the bar.

'You've never heard of *Donkey Oatey*?' he says, blinking disbelief out of his brown eyes, wiping flecks of white powder from above his lip.

'Should I have?' I stutter. 'My parents must have deprived me of that particular children's classic!'

He gives me a look I would recognise anywhere, one that involves raised eyebrows and scrunched-up noses. It is the 'are you having a laugh?' look.

'You've never heard of *Donkey Oatey*?' he repeats. 'Defining book of the seventeenth century and the Spanish Golden Age? The tome often described as the BEST BOOK EVER WRITTEN?'

'Oh!' I say, my body immediately relaxing. 'You mean *Don Quixote*!'

I pronounce it phonetically.

He starts laughing. He actually thinks I have made a joke.

'Just a little literary game I like to play!' I say, desperate to save face. He believes me. He carries on laughing. He throws his arms around me and snogs me senseless. 'The moment I walked in here,' he whispers, 'I immediately noticed you. You are the most beautiful girl in the room.'

Well of course I go home with him.

We kiss all the way back to his house – a house! – situated in a fashionable part of London. The windows are filled with expensive shutters and the front door is painted bright orange. I bet his neighbours are in rock bands and cult movies and on Booker Prize judging panels. I bet he bumps into David Walliams when he goes to buy a bottle of wine from the local off-licence. I bet if he had a dog (he doesn't have a dog, but stay with me on this one), the dog would be friends with Geri Halliwell's dog, and during long Sunday lunches at the massive oak dining table in his basement kitchen, everyone would make jokes about bumping into Fido's girlfriend on Primrose Hill, 'and her Chihuahua was there, too!'

Poor Geri Halliwell. I totally identify with Geri Halliwell. I just know that if I ever became a billionaire from being in a multimillion-selling girl band, I would totally be Geri Halliwell, the broken-hearted bulimic one, as opposed to, say, the stick thin one with the hot husband, or the crazy sexy one with several hot husbands.

He unlocks the front door, opening it into a hall full of limestone and beautiful lighting, with two bikes (two?) propped against a radiator. 'Just wait there!' he says, running into the living room, and then up the stairs, before running back down to the hall, out of breath and panting, like the pet dog he doesn't have. 'Sorry,' he says, taking my hand and leading me into the 'reception room' (living room). 'Just wanted to make sure the place wasn't a complete mess before you came in!'

I look around the place, at the minimalist furniture and the white floors, and the bookshelves holding the odd directional vase and, totally weirdly, picture frames that seem to have fallen over. They are the only things that look out of place here. This house has clearly not been messy since the builders employed by the expensive architects moved out.

'You didn't have to do that,' I say, politely. 'Your house is wonderful!'

In my head, I have already moved in.

He sits me down on a sofa that isn't covered in rugs because there are no beer stains or fag burns to hide. It is immaculate, cream, probably made to order at great expense. 'Do you want a drink?' he says, not waiting for an answer. 'Wine? Beer? A liqueur?' He leaves the room and I hear him padding down the stairs to what I presume is the kitchen, the clink of glasses echoing up the stairs.

Obviously, I have a look at the upturned photo frames. In one of them his arms are around a pretty brunette, both of them smiling as they sit on a boat, the Golden Gate bridge in the background. In another the same girl is standing, thumbs aloft, on top of some sort of hill, or maybe even a mountain. My heart sinks. There will never be a picture of me post-hike in any man's house. I will never be that girl. I will never be the immaculate, gorgeous, Everest-conquering girlfriend, who is currently probably away volunteering in an Indian orphanage. For a moment I feel hollow and dejected. Then I do what all skanky, coke-addled sluts with very little self-esteem do when placed in this situation: I tell myself that there is probably a problem in their relationship, as if this makes what I am doing – what he is doing – OK.

I don't do what I have been brought up to do, what all the women's magazines in the world have taught me to do. I don't leave the photo frames up, to show this two-timing scumbag that I know his game and I don't want to play any part in it. No. Do you know what I do? Yep. I return the frames to how he left them, and tell myself the mantra of the other woman: 'it's his problem, not mine.' I'm here now, so to hell with it. He comes back into the room bearing champagne flutes and a bottle of Veuve Clicquot, and all is immediately forgiven. I smile my sexiest smile, take a glass and throw it down my neck in one. 'You're quite a girl,' he says, coming over a bit Alan Partridge, seeming a little less sexy than he did ten minutes ago ('I'm here now,' I tell myself again, 'so to hell with it.') He removes a wrap of cocaine from his jeans pocket and places it down on the glass coffee table. 'Do you mind,' he says, 'if I do a line off your tits?'

Do I mind? I probably should. No, scrap that. I totally should. But that would spoil the mood, I tell myself (as if the fact he is trying to hide a girlfriend from me isn't enough of a downer). I'm here now, I tell myself again, so to HELL WITH IT. 'Why not?' I say, all casual, as if this kind of thing happens to me all the time. 'Go for it.'

I dislike almost every part of my body, but I am aware that I have a good pair of breasts on me, a fine rack, as blokes like this would bray. Of course, their noble purpose is to feed my offspring, but right now it looks increasingly unlikely that I will ever have any, so hey, why not use them as surfaces to do narcotics off? I mean, isn't that what every girl dreams will happen to them when they grow up?

Isn't it?

The problem with boobs, though, as surfaces to do narcotics off, is that they are by their very nature curvy, not flat, which means – as I soon find out – that if you are not careful, a lot of the narcotics will end up down your bra. This should be a sort of crazy, sexy, cool situation, but as I kneel on the floor, trying delicately to remove my bra so I can retrieve his drugs, careful that my boobs don't flop out too quickly and squish any powder in that sweaty bit between them and your stomach, I realise the situation is just crazy.

'Perhaps if you just lay flat on the floor,' suggests the

author, demonstrating for me the position I should be in, 'and cupped your bosom' – did he actually just use the word bosom? – 'then it would be a more stable environment for me to do the drugs.' A more dignified one, too, than the current kneeling position I found myself in? No, I don't think dignity even comes into it any more, given that he is currently directing me as if I am a piece of flat-pack Ikea furniture. This, I think, as I lie on the floor and stare at his elaborately corniced ceiling, is the life.

He starts kissing me again, slobbering all over me, trying to remove the rest of my clothes. 'Can I have a line?' I ask, as he wriggles on top of me. 'Don't you just want to get to it?' he replies, wriggling some more.

No, I think. I just want to do loads of your drugs and drink lots of your fine booze before calling a cab home.

'Can't we just have another drink first?' I say, trying another sexy smile while simultaneously attempting to cup my boobs and protect what little modesty I might have left. He stands up, goes and sits on the sofa. In an instant, his mood has changed, one moment frisky and playful, the next annoyed and impatient. 'If you really want,' he grumbles, refilling our glasses without even looking at me. 'But it's gone two a.m. and I have a lot of work to do tomorrow, so maybe it would be better if you just went home.'

I actually feel fretful and guilty, as if I have led him on. This man who has a girlfriend has made *me* feel as if I have done something wrong. 'Sorry,' I actually say, moving up to the sofa next to him and uncupping my boobs, in an attempt to lighten the mood. 'It would be much more fun to get to it.'

And so it is that we have uncomfortable, perfunctory, brief sex, not on his sofa – good God, we wouldn't want to leave a stain on the cushions now, would we? – but on the floor, my hips digging into the wood as he grunts on top of me. And when it's over, thankfully very quickly, he says that it is probably best I don't stay, as he needs a good night's sleep and anyway, I probably want to get home to my own bed. He orders me a cab. The wait for it is the longest ten minutes of my life.

And in the taxi home, I am just glad he used a condom, one he produced from his wallet, the presumptuous, arrogant bastard. But I don't hate him as much as I hate myself, allowing my body to be used as a drugs and sperm receptacle before being cast aside. The cab driver has Magic FM on the radio, playing sad love songs. I cry all the way home. This is my overdose moment. This is when I know that the drugs don't work, and that they have to stop. I cannot carry on in this perpetual cycle of self-medicating. I just want to feel healthy again. I just want to feel like me.

5

'I live my life vicariously through you . . .' and other phrases you don't want to hear when you're single

It's not like all my friends are fuckwits. Some of them, like Sally and Andy, are in happy, contented relationships, the odd one actually owns a house, and a few of them have even started to have *babies*. The first time a friend told me that she and her partner were pregnant, I had to remind myself that I was supposed to be thrilled for them, so horrified was I on their behalf because clearly this meant that their lives as they knew them were over. It was almost as if they had just told me they had a terminal illness, rather than that they were about to bring new life into the world.

These friends are people I have known since school,

girls who had exactly the same start as I did, but whose lives have somehow gone off in completely different directions. We are now so poles apart that I might as well be scanning their food in Sainsbury's. My mother asks how Jessica is, knowing full well that Jessica is married with a four-month-old baby and an Islington townhouse, and I see her eyes go all misty in recognition of what might have been; I see her trying to work out what it was she obviously did so wrong.

Although getting married and having babies by the time I turned thirty seemed like the obvious path for me, the norm, just something that was going to happen, I now see that, given only five years of my twenties are left, this might be quite an ask, akin to me becoming an astronaut on the Chinese Space Programme. The truth is, at this point I'm not even sure I want kids – or more precisely, I'm not sure kids would want me. I seem barely capable of keeping myself alive from one day to the next, let alone anyone else.

Chloe says that children turn people into dreadful drips, and while I can she has a point, I secretly dream of being a dreadful drip. I know it's not really the done thing to admit, but there it is, in black and white. I long for my life to return to the same state of dull mediocrity that existed before my parents got divorced and my sister and I started lodging with a family of silverfish; before I started having sex with men who liked butter and snorting cocaine off my breasts. At work, I listen to mothers and

113

fathers talk about weekends at the zoo, and recipes they are going to cook, and box sets they are watching, and I think it sounds heavenly, this totally normal, dull way of life. I love the idea of weekends filled with tedious tasks, as opposed to weekends spent counting the hours until it's Monday again and I can go to work and see people. Most of my friends are coupled up or busy – they time-table every weekend to the minute, while I spend hours loafing on a sofa watching *Keeping Up With The Kardashians*, feeling stupid because, although I know what I want, I have no idea how to get it. When I look back now, I want to laugh. How could I have hated long lie-ins and lazy weekends?

Of course, I never let on that I think any of this. 'Yawn, box-set bores!' I taunt, before announcing with *faux*-pride that I have never seen *The Wire* or *The West Wing*. 'Who needs faked drama when there's so much of the real stuff in your life?!' I caterwaul. In fact, the reason I haven't watched TV for over three months is a little more prosaic than that. I'm always out because I can't stand to be in. My flat is tiny and cold and damp and the silverfish are not good conversationalists. My sister is wrapped up in her new boyfriend, always at his – I may as well be living alone again for all the times I see her. The concept of us cooking together and watching *Coronation Street*, like normal flatmates, seems an alien one. The one time I did stay in on a weeknight, I wondered how people didn't go mad with boredom, how they managed to fill up the hours between 7.30 and 11 p.m. without resorting to drink. And speaking of drink, how on earth did they get to sleep without it?

My friends and colleagues with loved ones in their lives never go out, and when they do, it's to something like *the theatre*. This is probably one of the reasons my life veered away from the traditional path – the only culture in my life is in the fat-free yoghurt that has been sitting in my fridge for the past two months. The last time I went to the theatre it was during my A-levels, to an amateur production of *King Lear*, by the end of which I was tempted to pluck out my own eyes.

They will also make an exception to go out to dinner. I'm sorry, but I find going out to dinner about as appealing as that moment you are a bit sick in your mouth, and you realise you are going to have to swallow it back down so nobody in the room notices. It doesn't matter how nice the food is, it just gets in the way of the booze, and smoking fags, and you always end up sat next to some dork who wants to tell you about his past as a student revolutionary, or his present as – ha! – a corporate lawyer, and then at the end it costs an arm and a leg and you get embarrassed when you have to point out that while it would initially seem sensible to split it seven ways, you had neither a starter nor a dessert and you certainly didn't bother with a coffee, and then everyone else brings out wallets full of bank cards, paying with British Airways Air Miles credit cards ('We managed to fly to New York business class thanks to this baby!'), while you scrounge around among your monthly travel card and your Boots' Advantage for your Halifax Visa and pray that it doesn't get declined.

So maybe if I liked fine dining and theatre a bit more, and pubs and Justin Timberlake a bit less, I would be living in a four-bedroomed house in Notting Hill with my banker husband and our litter of small children. But then I would probably be miserable deep down inside, feeling trapped and unable to show anyone the real me.

'Hang on,' says Chloe. 'You're miserable anyway. Might as well be miserable in a nice house rather than a death-trap flat.'

That reminded me of the time I bought a homeless person a sandwich, telling Chloe that if I gave him money, he would only spend it all on drink and drugs. 'So?' she said, incredulous. 'What ELSE is there to spend your cash on?'

But anyway. I tell myself that the rollercoaster of my life is too much fun to get off yet, and that friends who have matched up with the first man they met during Fresher's Week will probably be happy until their mid-to-late forties only, when they will discover they have more in common than they first thought, namely, the local yoga teacher Dinah. But that is bitter, twisted, not really fair of me. I'm just jealous of them, of that I'm well aware. I still see them, obviously, once or twice a year. And every time I do I remember why our meetings are so rare. I realise what the problem is. It isn't that they might eventually grow apart from their husbands, it's that I have grown apart from them. It's that Sally, whom I've known since I was eleven and with whom I've been through so much, no longer has anything in common with me; or more pertinently, I no longer have anything in common with her. It's the things she says, the dictionary of the smug married, the fact that every time I see her and Andy, I feel like some Budgens version of Bridget Jones, ten years after it was actually acceptable to be anything like Bridget Jones. It's that every time I see Sally and Andy, I have to listen to things like this:

'We live our lives vicariously through you.'

Sally and Andy – Sandy, as they now like to be known – invite you round to 'their' house – everything now is theirs, ours or we – for a 'supper' party. The very fact that they are throwing a 'supper' party rather than a dinner party should set alarm bells ringing, but you accept anyway, because you have pulled out at the last minute the preceding six times (you had to, err, work late, you told them, when in reality you couldn't stand the idea of having to trek to Putney only to spend the evening consumed with jealousy and feelings of inadequacy because you are not enrolled in a pension scheme and you will never be able to afford a shoebox – no, really, the only footwear you can afford at the moment are the cheap 'ballet pumps' sold in Primark without a box, shoes that would probably cripple a proper dancer and will fall apart the moment they are exposed to rain).

You arrive at the door fifteen minutes late, clutching a bunch of droopy chrysanthemums – 'crisanthemimums', as you will later pronounce them – bought from the nearby Tesco Metro ('It's so sad,' Sandy will later say, 'that the march of the big supermarkets is spelling the end for our local shops') and a bottle of Jacob's Creek. Jacob's Creek is posh, right? 'I'm so sorry,' you splutter, 'had a mad day,' neglecting to mention that said day involved nothing more than cleaning your desk of all the files and press releases that were threatening to engulf the colleague to your right. Sandy smile, ushering you inside in a flurry of 'not to worries, we expected nothing less from you'. They ask you if you wouldn't mind taking off your shoes – they have just had new carpet put in. 'We stupidly chose a colour called "ash",' they say, motioning to their pristine charcoal floor. 'Realised when we got it that it was likely to get covered in mud when Mummy and Daddy come round with the Lab, but by then it was too late!' You decide to make a joke. 'Oh, I know what it's like,' you titter. 'My floor is covered in ash too!'

AHAHAHAHAHAH.

You take off your 'ballet pumps' and are instantly overcome with paranoia because it has been raining all day and the combination of soggy fifty deniers and a pair of cheap shoes has no doubt instantly turned your feet into some sort of breeding ground for stinking bacteria. You wonder how you are going to be able to pull your perfume out of your bag and spray your feet without anyone seeing. Plus, the 'ATMOSPHERE' written across your soles, in an attempt to make the Primark brand look classier, is fooling nobody. Next to immaculate kitten heels from Hobbs, LK Bennett and Russell and Bromley, you wish the ash carpet would just open up and swallow you whole.

'Come into the drawing room,' says Sandy. 'The what?' you want to say. 'You mean the sitting room? The living room?' No, they don't mean the living room, because there's one of those across the hall. This is the drawing room, the show-off room, the one in which they host pre-supper drinks, in proper wine glasses, and not ones from Ikea that have chips around the rim so that whenever you take a sip (or a gulp, if you're me), you risk ripping your mouth to pieces. 'Now Bryony's here,' says your host, walking you into the *drawing room*, 'the fun can start!'

Your heart sinks.

You look around the drawing room at the other supper guests, all in suits and pencil skirts and tights that don't have ladders down them. Or up them, depending on which way you are inclined to look at these things. The women wear twinkling diamonds on their engagement fingers, their hair so glossy that you imagine they get up at 5 a.m. to blow dry it. The men are all clean cut, their shirts pressed by the cleaner they pay to come twice a week.

'Bryony's a JOURNALIST,' says your host, in such a way that she clearly expects the room to let out a collective gasp.

'If you can call writing about boy bands and hotel heiresses journalism,' I mutter to my manky feet.

'Don't be modest!' continues the host, to which you would like to reply that you are not being modest, just truthful.

I think that my career choice is probably a large part of why my life veered off in such a wildly chaotic direction. When I decided I wanted to be a 'writer' (how lofty!), I was naive and more than a little bit snotty about friends who had set their sights on a career in law, or banking, or management consultancy, whatever that happened to be. They were selling their souls, I thought, and yet now I can see that they were selling their souls to be able to buy a nice house. Their chosen career paths introduced them to sensible people, eligible people, whereas mine has careered me into the path of alcoholics and flibbertigibbets to whom the word 'committed' means entry to a mental asylum. Who, exactly, is happier now, eh?

'Bryony,' says someone, 'I hear you're a bit of a party girl . . .'

Oh God, shoot me now.

'We were just having a totally yawnsome conversation about politics,' says someone else, 'but now you're here perhaps we can actually talk about something titillating . . .'

'Bryony,' says Sandy, with a wink and a nudge, 'tell everyone the Russell Brand story!'

Oh no. Not the Russell Brand story. Anything but the Russell Brand story. I grimace. Shake my head. The look of expectation on everyone's face tells me that they have already heard the Russell Brand story – being fifteen minutes late has actually enabled Sandy to brief their guests about the total fuckwit on her way – and they now fully expect to hear it from the horse's mouth. And because I don't want to disappoint these people I have never met, I end up telling them about the time I slept with a comedian who then dumped me for a supermodel.

I tell them that, a few months previously, I had been sent to interview a comedian on the cusp of fame, who at the time was presenting a spin-off *Big Brother* show. He wasn't really big back then, so I didn't know that he had a reputation, or that there were, by his own admission, hundreds of other girls with a Russell Brand story, all of whom were also probably asked to wheel it out at dinner parties. I tell them that this comedian on the cusp of fame had spent the whole of our interview asking if he could kiss me, and every time I said no, it only caused him to ask me more; that because he didn't look like a womaniser – he was dressed like Fagin and had hair so long that dreadlocks had begun to form under their own steam – it took me a while to work out that he was trying to seduce me; that after the interview was over, he got my number off his PR and proceeded to bombard me with texts and calls, singing James Blunt's 'You're Beautiful' down the line as I attempted to get a coffee from the canteen; and that after a few weeks of this, I eventually agreed to go on a date with him.

I told them all about the date, about how curiously traditional it was. This former heroin addict had taken me for lunch and then to the cinema to see a film about maths called *Proof*, and after that he had suggested we went back to his for some drinks. I told them how funny it was that, despite the fact he didn't drink, he had made sure his fridge was stocked with alcohol for me, and how, after a few glasses of wine in front of a Chelsea match, I had gone to bed with him.

I told them that we had seen each other another couple of times, and that just as quickly as he had started to text and call me, he had stopped. I told them that I had found it curious and wondered if he might be dead, and that this question had been answered for me when, a couple of days later, I opened the *Sun* and saw him holding hands with Kate Moss. Shortly afterwards, his fame erupted. 'So if you want to become a Hollywood star and start sleeping with supermodels,' I joked, 'then sleep with me!'

The room chuckled. 'That's Bryony for you,' announced Sally, sitting on the arm of Andy's chair, putting her arms around him. 'We always say, *we live our lives vicariously through you!*'

Are there seven more patronising words than these?

We live our lives vicariously through you, by which we mean to say: we are trying to make you feel better about what a complete and utter mess your life is, by pretending that we think it's fun and exciting while ours is superdull in contrast. But it's not! You just know, when you look at your hosts, that in actual fact they freaking *love* going to the garden centre on a Sunday morning. They would rather eat slugs than sleep with Russell Brand. When they say they live their lives vicariously through you, what they really mean is they are overcome with relief that it's you and not them who's having to go through the motions of being a single person in London in the early twenty-first century.

I mean, what am I to these people? A performing monkey? A clown, invited along to regale them with tales of one-night stands, casual drug use and an inability to pay my council tax on time? Someone they can go home and tell their friends about, this girl they once met who CAN'T AFFORD TO SHOP AT WAITROSE? Have I become an unwitting participant in some kind of educational programme set up to show these people how their lives could be if they really mucked them up, so that when they go home to their non-rented beds and snuggle up under Egyptian cotton sheets, they can count their blessings (not to mention the threads in their linen)? Why can't I talk about politics, too? I know who the Chancellor of the Exchequer is, I want to scream. I know my Miliband from MY BALLS! Were I not completely outnumbered by these buffoons, I'd probably start flinging smoked-salmon blinis at them.

'Bryony,' says our hostess, as we make our way to the dinner table, 'tell everyone about the wrong-knickers story . . .'

And do you know what? Instead of telling my host to FUCK OFF, I put on my performing-monkey hat, slap on my clown outfit, and as we tuck into our avocado with warm bacon vinaigrette, I start to tell them all the wrong-knickers story. I add dramatic pauses, throw in hand movements and even put on a comedy accent when pretending to be Josh, because – and here's the unavoidable truth – I really enjoy making my friends smile. While their laughter should annoy me, instead it puffs me up, filling the space where my self-esteem should be. Over time, I will become addicted to this scenario, me telling some embarrassing sex story to a room full of almost strangers who have never done it anywhere more exotic than the bottom of the bed, before returning to my manky flat, at least feeling like the funniest girl in the world. I start to do ever more crazy things so that I have ever more crazy stories to regale people with at dinner parties, or just in the pub – allowing men to snort coke off my tits, for instance, or having a threesome. I am deluded enough to believe that everyone is laughing with me. I never allow the possibility to enter my mind that they might be laughing *at* me. And even if they are, I don't care, because at last

I am something – I am the funny girl, the one who makes everyone else smile.

'We love seeing Auntie Bryony, don't we pumpkin?'

When I was growing up, I wanted to become many things. A unicorn, a dolphin, a marine biologist. At one point, an Arsenal footballer, although my inability to do anything even vaguely athletic soon put paid to that. I tell you what I absolutely didn't want to be, though – an aunt. It's not that I have ever wished infertility on my siblings. It's more that the word 'auntie' sounds so spinsterly. Aunt, as in maiden. Maiden, not as in young strumpet in a bodice, who is about to be swept off her feet by Robin Hood.

And yet, thanks to the few friends I have with babies, I have become an aunt. Whenever I seem them, it's all 'Auntie Bryony' this, and 'Auntie Bryony' that, as if their two-month-old child has a clue who I am. But the truth is, this unflattering moniker is used not for the baby's benefit. It's used entirely for the purpose of making his or her parents feel better because they didn't make you a godmother.

While some people collect godchildren like Advantage card points, I am still waiting for an invitation to sponsor the baptism of a child. This is a shame. I really like the idea of being a godmother. A fairy godmother, if you please. I just know I would be really good at it. Never mind that the only thing I do religiously is smoke fags and drink wine – it seems natural to me that my friends would want at least one party girl in their godparent portfolio, someone who can make them feel cool by proxy. In my head, I have bought all the gifts I would get my new godkid – tiny Converse trainers, mini Rolling Stones T-shirts, silly hats that make them look like teddy bears. I have imagined trips to the swings, where I would ply them with sweets that they otherwise weren't allowed, because I was the cool godparent, the one they always wanted to be with. And yet still, I can't shake off that auntie tag.

I don't know if this has anything to do with the time I babysat the six-month-old son of my friends Melissa and Tim. It was the first time they had gone out since they had the baby, and so it was a big deal. I felt flattered that they had asked me, quite sure it was proof that they were soon going to ask me to be godmother. As they got ready, Melissa told me that baby Miles had that week learnt to sit up. 'Just sit behind him so that he doesn't fall back,' she shouted from the bedroom, where she was painting her face with make-up for the first time in forever. I did as I was told. What I hadn't counted on was little baby Miles falling forward, right into the sharp leg of their coffee table.

Miles immediately started to screech, and I almost did, too. Melissa came barrelling in to the living room, crying, 'What have you done?' over and over as she grabbed her bawling son from me and held him to her. 'He just banged his head on the leg of the coffee table,' I tried to explain, immediately regretting my use of the word 'just'. A huge, purple bump had appeared over Miles's forehead. He had started screaming in several different tones, all at the same time.

'Oh my God, oh my God,' I tried to swallow the dose of stinging shame that had just been administered. I started to apologise, over and over again.

'We need to go to the hospital,' Melissa had started to tell Tim, who had also come running to the living room. 'We need to take him NOW!' He nodded in agreement as he tried to soothe his baby son. I felt nothing but horror and guilt.

'You stay here, Bryony,' ordered Melissa. 'In the unlikely event we get Miles seen quickly, and nothing is wrong with him, we might just be able to salvage this evening.' They left the flat, slamming the door behind them. I spent the next three hours sitting on the sofa in my own shame, checking my phone for any news.

When they finally returned, Miles was smiling as he clutched a rattle. I breathed a sigh of relief. 'He's fine,' said Melissa. 'But our evening is ruined.'

'Don't be like that,' chided Tim. 'It isn't Bryony's fault. Babies are always knocking into things; it's not as if she pushed him.'

He was right. I hadn't.

'I know, I know,' said Melissa, putting her arm around me. 'I'm sorry for snapping. You weren't to know he was going to fall forward. You don't have a baby. It's not like you have that in-built maternal instinct.' I closed my eyes for the moment. So it was OK then. I wasn't a child beater; I was just single. I left them to their evening. Auntie Bryony it was, then.

'I wish I was single again.'

A bare-faced lie told by coupled-up friends on the rare occasions when they come out with you *sans* their other half. Said evening is almost always on a Saturday, when their other half has had to attend a stag do in Belarus. 'Let's go out and get hammered!' exclaims Sally, and you are too kind to tell them that actually, on Saturdays, you usually stay in eating takeaway because you have gone out every night of the week, like most single people, and are now knackered and hungover. And because on Saturday night, all bars and pubs are full of people like them, fairweather socialisers who can't hold their drink and have their head down a toilet bowl by 9.30 p.m.

'Can you take me somewhere superfun and glamorous?' asks Sally, as if your life is one long episode of *Sex and the City* as opposed to, say, all seven series of *Only Fools and Horses*. So now you have to put your mind to finding somewhere to go, when all you really want to do is suggest she comes round and has a bottle of wine while we laugh at the silly costumes on *Strictly Come Dancing*.

'I could come round at five-ish and we could get ready together with some Prosecco,' Sally suggests. Is she actually fifteen years old? She arrives at five on the dot carrying a dry cleaner's bag that contains a cocktail dress, three different pairs of heels to dither over, and a bag full of cosmetics that is so large you wonder if it doesn't actually belong to a professional make-up artist.

'Let the fun begin!' beams Sally, stepping over the pizza leaflets in the doorway, asking if she can hang her dress in your wardrobe, meaning you then have to explain that your wardrobe is actually a clothes rail from Ikea. She tells you she thought she'd leave her clothes and make-up bag here, and pick them up some time next week – your flat is really big enough to accommodate all of her crap on top of yours.

Eventually, Sally inquires where you will be going that night, and you have to admit to her that you're not really sure; you thought she could choose. 'OK,' says an increasingly disappointed Sally. 'Why don't we go to Clapham?' At this point, your whole body lets out an involuntary spasm. Please no, not Clapham. Anywhere but Clapham. I would take Leicester Square over Clapham, land of the braying rugger bugger dressed head to toe in Hackett clothing, chinos and loafers with red socks.

'OK,' you say, brain too addled from last night's drinka-thon to think of anywhere else, 'let's go to Clapham.'

Although it's only a couple of miles as the crow flies, it takes almost two hours to get to Clapham. This is the other reason you do not go out on a Saturday: the public-transport system tends to shut down due to planned engineering works, or other such gubbins. You arrive in Clapham desperate for a drink, a sensation only intensified by the scene laid bare before you – queues snaking out of bars, smashed beer bottles outside packed pubs, men dressed as Vikings and golfers, braying into the cold winter's night. In the morning, it will look like the good residents of Clapham have survived some sort of zombie apocalypse.

'Isn't this just BRILLIANT?' asks Sally, bundling you towards a bar advertising an all-day happy hour, only a tenner to get in. The doorman stamps your hand with some unidentifiable shape that will take three days to scrub off in the bath. You head towards the bar, the queue five deep before you. Another reason you never go out on a weekend. Sally eventually pushes to the front, and returns twenty minutes later with a tray of Jager bombs.

The 'fun' really does begin.

Over the heavy thump thump of comedy dance music – 'Macarena', 'Saturday Night', 'YMCA' – you can just about hear Sally bang on about how envious she is of your life. In a way, you wish the music was louder, so that you didn't have to hear this disingenuous bilge at all. 'I JUST LOOK AT YOU AND THINK, MY GOD, SHE IS REALLY LIVING THE DREAM,' you actually make out at one point, and 'YOUR LIFE IS WHAT YOUR TWENTIES ARE SUPPOSED TO BE ALL ABOUT.'

Bugger me, she must be pissed.

'DON'T GET ME WRONG,' she screeches on, 'BECAUSE I LOVE ANDY, WE HAVE A GREAT TIME TOGETHER AND I KNOW THAT HE IS THE MAN I WANT TO MARRY. BUT SOMETIMES I JUST WISH I WAS HAVING FUN, HAVING THE KIND OF LIFE YOU ARE.'

Really? Living in a freezing cold flat with vermin? Having sex with men who forget to tell you they have girlfriends? 'WHICH PART OF THAT DO YOU ENVY IN PARTICULAR?' you want to shout back, but instead you just nod along. She's not finished. She hasn't even got properly started.

'YOU KNOW, AT TIMES LIKE THIS, I JUST WISH I WAS SINGLE.'

Seriously? No, I don't think so. Nobody actually wants to be single, unless they are a sociopath or happen to be going out with a sociopath. And Andy may be many things – a bit dull, seemingly passionate only about the fortunes of the Saracens, a bit too fond of boating shoes – but a sociopath he is not. The fact is, we are biologically created not to want to be single. Whether we like it or not, our sole purpose, essentially, is to get our rocks off with someone else and spawn with them. Us humans are social creatures, and it is simply not in our genetic make-up ever to truly DESIRE TO BE SINGLE.

'TOMORROW YOU WILL GET A LOVELY LIE-IN, BE ABLE TO DO WHATEVER YOU WANT,' she bangs

131

on, as if your lie-in won't consist of you wallowing in your own sweat and self-loathing, 'BUT I HAVE TO GET UP AND START PREPARING A ROAST, AND THEN I HAVE TO DRIVE TO STANSTED TO PICK UP ANDY, AND THEN YOU GET TO PUT ALL YOUR ENERGY INTO HAVING A FABULOUS, FUN CAREER, WHILE I STARE DOWN THE BARREL OF BECOMING A DUTIFUL BANKER'S WIFE, GETTING PREGNANT AND FAT AND SPENDING THE REST OF MY LIFE WITH A BABY HANGING OFF MY TITS, AS OPPOSED TO YOU, WHO WILL ONLY HAVE TO PUT UP WITH HOT BLOKES HANGING OFF YOUR TITS.'

She bursts into tears. You put your arm around her, tell her you're going to go and get her some more drinks. As you wait in the queue, you comfort yourself with the knowledge that the grass is always greener on the other side, and perhaps you don't want to be almost twenty-six with the rest of your life already mapped out for you.

'Though I sometimes wish I was single, I think you should meet this colleague of Andy's . . .'

Now look. Let's get this straight. I clearly want a boyfriend. I imagine what it would be like to have a boyfriend about once every fifteen minutes. I sometimes find myself fantasising about the feeling of being able to change my status on Facebook to 'in a relationship'. Once, to create an air of mystery about myself should any potential suitor want to stalk me online – but also because I was sick of being defined as alone – I took down the fact that I was single. What I didn't know was that 'Bryony is no longer single' would appear in all of my friends' feeds, prompting a flurry of 'WHO'S THE LUCKY MAN :-)' posts on my wall. So I had to explain that there was no man, lucky or otherwise, which made me seem about as mysterious as a cyclist in a high-vis vest and a helmet with flashing lights.

And yet, despite my obvious desperation for a boyfriend, I still find it irksome if anyone other than myself vocalises this fact, especially if that person happens to be happily settled down themselves. And so it is that, just as they lie about sometimes wishing they were flying solo, I also find myself manipulating the truth whenever I am in the company of couples.

'I'm happy being single,' I lie to them. 'I'm going to enjoy it while it lasts,' I lie to myself, because that suggests I think that this fallow period will one day come to an end. In actual fact, I often imagine I am going to be alone for ever, but I don't want *them* to think that. I want them to believe I am a strong, independent woman, a *bonne viveur*, the kind of girl who has her pick of men but eschews them all because she just doesn't want to be tied down. When my coupled-up friends think of me, I want them to think I am a Beyoncé song COME TO LIFE!

'You know Beyoncé's married, right?' says Chloe when I tell her this. 'And like, expecting her first child. I really don't think anyone is ever going to associate her with you.'

'Beyoncé,' I announce, haughtily, 'is an ESSENCE, not a human being.'

But even though I like to think I am channelling the essence of Beyoncé, I always get the same thing every time I speak to my coupled-up friends like Sandy. 'I'm so jealous that you're single,' they say, 'but while you're on the phone, I really think we should set you up with Andy's colleague so-and-so, who is, like, super handsome and has his own house and an Audi, and he broke up with his girlfriend of five years about four months ago, but he says he's really ready to move on and meet someone else now . . .'

Again, what is it with men? If I had been going out with someone for five years, there is no way I would be ready to move on within four years, let alone four months. This bloke is just like my dad. I don't want to go out with my dad.

'And we've told him all about you, what a party girl you are . . .'

Oh great, he's already shagged me and left me in his head.

'And showed him your Facebook profile picture . . .'

I am wearing a frog hat and smoking a cigar in my Facebook profile picture. (Don't ask.) 'And he thinks you sound like great fun . . .'

See, I told you he had already shagged me and left me.

'And wondered if we could all go out for drinks some time soon.'

'I told you,' I lie once more, 'I'm not looking for anyone right now. I just need some "me" time. Plus, I don't think a man with an Audi and a house is the man for me.'

'Why?' says Sandy. 'Is it because he sounds like TOO GOOD A PROSPECT? Is it because HE ISN'T A COMPLETE LOSER? If you carry on being this picky, you will never meet anyone. And you broke up with Sam like, a hundred years ago.'

'He broke up with me, actually. And I thought you said you were jealous of me being single.'

'For about five minutes a month when Andy farts in my face under the duvet I am,' says coupled-up friend, in a moment of exasperation. 'I just want to see you happy.'

Never, ever, say this to a single woman.

'I AM HAPPY,' I say, slamming the phone down and working out whether I want to a) cry or b) smoke a cigarette. Instead I crawl into bed.

'You'll only find love when you're happy in yourself.'

Oh fuck off. I mean *really*. Fuck off. Who do you think you are? Oprah freaking Winfrey? When you tell me I'll only find love when I'm happy in myself, I want to parrot it back at you in the tone of a five-year-old boy, while pulling a face. This 'advice' – and I use that word very loosely here – isn't just patronising, it's dangerous. It's a green light for me to be even more self-indulgent than I already am, which is, as you might be working out by now, really quite epically self-indulgent. Some days, when I'm telling my coupled-up friends all about the time I did this and the moment I did that, I realise that I display Lady Gaga-like levels of self-indulgence. I mean, I don't know how to be anything else. I am single. The only person I have to think about is me, me, me. You don't have to give me permission to go away and think about myself any more, really you don't.

And anyway, what does being happy in yourself even mean? How do you know when you are happy in yourself? Do you skip through life to a soundtrack of 'Zip-a-Dee-Doo-Dah'? Do you see more rainbows than other people? Do you wake up one morning and notice that you give off a gentle glow, one that attracts decent men rather than the type who want to use you as a surface off which to take drugs? And how, exactly, does one go about becoming happy in oneself? Is it through yoga? Meditation? Anti-blinking-depressants? If you could let me know, your advice MIGHT ACTUALLY BECOME VAGUELY USEFUL.

And since when were every couple you saw happy in themselves? Go for a walk in the park. Accept an invitation to a restaurant, if you really have to. Look around you. There are couples sitting in silence, pushing food around their plates. If they were happy in themselves when they met, they sure as hell aren't now. Let's think of famous couples, and see how happy they have been. Elizabeth Taylor and Richard Burton. Not happy. Eminem and Kim. Really not happy – he wrote a song about wanting to kill her. K-Stew and R-Pattz. So not happy. Charles and Diana. Never been more miserable. I mean, if anything, the more unhappy you are, the more likely you are to attract someone. Who wants to go out with someone who is deliriously, annoyingly happy, and bursting forth with smugness because of it? Not me, that's for sure.

'You'll find love when you least expect it.'

Well, this is totally unhelpful. I don't want to find love when I least expect it. When I least expect it – like when I'm on the loo, or getting my bikini wax, or rummaging through the bins outside for an important document I seem to have lost – is just not a good time for me.

I mean, why is love so selfish? Why does it always have to appear when it wants, with little or no consideration as to when it might be convenient for you – just before a friend's wedding, for example, or shortly after you have been dumped by someone.

Also, and here's the rub, if you are telling someone that they will find love when they least expect it, the chances are, they're expecting it almost all of the time. They are constantly on the lookout, like hawks in search of their prey. On the bus, in the supermarket, down the pub, just brushing their teeth of a morning, they have only one thing on their mind – the expectation of love. Tell someone that it will come along when they are *not* expecting it, and you merely put them on high alert. They tell themselves not to expect it. They only expect it even more. They are waiting, any moment now, for Cupid to fire his dart into them. Here's the thing. We don't want to find love when we least expect it. We want to find it *right now*.

'The problem is, men are intimidated by you.'

To be fair to my friends, this is mostly said to me by my mum, to which I want to reply, 'No, men aren't intimidated by ME, they're intimidated by me having a MAD MOTHER.' She's been saying it since I was fifteen and heartbroken because Theo only wanted to be my friend. 'He's intimidated by you,' she announced, but we both knew that this was wishful thinking. The truth was that after he had finished with Sally, he had moved on and was more interested in the blonde, blue-eyed chick who spent her summers in Scandinavia with her Swedish family.

Now, whenever I go through a break-up (or a man never gets in touch – a break-up would be something approaching progress, I like to think), she trots out the same line. I ask what it is they're supposed to be intimidated of. 'Your career!' states my mother, who has obviously failed to notice that this consists mostly of writing about Kate Middleton's collection of frocks. But I don't believe men are intimidated by a woman with a career, not in this day and age, or at least I can't without wanting to garrotte myself with my work pass. 'Mum, if a bloke is intimidated by me because I happen to have the good fortune to have a job, then he is probably a complete nobber anyway.'

'Don't talk that way, Bryony, it's so coarse and unlady-like!'

'Nobber, nobber, nobber!'

'It's no wonder you can't get a boyfriend when you use language like that!'

'Mum, has your old age caused some confusion and led you to believe that we are living in the nineteenth century?'

'All I'm saying is that it wouldn't hurt for you to be a little bit more traditional and aloof. Men love what they can't have.'

And here we come to the crux of the matter. When my mum says that men are intimidated by me, what she really means is they think I'm a freak because I sometimes text first. Granted, there have been times when my behaviour has been slightly deranged, bordering on stalkerish – refreshing Facebook feeds, wondering if the girl he is standing next to in that picture was humping him on the dancefloor twenty seconds after the picture was taken; looking at the girl in the picture's Facebook feed for clues of a relationship, which meant I was also stalking someone

139

I didn't actually know and hadn't actually ever met, like some sort of socially networked Glenn Close. But unless they ever do actually create that app that allows you to see who has looked at your page, how is anyone going to know you've spent all day looking at their profile?

I suppose there was the time I texted a bloke to apologise for my drunken behaviour, and then when I didn't hear from him for two hours, texted again to apologise for my rambling text message, and then when he was still silent for four hours, texted to ask if he was getting my texts, because my phone was playing up (in actual fact, the only thing that was playing up was me). But really, how rude is it to snog a girl and then not even get in touch the next day to say 'thanks for the memories'? And if I have been intimate with someone, why SHOULDN'T I be able to text them seven times the next day? Eh?

In this day and age, when women are CEOs and heads of state, I simply cannot reconcile that fact with not being allowed to text someone for four days. I can't believe it is still seen as slutty if I put out on a first date. And I'm sure my anger at this is the reason I usually put out four hours after I first meet someone in a bar, never actually getting to a date in the first place.

I know women who stick to the rules and tell blokes they are busy so they seem more alluring, when in actual fact they are staying in to watch *Made in Chelsea*. But I am not one of them. It seems so phoney, so archaic. The

Rules seem unjust and unfair, and abiding by them strikes me as a betrayal of the sisterhood. 'I'm not going to play games,' I tell my mother, because I am a woman with my own mind and any man who goes off me because I have texted twice in an hour can go fuck himself.

I suppose, if I developed self-restraint, only pecked someone on the cheek at the end of an evening, got on with my life as I waited for someone to call me, then made up some bullshit when they eventually did (claiming to be busy for the next two weeks, but maybe I have an opening for them at Christmas 2030), well, then maybe I might have a relationship. But if I have to act like somebody completely different in order to get a boyfriend, then maybe I don't really want one. Maybe I'll just embrace life as a spinster.

Bring it on.

6

How to survive the wedding season

I never receive post, or at least, I never receive post that I want to open. Sometimes, I think my sister and I should buy a twist on one of those 'NO JUNK MAIL' signs for our letterbox, changing it to: 'WE WELCOME JUNK MAIL – EG TAKEAWAY LEAFLETS – BUT PLEASE DO NOT DELIVER ANYTHING ACTUALLY ADDRESSED TO US'. No good can come out of letters addressed to us. They are a) bills, b) bailiff's demands for bills, or c) wedding invitations.

I don't want to seem like a party pooper or a killjoy, but whenever I see a wedding invitation, my heart sinks. It's the exquisitely thick cardboard with gold edges, cardboard so posh you just know it to be the product of the Amazon's rarest, most precious trees. It's the swirly-whirly writing. 'Mr and Mrs so-and-so invite you to the marriage of their daughter, Sally, to Andy, yada yada yada, please RSVP by blah blah, carriages at 2 a.m.' I mean, CARRIAGES? Have you just posted me back to the EIGHTEENTH CENTURY? No, I think I'll go home in a pumpkin, if there's enough signal in the castle you have hired to call and order one.

It's not just that I am a bitter single harpy who only once – ONCE! – was allowed a plus one, and even then, when I started to imagine the possibility of getting a boyfriend within the six months until the wedding, had my hopes cruelly dashed when I was told to bring Chloe. (This was proof, in my mind, that the only double act I was ever going to be part of was a comedy one, sent to entertain people with tales of drunken debauchery.) No, it's not just this – though, obviously, it is a large part of it. It's everything from the hen do to the money spent to the general mania that sweeps over a woman who has just got engaged. You only have to flash a diamond at them and bingo, they go from wanting to save the world to wanting to sit in judgement of it, like the fairy princess they believe themselves to be. Not everyone becomes demented, obviously. There are people who have quiet ceremonies in town halls followed by small lunches with close friends and family. But I hate them even more. At least with the fairy princesses, I have something that allows me to disguise my feelings as reasonable dislike, whereas with the sensible ones my wild jealousy is laid bare for all to see.

It starts with the hen do. Actually, it starts before the hen do. Almost as soon as you have received the cardboard invite, sometimes even prior to receiving the cardboard invite, you receive the email invite to the hen do from the Maid of Honour. Like being a godparent, I have never been asked to be a bridesmaid or a Maid of Honour (a Maid of DISHonour, perhaps), but I have no problem with that. Almost every Maid of Honour I have ever encountered is a control freak, uptight and joyless, the kind of person who genuinely thinks that novelty penis straws are outrageous and 'really great fun, yah', and who is desperate to hire a stripper because they haven't had sex with their own boyfriend or husband for coming up for three months now. Their email sign-off tells you that they are an assistant to the CEO of something or other, a job that you reason must entail very little, given the amount of time they put into organising your friend's hen do, sending you missives asking whether you prefer option one (chocolate making followed by dinner served by naked butlers followed by karaoke), option two (a trip to a spa in Hampshire, costing as much as your monthly rent) or option three (a weekend away in the south of France, costing three times your monthly rent).

If you go for option one, but ask to take part only in the dinner and the karaoke, because you're skint and you really don't want to spend three hours with strangers rolling chocolate bonbons that actually look a bit like dog poo, you receive a cool reply telling you to transfer the sum of £154.37 to the Maid of Honour's bank account, please, a sum which for some reason known only to the Fanny Fusspot in charge of events does not include drinks or transport. This means you must add another £70 on top of the £154.37 already paid, and say goodbye to the trip to Topshop that was getting you through the week. You wonder how on earth anyone could be friends with this bossy, humourless cow who works out sums to the penny, and decide that she must be some throwback from your chum's childhood, her oldest 'friend' whom she has never actually liked but can't get rid of, a woman who happened to have gone to the same nursery, primary and secondary school, whom your friend is stuck with for ever simply because of the catchment areas they grew up in.

Once you have transferred your £154.37 to the Maid of Honour, you think you might get a bit of peace and quiet, some escape from the endless 'reply all' emails that have cluttered up your inbox for the last three weeks. But now starts the conversation about providing Fanny Fusspot with a selection of pictures of you and the bride-to-be. There are also requests for you to a) write a 'brief' thousand-word tribute to the bride that can be compiled into a big book to give to her on the day of the hen do, b) buy the bride-to-be a pair of sexy knickers so she can start married life 'with a bang' and c) provide an embarrassing anecdote about the bride that can be incorporated into a game that will be played at dinner, between the main course and the dessert, and on the subject of food, could you please make your selection from the menu attached by 5 p.m. today, even though the hen do won't take place for another four months.

You dread the hen do. You wonder if you could pretend that you have suddenly come down with a dreadful case of Ebola. You wonder if, actually, you wouldn't rather come down with a dreadful case of Ebola than spend twelve-plus hours with a load of shrieking women wearing flashing deely-boppers, which, like the straws, are shaped like penises. There is something about being in groups of the same gender that turns everyone into the very worst versions of themselves, exaggerating every quality of the chromosome that defines their sex. You only have accidentally to come across a stag do on a night out to know that men don't get it any better, forced as they are to dress up as Widow Twankey, or Borat in his mankini, or worse, to wear nothing at all as they are wrapped in cellophane and tied to a lamppost. Plus, they are lucky if this happens in their hometown rather than a city somewhere in Eastern Europe that easyJet happens to fly to for 50p. At least us women are saved that particular fate.

So you arrive at the hen do, telling yourself it could be worse, when suddenly you are handed a black T-shirt two-sizes too small for you with the words 'SALLY'S HEN PARTY WEEKEND' written on them in bright pink. 'Yours to keep,' breezes the Maid of Honour, as if she has just handed you a bottle of champagne with a straw rather than a cheap T-shirt that will bring you out in a rash and is completely useless owing to the fact that you won't even be able to offload it to a charity shop. Sally arrives, and is handed the usual accoutrements – veil made of net curtains, bride-to-be sash made of some other flammable material. She looks embarrassed, nervous about what the day ahead holds. Deep down, she'd really just prefer a night in the pub and a game of Mr and Mrs, followed by a couple of hours dancing at some godawful disco to Shania Twain and Steps.

The day starts with the chocolate making, or the flower-arranging, or worse, the filming of an hilarious music video in which you all don glitter wigs and are taught a dance routine to the tune of Liberty X's 'Just a Little', and inside you are dying a bit and wishing that all those months ago, you had chosen the steak option instead of the salad one for the dinner tonight. You try to make friends with these women from various parts of Sally's life – the girl she works with, the ones she went to uni with, the person she met travelling in Australia – but they are all friends already, none of them terribly interested in taking you into their cliques other than to commiserate with you over the fact that you will probably never have a hen do, and to ask you for money for the 'kitty', so that everyone can get blasted on sugary, brightly coloured cocktails. It's one of the only times you will ever slip away from a night out early.

You start to dread the wedding day itself, so you put it out of your mind until two days before, when you remember the wedding list. You have lost the little card that came with the invite, detailing where it is being held and the name and password you must use to access it, so just when Sally really doesn't need to be hearing from a wayward guest, you text her to ask for the details.

'Don't worry,' replies Sally. 'You forgot to RSVP so forgetting the wedding list information is hardly a surprise! :-)' Her passive aggression almost vibrates out of the phone. You can't say you really blame her.

From a quick read of the list, you wouldn't know that Sally and Andy had been living together for two years in a townhouse in Putney. They want cutlery sets and solid silver picture frames, Peugeot salt and pepper shakers and rugs from Brora. They want picnic hampers and Alessi kettles and Magimix food processors. They would like a machine that washes your clothes and then irons them, before going to take the rubbish out, and if it's no trouble, some his and hers bath robes. They want napkin holders. Napkin holders! Nobody has used napkin holders since they spent Christmas circa 1995 at their grandparents' house. Yet the greediness of a wedding list is, I suppose, a bit better than the couple who asked for contributions to their luxury two-week honeymoon to the Seychelles, first-class flights included. The 'donation' website even included a barometer to let people know how much money had been raised. It was as if they were patients

148

in respite care suffering from a terminal illness, rather than middle-class newlyweds with a flat in Chiswick.

The problem is you have left it so late that the only gifts that haven't already been bought are a collection of baking trays or a car, put on there for a joke, or in case that rich uncle who lives in Canada is feeling a bit generous. Obviously, you can't afford the car but if you get them just the baking trays, you will look mean. So that leaves you having to go 'off list', which people hate ('If I wanted something, I would have put it on THE LIST'), or not bothering to buy them anything at all, an option that seems increasingly attractive, given that a) you have spent £154.37 on the hen do, b) you spent another £40 on the 'kitty', plus £30 on cabs, c) £200 has just been burnt on train tickets to the middle of nowhere and somewhere to stay once you get there, and d) you never asked them to get married in the first place. I mean SERIOUSLY guys. Just because you've decided to bankrupt yourself getting hitched, it doesn't mean you have to bring everyone else you know down with you.

And Sally and Andy aren't the only people you know getting married this year. When I was twenty-seven – the peak wedding-season age, I found – I went not to one, not two, but six weddings over as many months. If you take Sally and Andy's nuptials to be the norm, I spent £2,366.22 on these weddings. Every time I hear someone moan about the cost of getting married, I instantly want a decree nisi on our friendship, a dissolution of our union.

The Wrong Knickers

You didn't have to spend £3,000 on a dress you are only ever going to wear once, and there was really no need to blow several hundred quid on personalised potpourri wedding favours. I am going to forget this bloody potpourri on the table at the end of the night, leaving you horribly offended, and if, by some minor miracle, I DO manage to get it home, it is going to sit on a shelf with loads of other useless crap, annoying me, making me look back on your special day with nothing but resentment, until a year later when I finally chuck it in the bin. You didn't have to spend £20,000 on a wedding, but I DID have to spend £2,000 going to all of your weddings. You could have just gone to a register office and then off to the pub for a knees-up, but no, you felt entitled to a big wedding, and no wonder after all the cash you've spent on other people's big weddings. In that way, the wedding season is a self-perpetuating nightmare of showiness, the marital equivalent of the Olympics, where each host has to prove themselves bigger and better than the previous host in order to feel comfortable within themselves.

But I have a theory, and it is this: the larger the wedding, the less likely the marriage is to last. I once attended a marriage ceremony in Kenya. KENYA. This was on another scale, people. This was a wedding for which you had to get vaccinated (at a cost of £150). It had three legs to it – it was a *multi-destination* wedding. It entailed a few days outside Nairobi, white-water rafting; a week at the coast, where the actual marriage ceremony took place; and finally, a week in the Masai Mara on safari. You know it's a plush wedding when the guests get to go on the honeymoon, too.

I loved this wedding, I really did. I mean, I nearly drowned at this wedding, when I was thrown from a raft into the angry, bubbling Tana river, and I nearly got stampeded by a herd of unhappy hippos at this wedding, when I got out of the car to have a closer look. Now that's a wedding from which you feel you have got your money's worth, a wedding that gives a good return. I didn't mind spending money on this marriage, because it was ace. The only thing that upset me was that it was over within a year, the bride confiding that she knew her husband had been unfaithful before she had even got hitched to him. 'But once you'd all booked your tickets, I knew I couldn't back out,' she said.

'But look on the bright side,' I comforted her. 'At least we all got a nice holiday out of it.'

Sally and Andy's wedding day is tomorrow, and you have nothing to wear. Sure, you have a wardrobe full of frocks, but none of them are appropriate because they don't make you look like the Countess of Wessex at the Trooping of the Colour. It doesn't matter if you are the kind of person who usually wears wet-look leggings, leather jackets and T-shirts purchased for an eye-watering £50 from a Hoxton boutique. If you go to a wedding, you still have to dress like the Countess of Wessex at the

Trooping of the Colour. Everyone has to dress like the Countess of Wessex at the Trooping of the Colour.

To do this, you have to go to Hobbs. You have to shop like your mum. You have to wear a pastel dress – one with a floral print on it if you're feeling particularly daring – with matching jacket, nude tights and demure kitten heels, also in nude. You have to clutch a teeny-tiny bag that doesn't quite fit your B&B key in it. You have to wear a fascinator.

Whoever invented the fascinator was having a laugh. As if having to wear heels and Spanx was not uncomfortable enough, let's make women don headwear that looks like brightly coloured scaffolding a dove might meet a sticky end on.

I once got so drunk at a wedding that I passed out with the fascinator still attached to my head. When I woke up the contraption had almost become one with my scalp, and it is a constant source of amazement that I am not still attached to it to this day, having to turn up to meetings and do my supermarket shop with a fascinator on my head. It had to be cut from my scalp by the hotel receptionist as I sat at breakfast eating my egg and bacon. Needless to say, I have never worn one again.

Outfit ready, you make your way to Paddington, where you are planning to catch the 18.33 to your destination. As is everybody else. In a rare flash of organisation, you have reserved a seat, but in the chaos that is the Friday evening rush hour, the rail company has decided that all reservations are now null and void. It's every man, woman and child for themselves. It's like the 18.33 to Calcutta, with businessmen instead of chickens. You spend three hours in a vestibule sitting on your wheely suitcase, listening to a middle-aged man talking about terrible train journeys he has endured, as he gets more and more pissed on cans of lager purchased from the buffet car.

When the train finally pulls into the station, it's pitch black and you can't make out your arse from your elbow let alone where your B&B might be. In the gloom, you just about manage to see a couple who look your age, vaguely metropolitan, whom you presume must also going to the wedding. You don't know them, but they look like the kind of people who know what they are doing and where they are going, which is more than can be said for you. 'HEY THERE! HEY!' you shout into the distance. 'ARE YOU GOING TO SALLY AND ANDY'S WEDDING?' When you finally catch up with them, they look at you is if you're mad. And so things start as you'd rather they didn't go on, but as they inevitably will.

The couple are called Edwina and James. They went to university with Andy, they say, immediately marking you out as one of Sally's friends, i.e. not one of their set. Still, they kindly allow you to share their mini cab to the B&B. You sit in the front passenger seat, and spend the bumpy journey through hedgerows craning your neck backwards in an attempt to make conversation with two people who are clearly more interested in whingeing about his failure to pack the camera and the confetti, and her failure to let them just drive up in the Audi, which would have been so much more convenient, because even if they'd got stuck in traffic, at least they would have had their own seat.

When you arrive at the B&B, it turns out it is over a pub, and James suggests a 'quick pint. Never know, Weena . . .'

'You know I hate it when you call me Weena,' snaps Weena.

'Whatevs, Ween. Anyway, you never know, but our old muckers Taffy and Stimpy might be in the bar, too!'

You should really have legged it to your room at the mere mention of muckers called Taffy and Stimpy.

'JIMBOB!' bellows Taffy or maybe Stimpy, as Jimbob, Weena and I walk into the pub. 'WE WERE JUST TALKING ABOUT YOU OLD BOY!' Taffy and Stimpy are wearing chinos and polo shirts with loafers. They are enveloping Jimbob in bear hugs, giving him pats on the back that seem more like voilent thumps, as Weena watches with a look of pure contempt painted across her pretty face. You can tell that she only tolerates Taffy and Stimpy at weddings, christenings and bar mitzvahs. You just know that when she was a student, she witnessed Jimbob go on one too many benders with Taffy and Stimpy as part of the university rugby team, that there were not two or three but four people in their relationship: Weena, Jimbob, Taffy and Stimpy.

'WEE,' shouts Taffy or Stimpy, going to air kiss her. She looks as if she is going to punch him. 'Can't believe the Andi-nator is finally settling down. You next, eh?'

Jimbob rolls his eyes.

'And who is this fine filly,' says either Taffy or Stimpy, coming towards me with their arms wide open, like some sort of Eton-educated game-show host.

'Leave her alone,' snaps Weena. 'The last thing she needs after that train journey is an evening being pawed by YOU.'

You decide that inside Weena is a frustrated party girl fighting to get out. You are going to befriend her. You all join Taffy and Stimpy at their table, and under the circumstances, you hit the booze hard. Wine followed by beer followed by shots of flaming Drambuie. Why not, eh? Sally and the Andi-nator are getting hitched.

The next day you wake up with only an hour to get yourself ready and to the church. You feel sick. You are sick. By getting totalled the night before you have peaked too soon – why do you always peak too soon? – and now you won't be able to enjoy the main event. You eat the biscuits that come with the tea and coffee-making facilities – you have missed the breakfast you paid for, obviously – and force yourself into the shower. As the lukewarm water trickles over your body you get flashbacks of Taffy or Stimpy lauding you for your 'great bangers'. You think you might be sick again.

Once you have brushed your teeth, put on your

crumpled dress and covered yourself in several layers of make-up, you make your way uneasily to the reception of the B&B, where Weena, Jimbob, Taffy and Stimpy are all waiting for you, ruddy of cheek and bushy of tail. 'BRYERS!' they chorus. 'You missed a cracking walk this morning not to mention some A1 black pudding!' They have been up for hours. They truly are of a different kind.

In the people carrier to the church, you are sure Weena is shooting you withering looks. What did you do last night? Did you get so wasted that you tried to snog her? No, it can't be that – she is just the kind of repressed former boarding-school girl who would get wasted and snog you back. Did you try and snog Jimbob, then? No, you remember him passing out on a bar stool as you all got stuck into a round of 'Have you ever?' Oh God, it's all flooding back to you now . . .

'Have you ever,' said Taffy or was it Stimpy, 'got your bangers out in public?'

'Of course I have,' you lied. 'I'm a GAME GIRL!'

And then . . .

'Tell you what, Bryers,' says Taffy or Stimpy, interrupting the terrible realisation that is slowly, painfully dawning on you. 'You really ARE a game girl, flashing us your fun bags like that. What a CRACKING LAUGH!'

Fun bags! They actually used the phrase 'fun bags'. The people carrier pulls up outside the church. You are grateful to be sitting on the bride's side, because it means escaping these hopeless buffoons for at least half an hour.

The service starts, and as readings are made about eternal love and companionship, you become emotional. Not because your friend is getting married, but because you gave a pub an eyeful of your breasts purely so you could be thought of as a game girl by some upper-class oafs you will – hopefully – never see again after this weekend.

Really, what is WRONG with you?

The reception is the fun part, right? It's the bit where you get to let your hair down and relax a bit and celebrate after the serious stuff is out of the way. So why, when you arrive, are you filled with a strange mixture of dread and anticipation? Because of the seating plan, that's why.

The seating plan at a wedding tells you everything you need to know about how you are viewed by your peers in society. If you are near the top table, with the lawyers and the people who work at the BBC, you are A-List. If you are at the back of the room with the maiden aunts and the friends of the in-laws, then you may as well walk around with a big sticker that reads 'AFTERTHOUGHT' on your forehead. If you are not actually invited to the ceremony at all, and only to the evening do, you really have to wonder why you are friends with these people in the first place, so low down their foodchain do you rank. Being invited to the evening do only is so wounding that I would almost rather not be invited at all. Whenever this has happened to me, I always think, 'Why don't you just ask me to man the cloakroom and wash the dishes afterwards and be done with it?' I always go, obviously. Despite my umbrage, I wouldn't want to miss out on a good party.

When I get to the reception venue, the first thing I do, after swiping a flute of champagne, is check out the seating plan, praying as I go that I am not on the same table as Taffy or Stimpy. Please God, let me be next to some total hunk, even though I did a scan of the church and could see not a single one in attendance. Please God, don't stick me with some complete drip who works for a think tank and wants to talk to me about the media all night. Please, please, please, don't put me on a table full of couples. Please put me on the naughty table, the singles table, even though I have noticed that the more weddings I attend, the less available people there are.

'I've sat you next to a guy I think you're REALLY going to like,' Sally tells you, as she circulates the room. 'My second cousin Tom. He's a bit crazy and out there. I think you're going to get on FAMOUSLY.'

Oh no. Crazy and out there. This is not a good combination for me. It means that Tom and I will be doing drugs off dwarves' heads by 2 a.m. Even though there are no dwarves in attendance, we will find some. We will crash the nearest dwarves convention, if that is what it takes. Oh God. Snap out of it, Bryony. What this actually means is that you will get your boobs out again, probably. It means that Sally thinks you are a complete mess who can only be palmed off on her mental distant relative.

You make your way to your allotted table and stand in front of your chair as the other people on it make their way over. There is another single girl – DANGER, DANGER, COMPETITION FOR THE FEW REMAINING SINGLE MEN IN ATTENDANCE, ESPECIALLY AS SHE LOOKS LIKE JENNIFER LAWRENCE – and a gay couple. Of course there is a gay couple on the naughty table, because obviously gay men must all be classified as wild and crazy even if they are accountants and management consultants, as these two are. Taffy (or Stimpy) is there, too, though luckily on the other end of the table, a woman whose husband is away working in Hong Kong, and the girl from the hen do whom Sally met travelling in Australia.

But no Tom.

You are the only person in this entire cavernous function room who has an empty place setting next to them. The accountant on the other side is talking to the backpacker from Australia, meaning you are left twiddling your thumbs and trying to pick up the fag ends of conversations happening elsewhere on the table, and even on the table behind you because, hey, beggars can't be choosers. The starters come. No Tom. The main arrives. No Tom. The speeches begin, and halfway through the best man's, there is Tom.

'SORRY I'M LATE,' he says, his attempt at a whisper louder than most people's screams. 'HAD A TOTES MARE GETTING HERE.' He sits down, knocking his cutlery as he goes. 'Hi,' he says, as the already-nervous best man attempts to drown out the new arrival by talking even louder. 'I'M TOM.' He gets up again, goes around the table shaking every body's hand despite the speeches going on.

He's all right looking, Tom. Or at least he would be if his pupils weren't dilated and his nose wasn't a bit encrusted with blood. 'Haven't been to bed,' he will tell you when the speeches are over. 'Accidentally had a bit of a crazy night last night that didn't end until ten this morning, hence my lateness. Missed the train out of London, so had to pay a cab driver to take me!'

'A cab?' you say, incredulous. 'All the way from London to Somerset?' He nods manically. He is just like Hugh Grant in *Four Weddings and a Funeral*, had Hugh Grant's character been off his tits on cocaine.

You find it almost offensive that Sally thinks you might be a match for this man. It implies that you are a complete fuckwit, too. There is no way you want anything to do with him. You would rather try your chances with Taffy or Stimpy, though whichever one it is at the table seems to be snogging the face off the Jennifer Lawrence looka-like. No, you wouldn't touch this bloke even if there was suddenly an apocalypse and for some strange reason the seating plan placed you in such a position that it meant you were the only two people to survive it. You would rather mate with a cockroach than him, and that is that.

* * *

When you wake up the next day, it is with a start. You are not in your frilly B&B room. You are in a plain, grey room with double glazing and a table to your left, littered with cans of beer that have been turned into makeshift ashtrays. And to your right, there is Tom.

'Where the FUCK am I?' you say, realising with some relief that you both still have all your clothes on, Tom even managing to have gone to bed in his shoes.

'You're at the Travelodge on the service station just off junction 24 of the M5,' he says, as if this is a totally normal place to wake up on a Sunday morning, as if this is what he does every Sunday morning as part of his research into a book entitled *Travelodges of the World*.

'How did we get here?' You have literally no memory after about 10 p.m. the night before.

'Well, first we got a helicopter and then a private jet and finally we boarded a hovercraft. How do you think we got here, stupid? By taxi.'

'What happened?'

'Well, after the first dance we started doing shots and then there was a dance-off to "Crazy in Love".'

That fucking song again.

'And then there were some more shots, and then when the bar was closing, you said you wanted to carry on, and so I suggested coming here, and you said yes, and as I was ordering the cab, you tried to snog me.'

These are the words no woman ever wants to hear – you *tried* to snog me – because they imply you were not

161

successful. They imply that even a mad junkie isn't interested in you.

'No I didn't,' you say defensively.

'Yes you did. You were so wasted I thought it would have been rude of me to have obliged you.' Me, too wasted! Him, OBLIGE me! 'You were so drunk that you even forced Sally's dad to dance with you to Madonna's "Like a Virgin", which I get the impression you are most definitely not.'

'You're an asshole.'

'Four hours ago you were saying you loved me.'

'You must have hallucinated it.'

'Anyway, at least one guest has to make a show of themselves at a wedding. It's the rules. You served a noble role last night, one that you should be very proud of.'

You gather up your shoes, look for your tiny handbag, note with some alarm that it has failed to contain your B&B key, and make for the door. You make a vow to yourself – the only vow you will ever get to make at this rate – that for better or worse, for richer or poorer, in sickness and in health (but mostly, you're guessing, in sickness), if anyone asks you if you want to come to a wedding again, you will respond with a simple 'I don't.'

7

In which we learn that Father Time won't pay the council tax, and neither will our real dad

B uzz buzz.
There is somebody at the door.
Buzz buzz.
There is somebody at the door.
Buzz buzz buzz.
There is somebody at the door.
BUZZZZZZZZZZZ.
There is SOMEBODY AT THE FUCKING DOOR.
I rub my eyes and open them into darkness. Am I having some sort of terrible waking dream? I grasp around on the bedside table for my mobile phone, check for the time. BUZZ. It is 05.31 a.m. BUZZ BUZZ. 05:31 a.m. This, I think, is the definition of being 'woken with a start'. BUZZ-BUZZ-BUZZ-BUZZ-BUZZ, short pause,

BUZZ-BUZZ-BUZZ-BUZZ, shorter pause, BUZZ-BUZZ.

Bloody hell. There really IS somebody at the door, and they are playing a football chant on it. It isn't just a dream. It's a real, *bona fide*, person at the door. It is 05:31 in the morning, and there is somebody at the door. What is going on? Why is there somebody at the door?

'BRYONY,' comes an anguished wail from my sister's bedroom. 'WHAT THE HELL IS GOING ON?' She races into my room, jumps into the bed with me. 'Do you have drug debts?' she whispers, a look of morbid seriousness etched on her fatigued face. 'Is it a drug lord at the front door? You can tell me if it is. We can sort this out. We can tell mum and dad everything and they will settle the debts and then we can send you to reh—'

'Oh be QUIET,' I cut her off. 'I don't have drug debts, and there most certainly isn't a drug lord at the front door. Maybe it's some local drunks engaging in high jinks.'

BUZZ-BUZZ-BUZZ.

'Maybe it's a SERIAL KILLER,' gasps my sister, burrowing under the duvet. 'Oh God, we're going to die before we have fulfilled our potentials. We are going to die before we have had a chance to give our parents grandchildren. Before we have had the opportunity to do all the things girls our age dream of – having a successful career, owning a flat and a pair of Jimmy Choos!'

BUZZ-BUZZ-BUZZ.

'I don't think a serial killer would be so polite as to knock on the door. I think he'd just go straight ahead and break in and murder us in our beds before we had even noticed.'

BUZZ-BUZZ-BUZZ.

'For God's sake, Bryony, GO AND ANSWER THE DOOR.'

But there is no way I am going to answer the door to anyone who has turned up at 05.31 a.m. No freaking way. 'It could be Steve,' I whisper, clutching at ever-decreasing straws. 'Maybe he went out and got so drunk that he lost his keys, and now he's knocking at our door because he needs a bed for the night, or at least for an hour and a half until it's time to get up and go to work.'

BUZZZZZZZZZZZZZZZ.

'OK, I'm going to peak from behind the curtains and see who it is, and then I'm going to work out whether or not I want to open the door, or call the police.'

'MY GOD, WHAT IF IT IS THE POLICE COME TO ARREST YOU FOR TAKING DRUGS?'

'Given that I haven't taken drugs for like, a year, I think that's very unlikely.'

Confident that it's not the police, yet not entirely convinced it isn't a serial killer, I get on my hands and knees and crawl across the hall to the living room, where I can have a look at who it is. I don't know why I crawl. I guess I must have seen it in the movies, in horror movies where a wounded teenager is trying to escape an axe-wielding, mask-wearing madman who has entered their house. But I am not a wounded teenager, and I am not at risk from an axe-wielding, mask-wearing madman, because if I was, I am pretty sure he would have used his weapon to break through the door by now. If anything, the crawling is slowing me down. It certainly isn't protecting me should whomever it is at the door decide to look through the letterbox – in fact, it's putting me directly in their line of vision. I climb on to the sofa and twitch the curtains, just in time to hear the letterbox go and see two men in thick overcoats leave and get back into a large van on which I can, through the early morning gloom, vaguely make out the words 'DEBT', 'COLLECTION' and 'SERVICES' written. I climb back off the sofa and make my way to the mat below the letterbox. On top of it is an envelope beseeching me to open it URGENTLY, the word 'urgently' written in thick red type and underlined twice to hammer home the point.

I told you I don't like receiving post.

And so I open it, my heart hammering in my chest, my brain telling me that perhaps I would have preferred it to have been a serial killer at the door.

'You have failed to pay the outstanding amount shown above registered against you by Brent Council,' it starts, not even a 'Dear Miss Gordon' to soften the blow.

'You need now to settle the balance in full, IMMEDIATELY, or we will attend your address to remove your goods for sale by public auction or remove monies owed.'

What are they going to take? Our collection of Topshop frocks? Our make-up? The contents of the fridge – a tub of houmous, a wilted cucumber, both of which are probably past their sell-by date, and half a bottle of ketchup? My creaky old iPod, valuable only to geeks who view second-generation Apple goods as relics from a bygone era? We own almost nothing in this flat, not the beds that we sleep in or the crappy old television that we occasionally watch. Even the Hoover doesn't belong to us. I want to run after the bailiffs in my pyjamas. 'Come on in!' I will say with my most winning smile. 'Take whatever you want, and GOOD LUCK GETTING ANYTHING TO THE VALUE OF £854.67, YOU NOISY, SLEEP-DISTURBING FUCKERS.'

I go back to the letter.

'You should be aware that the outstanding amount is in relation to a Liability Order obtained from a Magistrates Court by Brent Council for non-payment of Council Tax. WARNING: REMOVAL OF GOODS INCURS FURTHER CHARGES TO YOU NOT STATED ABOVE.'

Oh great, kick a woman while she's down. TAKE THE CLOTHES FROM OUR BACKS, AND THE FOOD FROM OUR MOUTHS, AND THEN CHARGE US FOR THE PRIVILEGE, ALL BECAUSE I MADE ONE LITTLE, SILLY MISTAKE AND DECIDED NOT TO OPEN THE POST THAT THE COUNCIL KEPT SENDING US, ASSUMING MY SISTER HAD PAID THE COUNCIL TAX, AS PER OUR AGREEMENT

The Wrong Knickers

WHEN WE MOVED IN, ME TAKING ON THE WATER, GAS AND ELECTRICITY BILLS INSTEAD – which, now I think about it, I haven't paid, either. Surely it's a human right to have water, heat and light? Surely you shouldn't have actually to pay for them?

'Who was it?' says my sister, sitting down on the sofa and turning on our rickety telly to the overly awake and enthusiastic faces of the *Daybreak* presenters. My stomach is churning. I feel sick.

'It-was-the-bailiffs,' I spit out quickly.

'The what?'

'The bailiffs. I think they come really early in the morning so they know you'll be in. We haven't paid our council tax and if we don't pay it within fourteen days they will enter our home and take away our stuff and sell it at auction, and when they don't make enough money from that, they will come back and take us away and probably PUT US IN PRISON.'

My sister starts crying.

On *Daybreak* they are discussing the latest series of *Strictly Come Dancing*.

'Why didn't you pay the council tax?' snivels my sister.

'What do you mean why didn't I pay the council tax? You were supposed to!'

'I never remember signing a contract agreeing to it,' she weeps. 'Plus, I earn less than you!'

'Give you a massive clue. Flatshares don't work on a system of WHO EARNS LESS THAN WHOM. People don't say "Oh, I'm only on thirteen thousand a year, so I think I shouldn't have to pay any bills, and also, because you're on nineteen thousand, you should pay for my cereal, bread and jam." I earn barely enough to pay for myself every year, let alone also becoming a one-woman welfare system from whom you can claim benefits. We have our parents for that!'

'Actually, we don't,' says my sister, straightening herself out. 'At first I thought that Father Time would pay the council tax . . .'

'You what?'

'I kept putting off paying it because I thought that I would somehow find the money and it would all be fine, or at the very least *you would*, and then I called our actual father and he said that you – YOU, BRYONY, a woman of almost TWENTY-SEVEN YEARS OF AGE – had borrowed so much money off him over the past few months that he couldn't afford to bail us out of this particular conundrum.'

'I didn't borrow THAT much.'

My sister narrows her eyes at me. *Daybreak* has moved on to *The X Factor*.

'OK, like a couple of hundred quid. But otherwise, we couldn't have afforded to eat.'

'We don't eat, Bryony. We haven't done a single supermarket shop since living here, unless you count the one when we bought booze for the party, which, funnily enough, I don't. We live off Pret sandwiches, tortilla chips and dips. You couldn't spend a couple of hundred quid on that if you TRIED.'

'Well, I needed to SMOKE.'

'Whatever,' sighs my sister. 'The point is, what are we going to do now? How are we going to find nearly nine hundred quid in fourteen days? The bank of mum and dad has closed its doors to us. Neither of us gets paid for another three weeks. We have to think of something.'

On *Daybreak*, they have moved seamlessly from a feud between Louis Walsh and Sharon Osbourne, to a segment about payday loans.

I was bad with money before I actually earned any myself, destined to a life of financial folly before I was even a twinkle in my parents' eyes. I was born in the eighties and came of age during the booming nineties, when it was just normal to buy now and pay later, and to take out loans to go on exotic holidays nobody could afford. It seemed rude not to fly off to the south of France when the no-frills airlines went there for £30 each way, and bugger the fact you couldn't get a hotel for less than one hundred Euros a night. I was part of the Nintendo generation – the latest games console never enough, always waiting for the next version to come out, with flashier graphics and funnier games. We grew up bombarded with adverts targeted at us, for toys and music systems and, later, clothes and cosmetics, and I for one was never told no. I screamed or sulked too much if I was, so my parents, busy trying to balance jobs with family, gave in and did what was easiest and the least exhausting. When I look back now, I see an enormous Augustus Gloop of a child, and I feel a bit ashamed.

I expected a certain standard of living, a roundly middle-class one, and it's still a shock to me now that I should be experiencing anything less. When I got my job, I was cock-a-hoop at earning the gigantic-sounding sum of £15,000 per annum, but within the first month I had realised that this was, if not literally peanuts, then certainly not enough to live off anything but peanuts. And I am, apparently, one of the lucky ones. I have a job. I have a profession.

I have friends a trillion times brighter and better than I am who are not so fortunate – Sarah, with her double first from Cambridge, forced to work days as a receptionist and nights in a pub for lack of openings anywhere else; Tom who works in Topman and spends his evenings serving drinks to millionaire forty-somethings who sure are glad they weren't born fifteen years later, a sentiment meant to comfort Tom but which only serves to depress him more. Everything depresses Tom, even going on Facebook. He says he can't post an update without thinking of Mark Zuckerberg's millions and wanting to cry.

Even those of us who have become 'professionals' – I mean HAHAHAHAHA, how laughable is that? – wonder if our jobs will still be around in ten years' time, and if they are still around in ten years' time, we worry that someone younger and keener will be hiding around the corner, willing to do our jobs for even less. So I am pathetically grateful for my £15,000 a year, which will eventually go up to £17,000 and then – wow! – £22,000, my pay rising in such tiny steps that by the time I have reached a half-respectable wage to live on in London, I am in my early thirties.

'I don't know why you don't just ask for a payrise,' says my mum one Sunday afternoon, as I ask – no, beg – to 'borrow' another £40 off her, £40 we both know I will never pay back. If Mum was a bank, she would have been shut down by the government five years ago. 'You're a grown woman. When I was your age I had two children, a mortgage and SCHOOL FEES to pay. I bet you don't even have a pension.'

She's right, as ever. I don't. Who in their right mind would put a precious £50 away each month for the 'future', especially when the present is so bleak? No, don't even answer that.

And the thing is, I'm too scared to ask for a payrise. When I look back at my career during my twenties, the thing I will be most proud of won't be a promotion from the teen section to the main features section. It won't be an award-winning interview with a Hollywood A-Lister, and nor will it be a hero-gram from an editor, thanking me for my hard work on a story. It will be the fact that I survive not one, not two, not three, but four rounds of redundancies, even though my survival probably hinges on being paid so little that getting rid of me would make not the slightest bit of difference to the company coffers. 'Well, I suppose that's one upside of earning no money,' says my mum. 'Every cloud, and all that.'

And there is another reason I never ask for a payrise. I enjoy my job so much that I feel it would be a bit rude and unappreciative to ask to be paid more money for it. And so it is that I find myself sent to Dubai to review a hotel, only to be told that, because I don't have a credit card to secure extras (I don't trust myself with one), they will have to empty the mini bar in the massive room, which also has a kitchen, three sofas and two bathrooms. There I am, in one of the richest places on the planet, unable even to buy a mini packet of Pringles to eat while I lounge in one of the two baths. Instead, I ferret away croissants from the buffet breakfast, so I won't have to pay for lunch or dinner.

Then there is the time I'm flown to Los Angeles – the airfare itself is probably more than my monthly wage – to interview Justin Timberlake. Have I mentioned just how much I love Justin Timberlake? Every time I hear one of 'his songs, I feel like my clothes might fall off. I was ushered into a villa in the grounds of the Chateau Marmont, the kind of hotel in which A-Listers decide to take suites for six months, just because they can, and told that under no circumstances should I mention his love life, past or present. 'Whatever you do,' whispered the PR, 'DO. NOT. MENTION. THE. B. WORD.'

I took it he meant Britney Spears.

I waited in the living room of the villa for what felt like hours, a phalanx of security guards all around. Finally, His Lordship arrived. In front of me stood the most handsome man on the planet – even more handsome in the flesh, I think – with his hand outstretched for ME. 'Justin,' said the PR, 'this is Britne...' He stopped himself. I couldn't believe this was happening to me *again*. 'I mean, Bryony.' Justin's face fell. The interview was suddenly cut from an hour to twenty minutes, meaning I had flown almost 6,000 miles around the globe for what amounted to a tea break. 'I'm really spritual,' Justin told me, lighting a candle, 'and spontaneous. I mean,' he said, pointing to the villa's garden, 'let's go and do the rest of the interview in that tree!'

'OK!' I beamed, standing up. He looked at me with something approaching pity. His entourage started to snigger. 'Like, not *really*,' said Justin, and that was that. I sat back down. The interview ended.

Every time I think of asking for a payrise, I think of things like this. I think of the time I flew with Sir Richard Branson around the world, to Hong Kong, Sydney and LA, in upper class. I mean, this is no exaggeration, but I think the cabins were bigger than my bedroom back in Ladbroke Grove. The hotel room with views of Sydney Harbour certainly was. And all of this makes me laugh, this great paradox of my life. One moment I'm turning left and being lavished with champagne as I lie in my flat-bed somewhere over the Pacific Ocean, and the next I'm back in my dingy flat, wondering if my sister and her boyfriend might let me have some spag bol because I have hit the limit on my overdraft. I am, by now, a twenty-seven-year-old woman whose father still pays her mobile phone bill and whose mother still coughs up for her contact lenses. I remind myself that every month without fail I have to ask my mum for money 'just to tide me over until payday'. I even asked her for money as she sat in hospital by the bed of my dying grandmother. She had asked me to go and get some teas, and with not a penny to my name, what else could I say? I once even tried to pawn the Gucci watch I received as an eighteenth birthday present, only to be told by the man behind the counter that it 'wasn't in fashion enough to be worth anything over a couple of hundred quid'. A couple of hundred quid seemed like a lot of money at the time, but it would never have been enough to cover the costs of the counselling I'd need to counter the verbal assault launched on me when my mum eventually found out where it had gone.

For me, every month is the same. For the first two weeks after payday I live like a princess, buying bottles of wine at the pub – the drinks are on me! – getting cabs home and going mental in Zara, and for the two after that I live like a pauper, unable to top up my Oyster card unless I give up lattes and lunch until payday. At work, I have heard some people ask vaguely when payday is. They sit at their desks, sipping a latte they haven't paid for in copper coins, casually nibbling on a banana they have brought in, because, unlike me, they are sensible and buy bananas in bunches instead of paying 50p for one.

'Oh, when's payday?' they say, as if they're asking the date of something completely alien, like Ramadan or Diwali. When is payday? When is payday? This is like NOT KNOWING WHEN CHRISTMAS IS, OR YOUR BIRTHDAY. Payday is very clearly on the 28th of the month, or on the nearest Friday should it happen to fall on a Saturday, Sunday or Bank Holiday. The only possible excuse for not knowing the date must be down to something totally bizarre, like the ability not to spend your entire monthly wage fifteen days before your next one is due.

That is a feat I have managed once, and even then it was only because my darling grandmother had died and left me a nice sum of money. Someone sensible would have put it towards a potential deposit on a flat. I didn't, reasoning that a deposit on a flat was not as alluring as, say, a pair of Chloe jeans I had been lusting after for months and a handbag from Mulberry, both items I knew my glamorous granny would have approved of more than a huge mortgage on a bedsit in Crawley. There's no point saving for a rainy day in a country that has an average monthly rainfall above monsoon season in India, so off I went, blowing two grand in as many weeks on fripperies such as shoes and dresses, before reverting back to my normal poverty, ignoring the mounting pile of red bills as I went.

I didn't even pay back my mum the money she gave me to get teas.

It never once seemed strange to me that I carried a Mulberry handbag but not a functioning debit card, or that I kept up a ruinous £8 a day cigarette habit while bemoaning the fact I had to eat beans on toast for dinner. And so it was that the council tax didn't get paid, and the bailiffs turned up at our door one cold winter morning.

This is the fiscal situation in the Gordon household, and I think it is one that closely mirrors that of the UK as a whole: we are fucked. After she has paid her rent and travel costs, my sister is left with the grand total of £300 to spend every month. That is seventy-five quid a week. That is really very little when you live in London.

So I can't expect her to contribute to the eight hundred odd quid we owe the council or the bailiffs. I can't ask my mum and dad either. Every twenty-something knows that fifty quid here and there is acceptable, exactly the right amount to stop them going completely mental on you, but any more than two figures and you might as well accept defeat and move back home, a tail of debt between your legs.

But I can't afford to pay it, either. I'd use my overdraft but it's already gone, raised again and again until the bank took it away from me altogether, informing me in a letter – the fuckers didn't even phone me! – that they would also be replacing my Visa debit card with the piece of flimsy plastic attached to said letter, a piece of flimsy plastic bearing the pathetic legend 'SOLO'.

'Solo?' cackled my sister when I told her, tears of laughter streaming down her face as she attempted to comprehend what I had just told her, what I had just admitted after several months of suffering my fiscal fate in humiliated silence. 'The bank will only allow you a SOLO card. AHAHAHAHAHAHAH. Even our fifteen-year-old brother grew out of a Solo card, like, TWO YEARS AGO. Oh man, this is brilliant. You only have a Solo card. How the heck did you manage that?'

'Because I kept going over my overdraft limit. And every time I went over my overdraft limit, I would be charged, which would then send me even further over my overdraft limit, incurring yet another charge, and so on and so on until I'm reduced to carrying around a bank card that's so piss poor, they haven't even bothered to emboss the numbers on it. That's how lame this Solo card is.'

Let me tell you about a SOLO card. I think it's called a SOLO card because there's only one outlet in the whole country that accepts it, the others laughing you out the door and suggesting you come back with Luncheon Vouchers, or book tokens, or that you instead pay with buttons. You can use your SOLO card to get money out of a cash machine, but you can't do much else with it. You certainly wouldn't want to try anything as daring as using it abroad. If you try to pay with a SOLO card for a ticket on a train, the conductor will throw you off at the next stop and you will have to call your mum by reversing the charges, and ask her to come and pick you up, so that you don't have to walk to your destination. I know this, because it once happened to me.

So here I am with no overdraft, no functioning debit card, no hope. Bailiff day is drawing closer, and yet I am no nearer to working out how to pay them off than I was when I read their menacing final demand. I could sell my body, become a high-class call girl – the only problem with this (no, no, one of the many problems with this) is that I am not entirely sure anybody would pay me for my time. Every time I saw a client, I would feel the need to explain to them why I was in this mess. There I would be, sitting on the edge of the bed in a pair of bright red stockings and crotchless panties, and as I leafed through the bank notes he had just put down, I would start up. 'You know I'm not normally this kind of girl,' I would begin. 'I mean, I actually have a day job, a proper job, one that involves sitting at a desk rather than straddling it.' Quick side glance at the hotel room's 'office' space. 'It's just that, you see, I've become a victim of the economic crash just like everyone else, and now I'm having to make ends meet. How I long for the days of boom and BUST.' Gratuitous forward lean to show off my boobs in their balconette bra. 'And so here I am, trying to scrape together the eight hundred odd quid to keep the bailiffs from BANGING DOWN MY DOORS.' Coquettish giggle.

No, it would be completely hopeless.

Instead of selling my whole body, perhaps I could just sell bits of my body – kidneys, a bit of a lung, a cornea perhaps. Actually, I'm not sure my lungs would be much use, and I know my corneas wouldn't be, given that I'm almost blind without contact lenses, so somehow I will have to persuade my sister to part with hers. Alternatively, less desperately, I could just beg the bank.

I pop into my local branch during my lunch break, queue for half an hour behind people who still have things like chequebooks, and ask if I can talk to someone about the possibility of a loan. 'You can see someone in half an hour,' says the man behind the counter, not looking up from the pile of notes he is counting. 'Please be seated in the waiting area until a colleague can come and see you.'

I try to get eye contact with him. There is not a flicker.

'Is there any way I could see someone earlier? It's just I have to get back to wo—'

'Counter number eight,' snaps the man into his microphone. He looks straight over my shoulder to the queue behind me as he speaks.

In the waiting area, I wonder how banks have managed

to get away with their totally lousy work ethics. Open from nine to five only, shut Saturdays and Sundays and, naturally, Bank Holidays, though truth be told, almost every day is a holiday if you happen to work behind the counter in a bank.

If a clothes shop held those hours, or a grocery store, they would have gone out of business within a week. But banks hold all the power, because they hold all the money, and so it is that I find myself sitting in their waiting area with fifteen other people, all of us forced to waste two hours of our working days just so the shirkers the other side of the bullet-proof glass can knock off at five on the dot. I sit there fiddling with leaflets about mortgages and insurance and ISAs. I don't know what an ISA is. I look at posters featuring happy children tearing open presents. 'Personal loans for everyone!' it reads. 'It's up to you what you spend it on.' This makes me feel better about myself, for a short while. If there are people taking out personal loans to buy presents for other people, then it must be totally OK to take out a personal loan to fend off the bailiffs.

But when I finally get to see someone about these personal loans for everyone, I discover that, actually, they are personal loans for everyone but me. The man I saw half an hour earlier has come out from behind counter number eight and is taking all my details down on a computer. He asks my employment status, my salary, my address, my date of birth. Then he hits a button, 'which will enable me to tell you how much money you can borrow'.

We sit silently with rictus grins on our faces as the computer grinds into action, the whir of its internal fan adding to my sense of anxiety about the size of the financial problem I face. WHOOOOOSHHH, goes the computer. WHIRRRRRR. The man from behind counter number eight tilts his head from side to side in time to the sound of his computer. He taps his biro on the desk and looks at his watch. 'Sorry,' he says, not really meaning it. 'You know what it's like with computers.'

'I do,' I nod. If in doubt, blame the computer or even better, the email being down. Even though we all know nobody's email has really been down since 1998.

Eventually, the computer stops making a noise. 'Ahah, here we go,' says the man from behind counter number eight. 'Right.' He chews his bottom lip and stares at the screen for a bit. Then he turns to me and with a well-practised voice that contains hints of both pity and contempt, he tells me that I have been turned down for a loan.

'You might want to try again in six months or so,' he says. 'Is there anything else we can help you with today?' I don't know how he expects me to answer that question. 'Actually yes, there is. Seeing as the bank won't lend me eight hundred pounds, would you mind loaning it to me out of your own pocket? I promise I will pay it back when I can. You know where I live because all of my details are on your computer there, and I could leave this Gucci watch as security.'

'No thanks,' is what I actually say, packing up what little dignity I have left. 'You've helped me quite enough today.'

I head back to work. I know what I have to do.

I am a fool, an idiot, a wilful ignoramus. I have taken out a payday loan, against the advice of the people on *Daybreak* who alerted me to the existence of these legal loan sharks in the first place. When I knew they were easy to access, it was only really a matter of time – in that way, these loans weren't that different from cocaine for me. 'Need a little cash until payday?' said the adverts, when I looked on Google. There were hundreds and hundreds of companies who wanted to give me money, and they wanted to give me that money literally at the touch of a button.

It took me five minutes to get the cash together to keep off the bailiffs, and it felt good. Never mind that I had merely transferred my debts to another organisation, an organisation that wanted to charge me an APR of 4,214 per cent, which when I briefly thought about it, did sound like rather a lot. Like an ISA, I didn't know what APR was. Ignorance, for the time being, was bliss. It meant I could buy Marlboro Lights instead of Mayfairs. It meant I could go out five nights a week and not expect a wake-up call from the debt collectors. Not the ones I was used to, anyway.

The best thing was I didn't have to pay the loan off the next month. I could just chuck the company a small amount of cash and defer it for another month – and another, and another, and another. The money could roll over and over and over, until I ended up paying £3,000 for an £800 loan, which, over the next year or so, is exactly what happened. I was never going to learn, not at this rate. I had become a financial buffoon, trapped in a cycle of endless, knowing stupidity. There I was, approaching thirty, and I hadn't even worked out how to budget properly. BUZZ-BUZZ-BUZZ went the bailiffs in my brain, trying to recover what grey matter they could from the mess that was my head. It was time to take control of my life.

8

Body beautiful, mind miserable

When Chloe suggests we go on a 'body and soul' bootcamp in St Lucia for a fortnight – as if two weeks of brutal discipline is going to make up for nearing a decade of self-destruction – I realise I have to tell her about the payday loan. The shame of it is burning a hole not just in my wallet but in my very being. I feel like Kerry Katona, and then I feel worse than Kerry Katona, because at least Kerry Katona had assets from which she could be made bankrupt, whereas me . . . I have NOTHING. 'I can't even be made bankrupt!' I wail, in the queue for teas in the canteen. 'How pathetic is that?'

'Relax,' says Chloe, ordering a green tea. 'When I was in my twenties, the only thing I had any control of was my weight. Now I'm in my late thirties I have swapped control of my weight for control of my bank account. And I know which I'd rather.'

That is one of the strange paradoxes about Chloe – while she is glamorous and cool and a bit rock 'n' roll, she also has a savings account. I can't imagine ever being in control of my finances enough to have a savings account or, now I come to think of it, being in control of my weight. At the age of sixteen I had tried to be anorexic, but like so many other areas in my life, it hadn't worked out for me. I had read all about the eating disorder in *Just Seventeen* and had started the week with high hopes for my career as an anorexic. It seemed to me a noble and honourable pursuit. But by Wednesday I had realised I was too greedy ever to make a proper go of it, too adoring of frankfurters and ketchup. I didn't have the willpower or the strength. And so it was that my flirtation with anorexia ended after just forty-eight hours, my admiration for those who managed it plentiful. I didn't pity anorexics; I envied them. How they could be as strong as iron while weighing little more than a baby bird seemed amazing to me.

For most of my teens and early twenties I weighed only nine stone, but I never felt anything other than fat. Fat seemed to me to be as much a mental state as it was a physical one – almost every woman I had ever come across thought she was ginormous, so it seemed natural that I should think I was, too. When I observed my mother and her friends, they were always talking about diets, and discussing going for the burn while watching the Jane

Fonda workout. I learnt that 'You look like you've lost weight' was the ultimate compliment, and that the response was almost always something along the lines of 'oh God no, I feel huge, but thank you'. I don't think I ever heard a woman say that she was happy with her body, or express any affection towards it. The opposite in fact. They moaned about their noses, their feet, their wobbly arms and their love handles. 'Hate handles more like,' they would all laugh, before moving on to a discussion about the latest diet from America that they had read about in the *Daily Mail*.

I don't blame my mother for the fact that I felt fat. Nor do I blame women's magazines or fashion models. It goes deeper than that, doesn't it? Female self-loathing has been handed down throughout the generations; it has been ingrained in our psyches, etched on our DNA. Had any of my mother's friends, or my friends for that matter, ever announced that they were happy with their bodies, I am pretty sure they would have been cast out from their social circles like lepers, condemned for their monstrous ego behind their back, which now we mention it, could do with some serious toning.

Being thin was the ultimate goal, although I have no idea why. Did I think it would make me more successful in my career, or help me find lasting love? I guess I just believed that it would make me happier, although the truth is that the battle to be thin only ever made me feel miserable.

The Wrong Knickers

So 'mad as a box of frogs' was the default setting with which I went into my twenties. When one day I look back on that decade, I will realise that the unhealthiest relationship I have is not with a man, but with food. But I don't have that hindsight now, that maturity. I can't see that my body is at its loveliest, my boobs will never be perkier and there will never be a gap so large between my thighs. I have no idea of the things my body will go through in a decade or so, and that then, when I really do need to lose weight, I will be too busy and tired and resigned to do anything about it. I will squander my aesthetic golden years, I will spend them in denial, and in the quest for thin I will actually take a perfectly good body and probably make it worse, making bright skin grey and doing God knows what damage that I cannot see.

You know those bits in the Sunday supplements, where celebrities reveal their diet and a nutritionist analyses it, telling them that while they eat oily fish, kale and pomegranates, and drink hot water with lemon every morning, they really could do with more roughage in their lives? They make me laugh out loud, they do. I've tried drinking hot water with lemon in the morning, but it does nothing for me. It contains no caffeine, no sugar, nothing other than a citrus zing to pep you up. And if a nutritionist was to analyse *my* diet, I'm pretty sure she would send me straight to hospital and put me on a drip, giving me three weeks to live in the process.

But in an effort to realise how screwed up my eating is, one week I write down everything I consume. It's probably best you do not read it while you're eating:

BREAKFAST

I know that breakfast is the most important meal of the day. It's just a shame that it happens to fall when it does. Who can eat before midday? Who can bear to put anything down their throat other than coffee? I can't – I'm usually too hungover to try, and I don't want to waste precious calories on something as dull as cereal. So instead I have a black coffee with five sugars and three Marlboro Lights.

MID-MORNING SNACK

I've heard this should be something like pumpkin seeds. I used to feed pumpkin seeds to my Russian dwarf hamsters, give you a massive clue. My mid-morning snack is actually a soya latte, because I have heard soya milk is better for you than dairy. And some more fags.

LUNCH

Obviously, I have whatever the soup special is at Pret a Manger, every day for the entire week. Sometimes, as a treat when I'm really hungover, I allow myself a sand-wich. It's a wonder I'm not hungover all the time, given how little I eat and how much I drink, but as I like to say, 'You only live once, even if you don't live quite as long as you should because you have a shoddy diet . . .'

MID-AFTERNOON SNACK

A multi-vitamin and mineral pill, with an Omega 3 capsule chaser. Some edamame beans, without the salt.

DINNER

Quavers. Quavers are my one concession towards carbs. When I tried the Atkins, I discovered that if you cut them out of your diet entirely, you start to smell a bit like an open sewer.

WEEKEND DIET

Well, obviously, I'm starving by the time the weekend rolls around. I'm ready to feast. I eat fish and chips and pizza you can order by the yard. Once, I order so much pizza that when the delivery man arrives, he asks if I'm having a party. 'No, it's just for me,' I say, having to turn the box sideways in order to get it through the door. I buy burgers and battered sausages, and snack on pork pies. I dip them in lashings of low fat mayonnaise, because if it's low fat, then that's OK, right? Hmmm, mayonnaise.

I think about food all the time, but the irony is I have no idea how to cook it. I wear this inability to rustle up a green salad like a badge of honour – I am pretty sure it makes me a proper modern woman and shows that I'm too busy smashing through glass ceilings (or falling off nightclub tables) to waste my time making macaroni cheese. On the rare occasions I go to the supermarket, I often marvel at the trollies and baskets in front of me, the herbs and spices and grains and pulses and pieces of meat on the bone to be roasted. I have heard rumours that you can make soup yourself, rather than just buying it in cans and plastic containers or from Pret a Manger, but the mind boggles when you think how this process would actually work. I have heard people talk of boiling chicken bones for stock, but to boil chicken bones you would have to cook a chicken and I have no idea how one does that. I look at things like fennel and butternut squash and aubergines, and think what the fuck do you do with them them? It's like trying to solve a particularly hard equation, or work out the meaning of life.

I know that, like having a boyfriend, if I could cook, my life would instantly be better. But it's a vicious circle. If you don't have a boyfriend, you have nobody to cook for, and what's the point of cooking for one? All that time, effort and energy spent on something only you are going to eat? It would be like painting the Mona Lisa and hiding it in your basement for the rest of time (except, of course, I don't think I could ever manage the culinary equivalent of the Mona Lisa). I can sort of do a spag bol, as long as you don't mind it being more spaghetti than bolognese (the very idea of mince makes me queasy, OK?), and I can cook a steak and fry some spinach alongside it, as long as you don't mind your steak blackened on the outside but bloody in the middle. I can chop up broccoli and cauliflower for you to dip in some houmous, but don't expect me to cook either of these vegetables for you unless you fancy them boiled to the point that their nutritional values are negligible, their vitamins and minerals leeched from them into a rusty old pan.

I tell myself that cooking is something that will happen

later in life, like the menopause and an appreciation of classical music and, if Chloe is to be believed, savings accounts. I will wake up one morning and magically Radio 3 will be blasting out around the house, as opposed to some witless goon on Radio 1, and there will be a pot of something 'slow cooking' in the oven. I mean, slow cooking? Just really, who can even be bothered with it?

I did once try to do a Sunday lunch, as I felt this might be a good PR exercise, a way for people to see a more grown-up me, a less vapid, shallow one. I roped Chloe in, because I felt it would be good for her too – if nothing more, it was a way to fill up half of the weekend.

We decided to do it at hers, as she has a dining table (one used exclusively as a resting place for bills, receipts and bits of random paper that have nowhere else to go), while my sister and I are forced to eat off a coffee table. We invited Steve, my sister, James and his new boyfriend, Richard. 'You're bringing the food,' grunted Chloe. 'I don't do supermarkets.'

'Easy!' I said, enthusiasm bouncing off me. 'What could possibly go wrong?'

I don't know. Maybe my sister left the fridge open by mistake, or perhaps the temperature had been turned down accidentally when I had loaded in the packet of beef I had bought from the butcher. He had told me it was a perfect joint of meat, that OF COURSE it would keep until Sunday if I stuck it in the fridge as soon as I got home, and yes, it would survive a short journey across town, too. I handed over a twenty-pound note, and imagined the praise bestowed on us when our friends tasted Chloe and Bryony's amazing roast.

'It looks like Lady Gaga,' is what Chloe said when she removed the beef from the plastic bag.

'What do you mean, it looks like Lady Gaga?' I responded, as I sat on the floor fiddling around with the nobs on her sparkling clean, never-before-used oven.

'I mean, it seems to have hair. And eyebrows. It looks like Lady Gaga when she wore that meat dress to the MTV awards.'

I stood up and took a look at the meat. I closed my eyes and dry heaved. The meat that would definitely keep did indeed look a bit like Lady Gaga, if Lady Gaga had follicles made from mould. 'Oh Jesus,' I said, turning away and clutching my stomach. 'He said it would keep!'

'Well it hasn't. And we have guests turning up in like,' she checked her iPhone, 'an hour. And if we serve them this, they will all be starring in their very own episode of *Come Die With Me*.'

'What are we going to do? Can't we just cut off the mouldy bits?'

'Bryony, if we were to cut off all the mouldy bits there wouldn't be enough meat left to serve one person, let alone six.'

'OK, so we improvise.'

'How? Serve them vegetables, potatoes and wine and

hope that they don't realise that there is no roast on their plates?'

I took a deep breath. 'We're going to have to order in takeaway and pretend that we have cooked it.'

'Oh right, we'll just call up the takeaway Sunday roast shop and have it delivered.'

'No, we'll call the pub down the road. We'll go there and pick it up. Right now, it's all I can think of.'

And so it was that hidden in the bottom of the oven we had one portion of chicken, one of lamb, a beef, and a suckling pork for good measure, because that was all the pub could do without running out of meat for their existing customers. For this lie, which we were sure nobody would buy, we spent the grand total of £100. Steve arrived first. I don't know why I had thought it would be a good idea to invite him at all – he fancies himself as a bit of a Gordon Ramsay in the kitchen, or at the very least, an Antony Worrall Thompson. 'So,' he said, plonking down an expensive-looking bottle of red wine on the nearest surface. 'What kind of roast are we having?'

'A sex one,' said Chloe, sarcastically.

'We're having a mixture,' I jumped in.

'A mixture?' said Steve. 'Wow, you really have been hard at work, which is funny, because I can't seem to smell any cooking.'

'Don't you know it's terribly rude to turn up and criticise your host's culinary skills?' said Chloe. I wasn't sure her and Steve got on terribly well.

'I wasn't aware that Bryony or you had any culinary skills.'

My sister – well, she was too much of a food ignoramus to figure out that most people didn't cook four different varieties of roast for their guests. James and Richard only cared about the wine. Steve liked his pork, but remarked that it was 'a little bit dry'.

'You're lucky to have been fed at all,' snapped Chloe.

'Well, I'm looking forward to seeing what you've made for dessert,' he said, leaning smugly back in his chair. Chloe and I looked at each other. We stood up and went to the kitchen area. 'Jesus,' she hissed in my ear. 'The fucker expects *dessert*, too?'

'I think it's fair to say,' I whispered, as I put my coat on to go and buy some ice cream from the nearest newsagent, 'that we won't be doing this again in a hurry.'

And then there is – haha – exercise. Kickboxing. Hiking. Spinning. Abseiling. Climbing. Swimming. Power plates. Zumba. Aqua-aerobics. Tennis. Table tennis. Tai Chi. Circuits. Turbo training. Legs, bums and tums. Pilates. Yoga. Hot yoga. Slow yoga. Fast yoga. In my never-ending quest for the body beautiful, I have spent a small fortune signing up for all of these classes, only to dump them anything from a fortnight to two months later, my initial enthusiasm quickly dwarfed by exercise-induced boredom. All of these classes were going to save me, they were going to get me on the straight and narrow, except that they have never left me anything other than out of pocket and desperate for a packet of pickled onion Monster Munch. I keep waiting for the endorphins everybody bangs on about, but the endorphins never kick in; the only happy hormones I experience are when I get home and eat a bowl of pasta. The other day, I wrote down all the terrible exercising experiences I had gone through, and just reading it made me break out into a sweat:

RUNNING

I call it running, but what I do is more like 'fast walking'. Once, while I was taking a turn around Hyde Park during my lunch break, I got overtaken by an octogenarian running club. On my iPod there are gym playlists and stretching playlists, running playlists for sunny days and running playlists for wintry days. But the only sound I am really familiar with is the sound of failure; on all of my 'jogs' I am convinced I should be followed around by a band of men playing comedy falling over noises on their trombones.

I spent more time choosing my running kit than I ever have actually running. I have to wear not one but two sports bras to control my boobs, and then I can't breathe properly because I feel so restricted by them. I can't breathe properly even when I'm sitting at my desk – that's what happens when you smoke twenty a day – so imagine what I'm like when I go for one of my jogs. My lungs feel like they are going to explode. Some people talk about the sense of freedom they feel when they go running, but I think they might be psychopaths. The only thing I feel I might be freed from when running is this mortal coil – which reminds me of something Steve said when I came back from that run in Hyde Park, red-faced and sweating. 'Good grief, Bry, you look as if you've been in the blast of a nuclear bomb.'

SURFING

By now you are probably thinking of me as the kind of girl who has only ever surfed the net, or perhaps, at a push, the cultural zeitgeist. Not true. Desperate to be the kind of girl who could casually drop in to conversation her ability to surf, thinking, stupidly, that it might win me back Sam, I actually paid to do a course in Cornwall one Bank Holiday weekend.

I got it all wrong. Do you know how far away Cornwall is? I may as well have booked a course in Hawaii for the time it took me to get there. The train I boarded was the train everyone had decided to board; it was one of the hottest weekends of the summer and the air conditioning broke down. The journey was supposed to take, at a push, six hours, but we broke down somewhere near Newton Abbot and all had to change trains. Eventually, I arrived in Newquay ten hours after I had left Paddington.

Now I'm a girl who likes a party, but even for me, Newquay was too much. Teenagers vomited on every corner, at each turn there was a stag or hen do shrieking and bellowing at passers-by. As I lay in my single bed in a dingy hotel, listening to the sounds of the nightclub below, it occurred to me that the place was like one of Dante's circles of hell.

The next day, after two hours' sleep, I turned up at Fistral Beach exhausted. I was surprised to see that the rest of the group were bright-eyed and bushy-tailed, raring to go, despite the fact the temperature seemed to have dropped twenty degrees overnight and it was now freezing, with a mist enveloping the sea. Squeezing into a wetsuit was an exercise in itself, and when I'd finally managed it, I collapsed on to the wet sand like an asthmatic walrus. I couldn't even pop up on to the board on land, let alone in the water, and when I found myself washed up on the beach next to a hypodermic needle, I decided to spend the rest of the weekend eating fish and chips and drinking Rattler in the pub with the other dropouts from the course, all two of them.

YOGA

I mean, is there anything more boring than a yoga devotee? I don't think I have ever met a truly fun person who can do a perfect downward dog – not on purpose, anyway. There is a yoga studio around the corner from where my sister and I live, and every day I see them pouring out with their mats and perfect, sleeked-back hair, looking calm and serene as they think about their lunch of tofu and buckwheat noodles with a heavy topping of smug self-satisfaction. 'We should try that,' said my sister one day. 'Look how *at one* they seem to be. I bet if we did yoga, everything else would fall into place.'

Like the downward dog's bollocks it would. But if we didn't try, we wouldn't ever find out, I supposed, so we booked ourselves in one Sunday morning to do something called 'Bikram Yoga', which, it turned out, involved doing yoga in a sauna. At the best of times, I'm not sure I would be any good at yoga, but I definitely knew there was no hope in forty degrees of heat the morning after an accidental bottle and a half of white wine. As we arrived, everyone was high-fiving each other – I already felt the prickly heat of being an outsider at this point – and then, as if it couldn't get any worse, we saw Steve, with a pink mat rolled up under his arms, chatting up the instructor, who happened to look a bit like Christy Turlington.

'STEVE?' shouted my sister, across the room. 'What are YOU doing here?'

'The question,' said Steve, sauntering over to us, saying hi to everyone as he went, 'is surely what are *you two* doing here? I come every week. Have done for months now. It's really, you know, "cleansing".'

'I think I just heard you use the word "cleansing", Steve,' I said, scrunching up my nose. 'Are you feeling OK?'

'After this class, I will be!'

'I reckon you only do it because you fancy all the hot yoga chicks,' said my sister.

'Shut up and lie down your towels next to mine,' hissed Steve. 'And please. Don't. Make. Too. Much. Fuss.'

It was like he had read my mind. As every painful minute progressed, I thought my limbs might simply stop working. My body simply couldn't and wouldn't bend. My sister, meanwhile, well obviously she was brilliant at it. Off she went, into the child pose, the Lords of the Dance pose, the One Legged King Pigeon pose (I mean, AHAHAHAHAHAHAHAHAHA) while I dissolved in the heat like a slug. 'That was amazing,' said Naomi, high-fiving Steve, 'I'm coming back next weekend.' Me? I refused even to walk past the place again.

KICKBOXING

I have saved the best for last, I like to think. Have I ever told you about the time I lost a tooth after a night snogging an Australian kickboxer with a back full of tattoos and a penchant for wild sex parties? No? Well, let me tell you now. Not having a degree in dentistry, I cannot tell you if the two events are related to one another, if his forceful snogging is the reason I pay £200 to have what remains of my tooth yanked out by an Iranian who works out of a small room above a betting shop somewhere in Kensal Rise. I suppose, if I really was Cool Girl, I could have asked the Australian kickboxer to pay for some decent dental care and get the tooth filled in, rather than leave the space vacant – as it is to this very day – a space that has led to some interesting conversations with all the men who have come since and discovered the gap in the course of their initial, friendly investigations into my mouth.

Anyway, though I'm sure the Aussie kickboxer would like to think that his tongue was powerful enough to dislodge a woman's tooth, I think it was probably just a happy coincidence that makes a reasonably good story all of these years later. I don't remember the kickboxer being a particularly bullish kisser. In fact, strangely for a man whom I will soon discover likes group sex while wearing a mask, he doesn't seem to use his tongue at all. He just places his massive lips over mine and sort of sucks. It is a bizarre way to kiss, and probably part of the reason that I find myself back home from our date at the chaste hour of 10.30 p.m., starving because the date took place at a vegetarian restaurant, me pushing tofu around my plate in between his attempts to Hoover my face. Part of the reason, but not the whole reason.

An hour and a half into our date, emboldened by nothing more than a shot of wheatgrass and a carrot and ginger juice, the Australian kickboxer suddenly asks if I fancy coming to a 'special party' with him. My ears prick up. By special party, does he mean one where people drink and smoke and have a good time? By special party, does he mean one in a pub, where there are bar snacks like crisps and ohmygod pork scratchings?

If that is the case, YES, I will go to a special party with him!

'It's quite unusual,' he continues, perusing a menu of green teas. I decide that unusual to him is probably drinking two lager shandies on an evening out. 'It's a bit out there.'

'Out there is normal for me,' I say confidently, because compared to this, a wine tasting is out there. 'Hit me with it!' I beam, imagining glasses of wine the size of soup bowls, and tubs of salty peanuts. 'I'm ready for anything!'

'OK,' says the kickboxer, a smile the size of New South Wales stretching across his face. 'Well, it's sort of a sex party.'

'A what?' I ask, sure that this is simply his way of inviting me back to his.

'You know, a party full of beautiful, like-minded people who enjoy spending time with one another.'

I stare at him.

'If you're worried about discretion,' he says, motioning to the waiter for the bill, 'everyone wears masks. They provide them on the door.'

The door? Oh, hello, welcome to the sex party, please let me take your coat and here's a mask and some condoms. Enjoy your evening! And how, exactly, does the mask make things better? Had I drunk anything stronger than organic elderflower wine, I might venture to say to him that if you can only have sex with people whose faces you cannot see, this is not necessarily a good thing.

And furthermore, if you are going to suggest group sex to a woman, don't immediately tell her that she might like to put a mask over her clearly hideous face to improve the experience.

'I've been quite a few times and it's all very classy.'

I almost spit out my drink attempting not to laugh. It doesn't matter what spin you try to put on a sex party – even the people attending it must surely know that of all the many things it is, classy is not one of them. Slowly, he seems to twig that he has got the wrong girl. Simultaneously, I'm trying to work out what vibes I must give out for him ever to have thought I was the *right* girl.

'I'm sorry,' he says, pulling out a wad of notes from his wallet and placing them on the table. Is he going to try to PAY me to go to the sex party with him? 'I must have got the wrong end of the stick with you.'

'No, no,' I say, when in actual fact I mean, 'Yes, yes, you have.' Why is it that I feel I must be polite to everyone, even presumptuous little tossbags who want to share me round a group of people like a plate of smoked-salmon canapés at a drinks party? 'I just hadn't really factored in for a sex party tonight,' I actually say. Goddamn it, woman. Stop trying to be polite! 'I'm kind of tired.' No, really stop. 'Maybe another time, eh?' Eh? EH? NO! Definitely not another time. Not even if you DID pay me.

The kickboxer hands the notes to the waiter. 'Let me get this,' he says, his voice suddenly chilly. I don't try and go halves, not when all I have eaten is a roasted pepper.

'Well, it was nice spending time with you,' he says, as if I am a penpal. He stands up to leave. 'I'll see you at class on Monday.' He shakes my hand. He ACTUALLY SHAKES MY HAND. 'Do you want me to walk you to the tube?' he asks as a sort of afterthought. I tell him that it's fine, because a) I don't think I can bear to spend another three minutes with him and b) I don't want to go to the tube. I want to go to McDonald's to buy some food.

So here I am, back at the flat, with the item I have lusted after all evening – a Big Mac. I want to place my lips over this Big Mac and devour it in the same way that the kickboxer has been doing to me all evening. I want to make love to this Big Mac. I want to become one with it, which is just as well, because as soon as I bite into it, I hear a crunch and feel a bolt of pain and the next thing I know, I'm spitting a load of enamel into my hand, enamel that has charmingly bonded itself to a gherkin.

'WHAT WAS THE HOT AUSSIE LIKE?' says my sister, bouncing into the kitchen before noticing the blood pouring from my mouth. 'OHMIGOD HE MUST HAVE BEEN GOOD! TELL ME TELL ME TELL ME!'

'TISSUE,' is all I can say, as I gulp back blood.

'WHAT? TELL ME TELL ME TELL ME?'

'TISSUE! TISSUE! TISSUE NOW!'

She disappears into the bathroom but returns empty handed. 'We've, erm, run out of loo roll.' If I could speak properly, I would complain that it was her turn to buy the loo roll, that I have bought the last thirty loo rolls and really, is it SO much to ask her to spend two quid on a packet of Andrex, or even less on some cheap stuff from the local offie that probably makes your bottom bleed but is STILL better than having no loo paper at all, and while we're on the subject, could you PLEASE throw away empty loo rolls rather than chucking them on the floor of the bathroom because as far as I know, nobody is planning to make Tracey Island out of them? But I don't say any of this because I have been rendered mute. Metallic liquid is filling my mouth, and all I can do is dribble as I attempt not to swallow my own blood. If I could talk, I would probably tell a cautionary tale about the effects of getting involved with unsuitable men: don't do it, and if you do do it, your teeth will fall out. You will not be able to speak and moan about getting involved with unsuitable men. Let that be a lesson to you all.

'JUST GET ME SOMETH—' and suddenly my sister has shoved the J cloth that has been hanging over the sink for the last three months into my mouth. Another cautionary tale: be careful what you ask for. I taste metal and washing-up liquid with a hint of onion. I think I am going to vomit. I am going to vomit, and then I am going to spend the rest of my life a toothless spinster who smells of damp old J cloths.

'So how did the date go?' asks my sister, her face telling

me that she already knows the answer. 'Please tell me your bleeding mouth is not the result of you trying out your kickboxing moves on each other. You're an amateur, and he's your teacher . . .'

'WAS,' I manage to get out of my mouth, bloody saliva pouring forth with it.

'Wow, it obviously went super well. When you've managed to remove all the broken teeth from your gob, perhaps you can tell me how it is that the date you were so excited about just five short hours ago has ended with you needing dental work and jacking in the semi-professional career in kickboxing you've been yabbering on about for the last few weeks.'

Kickboxing. It had left me feeling, if not literally bruised and battered – I had spent most of the classes doing little more than admire the curve of the Australian's biceps, the muscular bulge of his calves – then meta-phorically so. And yet it had seemed like such a good idea at the time, the perfect way to let go of some of the aggression that had been stored up inside me after the Sam situation, the Josh situation, the divorce situa-tion, the never-having-any-money situation. And it all started so well. I had returned from the first class with a slightly aching right hand and a crush. The Aussie instructor had a shaved head that somehow made his huge green eyes look even bigger. He was strong and capable and just the kind of man I needed in my life. On his back was a tattoo of an angel that to me made him look brave; a passer-by would probably have just thought he was a budget David Beckham. The fact he was Australian added an exoticness to my crush, as if Australians were not two-a-penny in London, and in certain areas – Shepherd's Bush, Acton, Earls Court – easier to find than in Sydney. 'The instructor is soooo dreamy,' I had told anyone who had cared to listen, and a fair few who hadn't, too.

But who cared about their uninterest? I knew there was a possibility that the instructor was interested, from the way he stood behind me, holding my body in the correct position, helping me to hit the punchbag in the right way. The way he used me to show the other members of the class a move, even though I didn't have a clue. Three weeks in I had swapped my baggy tracksuit bottoms and T-shirt for a slinky number I had bought for £100 from Sweaty Betty. I started to turn up for the class in full waterproof make-up. Like the start of some terrible seventies porn film, I asked if he would mind giving me some private tuition. Who cared that it cost me an extra £30 a week if it meant I got to spend more time with him?

And one evening, after an hour of me giggling as I attempted to punch and kick his boxing pads, he asked if I fancied grabbing a quick drink in the nearby pub. Of course I did. It didn't bother me that he drank only orange juice, because I was hopelessly tipsy after my first glass of wine, inevitable given that all I had eaten that day was a piece of toast and an avocado salad from Pret a Manger.

The Wrong Knickers

He asked me about my love life and, though I knew it was bad form to talk about exes, I did anyway, poo-poohing them all and telling him what a great, wild time I was having being single, a total lie told because I thought it made me look more attractive. He had kissed me as he put me in a taxi home and asked if I fancied dinner. Dinner, followed by a sex party, I now realised. That's what you get for trying to be the cool girl.

The Iranian dentist said my teeth were in 'real bad condition. You eat lots of sugar? No, why I ask this, you obviously eat lots of sugar! You must stop eating so much sugar!' I closed my eyes and told him to get on with whatever it was he had to do. When you have a tooth removed, you have to be careful that you don't end up with something called dry socket. Chloe jokes that with my reputation, there's little chance of that happening, but the Iranian dentist was adamant that it was very serious indeed. That it would lead to 'much pain', as if his drill hadn't seen to that already.

I thought it was unlikely I would end up with dry socket, which when I looked into it appeared to be a random inflammation of the extraction site. Only 5 per cent of people who have a tooth out end up with it, so I reasoned I was relatively safe. The night of my tooth extraction, I wedged some more cotton wool in my gob to protect the exposed bit of gum, and promptly went out with Chloe and Steve to the pub. With my puffed-out cheek, I looked like one of my Russian dwarf hamsters, but I didn't care. After the week I'd had, with the Australian kickboxer and the sex party and the J cloth and the missing tooth, I was desperate for a drink. Completely and utterly desperate.

I drank through the cotton wool and smoked through the pain. The next morning, there was a dull ache in my mouth. I put it down to the tooth extraction, but within three days, the dull ache had turned into a pounding pain throughout my head. It was unbearable. I was mainlining Codeine. I was writhing in pain. Had I not thrown that manky J cloth in the bin, I would have happily bitten down on it to try to quell the pain. After a sleepless night crying into my pillow, I returned to the Iranian dentist.

'Dry socket,' he said immediately. 'You smoke? You drink? These risk factors for dry socket. You need to be healthy!' He beamed at me, a mouth full of gold fillings. 'You eat fresh fruit and veg, very little red meat, you floss every day, you be fine!' I left feeling like a prize idiot. So much for taking control of my weight and my finances. I couldn't even control my own body.

9

My embarrassing but necessary indie phase

In the unlikely event I ever become notable for anything other than being able to drink my own body weight in strong continental lager, there will be blue plaques commemorating my habitation littered all over London. On the bedsit in Bethnal Green, outside the cold, silverfish-infested dump in Kensal Green, and on the front of an ugly prefabricated building in deepest darkest Camden.

A change is better than a rest, my mother always said, whenever it was announced that we couldn't afford to holiday 'abroad', and so shortly after the bailiffs have woken us up at the crack of dawn, we decide to up sticks and move somewhere else.

'The place just feels . . .' my sister shuddered for effect, 'TAINTED. I don't want to be here any more. We need to start afresh somewhere else, somewhere where we pay our council tax on time and our TV licence in monthly direct debits and we set up a "household" account in order to be organised.'

Instead of making actual changes in our own lives – cutting down on nights out, taking up a hobby like sewing or charity work – it is so much easier just to move. Every new flat represents new hope. It's always the last place we're going to live as single girls, the last place we'll rent before we magic a £60,000 deposit into our bank accounts, enabling us to buy somewhere. It's always the place we're going to take care of, the place we're going to buy fresh flowers for without leaving them to die in manky, smelly water, the place where we're going to throw lovely dinner parties and put up art on the walls, replacing stock Ikea prints of the New York skyline and a black taxi driving over Westminster Bridge. Except, of course, it never is.

Steve decides to join us in our search. He has been defeated by damp and mould and wants out of this cursed block of flats just as much as we do. 'I can't believe I'm actually going to live with you two,' he says, shaking his head in disbelief. 'I imagine it's going to be a bit like living with teenaged children. I'm going to feel like your uncle.'

'I'm just so glad that they will have a sobering influence on them,' says my mother, who for some peculiar reason has got it into her head that Steve is a man of letters, a paragon of virtue, rather than an alcohol-dependent Joey from *Friends*. 'Why don't you move somewhere nice, like Fulham, or Putney, or Clapham?' she continues.

'That sounds lovely Mrs Gordon,' says Steve, oil oozing from every pore.

'Oh, please call me Jane,' she smiles, her eyelashes fluttering in the breeze of a young man.

'Shut up, Steve. Because, Mum, Fulham and Putney are expensive and boring and Clapham is full of rugger buggers and yummy mummies pushing their stupid monster truck buggies around,' I sneer. 'I'll strip naked and run through Piccadilly Circus before you catch me living in Clapham.'

'It was only a suggestion,' sighs my mother.

We end up in Camden, of all places. Camden! With its spit and sawdust music venues, its population of chain smokers who dress like pipe cleaners, and its market full of stalls selling legal highs. At least in Fulham or Putney or Clapham there may have been a flicker of hope that our lives might change, a small chance of stability. But by choosing Camden we may as well move straight into the Priory. We are doomed from the very start. What are we thinking? No, don't answer that. We are thinking pubs, all-night bars, off licences that will sell you fags and six cans of Fosters for five quid at three in the morning. There is not a hope in hell that this flat will be a place for dinner parties, or that it will end up as anything other than a place to rest our heads and a venue for all-night piss-ups. We may as well tell the landlord to spend the deposit now, possibly on an array of deep-cleaning equipment.

The flat is grey and dull, which my mother interprets as an 'excellent blank canvas'. There is a dodgy-looking oven next to an evil-looking boiler, both of which will probably kill us with deadly carbon monoxide if not treated with the right amount of respect. The electricity is on a coin meter (my mother: 'It means you will be able to keep on top of your bills!') and the door to my bedroom is broken, the handle falling off whenever you do something out of the ordinary, like try to open or close it. 'Well, I think you've made a really good choice,' announces my mother as she scurries out the door at such speed she forgets her brave face in the hallway. 'I think you will be really happy here.'

It isn't long before it all starts falling apart – let's face it, it was never that together in the first place – before the electricity starts going out in the middle of *The X Factor*, leaving us desperately scraping around for ten-pence coins so we don't miss Dermot announcing the result of the public vote. Steve spends so long in the shower that there is never any hot water, and he leaves little man hairs in the bath that make me long for the days of our pet silverfish.

If we ever stayed in before, now we most certainly don't. We move to Camden just as the relatively elderly Primrose Hill set – Kate Moss, Sadie Frost, Jude Law et al. – are being usurped in coolness by Amy Winehouse, the Arctic Monkeys and strange-looking people like Noel Fielding. There is just too much going on around us – pubs like the Hawley Arms that feature daily in the gossip columns of the *Sun*; secret gigs in kebab shops next to the tube; pub quizzes hosted by obscure indie bands you would only ever read about in the NME.

But I have never read the NME. I have always been a *Smash Hits* kind of girl, a *Just Seventeen* kind of girl. I have always hankered after muscular, healthy-looking boy band members. I have only ever listened to catchy, easy pop that bounces merrily off the ears, allowing you to daydream about being swept off your feet. I don't under-stand indie music, never have done; it has always seemed so noisy, so lacking in melody. I think the measure of a good song is can you imagine your life as an accompanying music video? Can you see yourself as the shining star of an empowering Beyoncé song, or the coy-looking lovely in a One Direction single, who starts off looking sad and lost but gets to snog Harry Styles as the tune reaches its crescendo? If it doesn't do this, I am not interested.

But once I move to Camden, things start to change, because if you want to be part of the cool gang in Camden, you can't be into boy bands, not even ironically. I down-load albums by the Strokes, the Kooks and the Kills. I listen to them over and over again, hoping that on the seventy-ninth outing, I will finally get it. I never do, but that doesn't stop me pretending. As Steve and I frequent the pubs around us, we slowly make indie friends. Camden is the kind of place where you are so pissed on Jack Daniel's that you end up speaking to anyone who might happen to be standing next to you at the bar. We meet Rebecca Raves on one such evening. We are too flattered by the attention shown to us by such a hipster to realise that the only reason she wants to befriend us is so that we'll write about her in the paper.

'Is that your real surname?' I ask one evening, as I cackhandedly play a game of pool against her before she starts a long stint DJing at her weekly club night. 'I don't tell anyone my real name,' she says, mysteriously, motioning for the door because she obviously wants a cigarette. 'What does a name even matter, anyway?'

I nod along. It's just easier that way.

'I bet her real name is Margaret and she comes from Woking,' says Chloe, after she has met Rebecca Raves for the first time. 'And what's with the holes in her tights? Can't she buy some new ones from Boots? Why does she wear so much make-up? Has she never heard of a hair-brush? I can't stand it – she somehow makes being unwashed look good. I hate her.'

'Rebecca's asked if I want to go to Glastonbury with her,' I tell Chloe.

'You're joking, right? You? Glastonbury?'

'And you, too,' I say. 'I think we should both go. You've got to try everything once, right?'

'No. Wrong. You don't have to try everything once, you really don't. See – crack cocaine, sky diving and let us not forget LIVING IN CAMDEN. I'm not paying near on two hundred quid to stand in a cold field covered in mud watching some band I've never heard of, some band I never want to hear of. If you're going to make me sleep in a tent for four nights, you're going to have to pay me.'

'You're such a spoilsport.'

'You're on your own, kiddo.'

'I'll show you,' I sulk.

'Yeah, you will,' sighs Chloe. 'Trench foot. That's what you're going to show me.'

* * *

You can't, of course, just *go* to Glastonbury, any more than you can just go to Hogwarts without casting a magic spell and standing on a platform that doesn't actually exist. It would be easier to get to Everest or North Korea or Chernobyl. It's not the transport links that are the problem; it's getting tickets for the damn thing. To do so, you have to sit in front of three computers with six mobile phones on the go, refreshing the website and ringing the box office again and again until everything crashes and by the time it's back up again all of the tickets are sold out, meaning you have to go into a ballot for the next round, leaving you feeling as if you're taking part in some sort of musical version of the *Hunger Games*. This is no exaggeration. You are pretty sure that once you factor in the rain, the mud and the dodgy sanitation, you might well not survive the weekend.

What's worse, you don't even know what you are trying

to buy tickets for. The line-up won't be revealed for another three months, and the only acts you can be sure of appearing are Shakin' Stevens and the Wurzels, which means that, essentially, you have been attempting to spend almost £200 to see the Wurzels.

'I can't get a ticket,' I tell Rebecca when I next see her, my voice tinged with anxiety that this will spell the end of our non-friendship.

'Don't worry, babe,' she says. Only someone as cool as Rebecca could get away with using the word 'babe'. 'I can get us tickets 'cos I'm DJing.' Cos. She would never waste her energy saying anything as complicated as 'because'.

'Oh wow!' I almost squeal. I try to catch myself. I don't want her to think I sound like some smitten schoolgirl. 'That's so cool. You must be well chuffed.'

Chuffed? Did I actually just use the word 'chuffed'?

'Nah, they usually ask me. Do you think maybe that if you come, you could hook me up with your music editor?' Still I do not see that this so-called 'friendship' is based entirely on my need to be cool and her need to get publicity. 'So anyway, we'll leave on the Wednesday so we can get a good pitch for the tents and bed in. It'll be great. You'll love it.'

I know for a fact I won't. Glastonbury won't be my first festival. That honour goes to Reading, which I attended when I was just eight years old. When I tell Rebecca this, she is really impressed, especially when I mention that I got to watch the Pixies. But I leave out most of the details – the fact that I only went because my posh Berkshire uncle had been invited by his friend, who happened to run the festival at the time; the fact that, when he told me were going to see the Pixies, I actually thought we were off to meet some magical fairies. I didn't mention that I was wearing a Devon Pony Sanctuary jumper, a floral Laura Ashley skirt and a pair of patent Mary-Jane shoes with polka-dot ankle socks. I didn't mention the naked woman with a dog tied to a stick, who looked at me and started laughing wildly, screaming to all her friends, 'WHAT THE FUCK IS SHE DOING HERE?' I spent the rest of the night crying and have been scarred ever since.

I put the prospect of Glastonbury to the back of my mind. I am not counting down the months and weeks and days as some people on Facebook seem to be. I am not 'totally stoked' about the chance to see Blur and Bruce Springsteen, because do I look forty-four? The week before, I visit a branch of Millets and spend all the extra money I have from a small payrise on the kit I'm going to need: a pop-up tent, a blow-up airbed, a sleeping bag. I'm in way over my head; it's like preparing for a PGL kids' adventure trip, except with booze and fags and very probably, drugs.

I spend almost £100 on a pair of purple Hunter wellies that will stick to my thighs and give me welts and make me feel fat – a pair of £100 wellies that will have to be cut off me when I eventually return to London, a shrivelled husk of a woman, a shadow of my former self.

I spend the night before preparing a 'capsule festival wardrobe', the kind I have read about in *Grazia*. I select cut-off denim shorts and brightly coloured T-shirts, neon hoodies and floaty sundresses. I buy a snazzy jacket from Topshop that has the vague appearance of being waterproof, but which I soon discover is nothing of the sort. I pack dry shampoo and enough wet wipes to fill a maternity ward. I feel the nervous trepidation of a woman who is about to embark on childbirth for the first time.

When we arrive at the site, the first thing I notice is that I have forgotten to pack any contact-lens solution. Or my glasses. It's all very well having three different types of frock and sixty-seven different tops with you, but what good are any of these if you are so blind you cannot see any of them? 'Don't worry, babe,' says Rebecca, who I think might already be stoned. 'We'll find you some. There's bound to be some in this place, right?'

You'd think so. I can buy comedy Viking horns and clothes made of hemp, glow sticks and stick-on tattoos, and real tattoos come to that, but blow me if, anywhere within the 1,100 acres that make up the Glastonbury Festival, you can buy a handy travel size of saline solution. There is a pop-up chemist, which I spend four hours of the first day trying to locate, but when I do find them, they are about as much use as a sticking plaster on a broken leg. 'We've got some hayfever drops,' they say in a manner that leads me to believe they actually think they are being helpful. I buy them anyway, reasoning that the tiny bottle might come in handy at some point. Only I could go to the world's most famous music festival and moan that there isn't a well-stocked chemist. Only I could go to the world's most famous music festival and worry because I haven't brought my reading spectacles.

That night Rebecca takes me to the stone circle – a mass of rocks – and someone gives me an E. If there is one thing that is good in my life right now, it's the fact that I'm drug-free, but I'm so desperate to impress Rebecca that I accept the little tablet with a smiley face etched into it. As you know, I have never done ecstasy before. I've always been too fearful of my brain swelling up and oozing out of my head, but here I wonder if such a fate would be that bad. I'm cold and ill-prepared and my phone has already run out of battery. It seems particularly tragic that I should be almost twenty-eight years old and 'dropping' an E, but I swallow the pill with pleasure. And then I wait. And I wait and I wait and I wait.

What did I expect would happen? I had imagined a rush of warmth, a haze of love, a glow of gorgeousness. I had imagined bounding up and dancing around the stone circles. I had pictured embracing Rebecca, telling her I really loved her, her reciprocating and revealing that yes, her real name was Margaret and she was from Woking and to hell with it! But it doesn't happen. I am just chilly.

The only thing I would love to get my hands on right now is a pair of gloves and a nice woolly hat.

'Becca,' I shout in her general direction. 'I'm kind of tired and think I might go back to the tents.' But she isn't paying any attention. Her arms are wrapped around a bloke with longer hair than hers. He is tracing shapes around her face with his finger, telling her she is beautiful. 'Bry,' she shouts, not turning away from him. 'This is Leo. Leo's in this really cool new band.' Leo doesn't say hi. Instead he starts covering Rebecca in kisses, smothering her as she squeals in delight.

'OK, Becs,' I say, standing up unsteadily. 'I'm going now. See you in the morning!'

'Bye!' she giggles behind a mop of hair – I can't work out if it's his or hers – and I start to make way back towards the tents. Except it soon becomes clear that I don't know my way back towards the tents. I walk in ever-decreasing circles, past falafel stand after falafel stand, or is it just the same falafel stand? I start to feel woozy. Things don't seem right. The next thing I know, I'm falling to the ground next to a bin full of half-eaten falafel wraps.

'You OK, love?' says a man in a high-vis jacket, hovering over me. 'Do you want me to take you somewhere?' Yes, yes, I do! Take me away from here, far away! Take me home to the relative peace of Camden! Take me to the train station if that's too far, put me on the first carriage out of here!

221

'Campsite C,' is what I manage to blurt out.

Back in my tent, I think I'm dying. Everything has turned purple. When I close my eyes, there are wild colours. I think I want to call my mum and tell her how much I love her. Then I remember that my phone is dead. And realise that I'm not dying, just coming up on the E tablet I took an hour or so earlier. This is great. This is brilliant. The first time I take E, I end up alone and cold in a one-man tent with, I now realise, a puncture in my airbed.

For the next eight hours, I lie on my airless airbed, listening to the couple in the tent next to me having sex. It could be Rebecca and Leo for all I know or care. At some point, it starts to rain. The tent amplifies the weather and makes it sound as if outside it's hailing and sleeting, when in fact it's probably just drizzling. The drip-drip of the rain makes me realise I need a wee. I need a wee, but the nearest loos seem like half a mile away. I lie there, my bladder feeling fuller and fuller, my contact lenses feeling dryer and dryer on my eyeballs, wondering if I will survive the night.

The rest of the festival is a blur, and not just because my contacts get dirtier and dirtier as time goes on. I decide that the only way to get through this horrific torture is to drink heavily. It occurs to me that the reason people take so many drugs at festivals is because the only way to get through them is to be as high as a kite. I see no bands, none that I can remember anyway, and spend much of the weekend gatecrashing Rebecca and Leo's ecstasy-induced love fest, leaving their sides only when it's clear they're about to start humping one another. When we finally come to leave, I cadge a lift back in Leo's van and am so deranged, so crusty with tiredness, that I decide to take my contacts out and put them in my mouth, having once read that saliva can do the same job as saline. It doesn't. When I put them back in, my eyes turn into a streaming mess.

For the next week I feel as if I have jet-lagged myself without having gone any further than a field in Somerset. The doctor tells me I have viral conjunctivitis. I try to paint my eyes with mascara and liner, but it's hopeless. For the next fortnight I look like a drag queen from *28 Days Later*. 'I wish I'd listened to you, Chloe,' I admit. But I still don't learn my lesson.

Indie Barman becomes the closest thing I have had to a boyfriend since Sam, which was almost five years ago. Had you told me when we broke up that I would be single for that long, I would have lain down and wept. But time flies when you're having forced fun.

So Indie Barman is sort of my boyfriend, despite the fact I have neither his phone number nor his email, nor the faintest clue where he lives. We meet through Rebecca Raves and Leo, now going steady after their whirlwind festival romance at Glastonbury. Indie Barman plays the drums in Leo's band. His real name is Dylan 'as in Bob', he explains helpfully, but he will go down in lore forever as Indie Barman, given that is all Chloe will refer to him as. 'He's not a drummer, Bryony,' she says, after her first meeting with him. 'He's a barman in a pub who happens to play the drums for a crappy band in his spare time. Also, any man who introduces himself as "Dylan, as in Bob" loses the right to be called by his proper name, in my book.' So Indie Barman it is.

He wears leather jackets, skinny jeans, Converse and T-shirts bearing the legend of bands such as the Cramps. I don't really know their work – and with that kind of name, I don't think I want to – but I soon perfect a nonchalant ability to pretend airily that I do. He has shoulder-length black hair that falls almost into curls, framing his bright blue eyes and beautifully structured face. Although he has the look of the strong silent type, the mysterious hipster, he's cheeky as hell, the kind of man for whom the word 'scamp' was surely invented. Naturally, I fall for him immediately.

'He looks like he needs a good wash,' says Chloe.

'I can assure you, he's VERY clean,' I lie.

The first time we get together, he has just knocked off from his shift at a pub in Primrose Hill, the kind where you hear minor members of rock royalty snorting coke in the bogs. He slides into our booth with a 'whisky mac' as he calls it, which should be my first warning sign that he is a bit of an arsehole. Instead, it just makes me want to jump his bones.

He immediately puts his arm around me, making me flush bright red. 'So who's this lovely young lady?' he says to Leo and Rebecca, who rolls her eyes to the heavens at the cheesiness of it. We are introduced – he is Dylan, as in Bob, I am Bryony, as in . . . no, I can't think of anyone – and we spend the evening bantering, pulling each other's pigtails. 'I don't know whether to strangle you or kiss you,' he says at one point, as we get more drinks from the bar – an opportunity we both jump at as it means we can be alone – and well, I think you can guess which one he decides on.

We go back to mine because he's 'in between places'. I'm keen to play it cool, keen to peck him goodbye and wait and see, but he seems determined, the reason for which, I would soon discover, had less to do with me and more to do with him needing a place to stay for the night because he had been chucked off the latest sofa he had been sleeping on. And it was going well, it really was, until he tried to go to the loo in the middle of the night and discovered he was locked in my room, the handle broken as ever. 'I usually just have to wait for my flatmates to wake up in the morning and let me out,' I say, wanting the ground to swallow me up. 'Jesus,' he says, jumping up and down on the spot. 'You've locked me in here! You're like Kathy Bates in *Misery*! Next you'll be sawing off my legs!' They always hurt me, these gentle digs about being a maniac, because deep down I know I am only ever two tequila shots away from turning into one.

In the end, he climbed out the front window and peed in the garden. And despite the traumatic experience of being locked in, he came back for more. The next night, and the night after, and the one after that. I was convinced this was it, that he was the one – it never occurred to me that maybe he just needed a place to stay, and that getting a shag out of it was merely a bonus. I was too busy imagining rock 'n' roll weddings, changing my name to Bryony Bangs or some such, picturing the bridesmaid dress I would put on Kate Moss.

And then just as quickly as he had come into my life, he was gone again. Vanished. Vamoosh. 'They're just working on the album,' said Rebecca, not entirely convincingly, given that Leo was constantly by her side, a rock 'n' roll limpet, and didn't seem to be working on anything other than Rebecca. 'You know what these creatives are like. You have to give them time.'

So I gave him time, and spent a lot of *my* time refreshing the band's Facebook page, noticing that Dylan as in Bob was updating it three or four times a day – not with tracks, but YouTube links to old Nirvana records he liked. Was this the work of a busy man? I didn't think so.

I suppose that someone with higher self-esteem would at this point have written the whole thing off and got on with their lives. I suppose that someone with higher self-esteem would never have gone there in the first place. But I wasn't someone with high self-esteem. I was desperate to see him, to check that I hadn't done something wrong, like farted in my sleep the last time I saw him. I didn't know how I was going to broach that particular subject with him – 'Hey Dylan as in Bob, so I was wondering, is the reason you've disappeared because I let off a massive parp and you were totally horrified?' – but I knew I had to see him, to get some reassurance that he didn't totally detest me.

'We have to go and have a drink in his pub,' I tell Chloe, one lunchtime.

'We absolutely don't,' she replies. 'Do you know how mad you'll look if you turn up at his pub when he hasn't been in touch for two weeks?'

'That's totally unfair. Why is it mad if a woman turns up at a pub to check that someone is OK. If a bloke did it, you would think he was caring. A girl does it, and they should be committed!'

'But you don't want to check he's OK. You know he's OK, because you spend all day watching him faff around on social-network sites. Be honest with yourself, Bryony.'

'I *am* being honest with myself,' I lie. 'Why can a woman not go for a drink in a pub near her home?'

'Because there are loads of pubs near your home that this total loser doesn't work in.'

'But it's a nice pub. It has a good Jukebox and nice ales.'

'Since when did you drink ales?'

'I can drink ales if I want. I think it's my womanly RIGHT to drink ales in this pub. I can't avoid it for the rest of my life just because HE works there. He doesn't OWN it.'

When you're desperately clutching at straws, it's so easy to convince yourself that you're not.

'OK,' says Chloe, shaking her head. 'I'll come with you to this pub to shut you up, and to laugh at you as you make a total tit of yourself.'

'You're such a good friend.'

'I'm better than you'll ever know, Toots.'

I often find that a lot of thought, energy and time has to go into appearing effortlessly casual. I can't just turn up at this pub I have told myself I have every right just to turn up at. I need to make a plan. We will go on a Thursday night – Friday looks too try hard – and pretend that afterwards, we're going to a gig. This means I have to find a gig for us to pretend to go to. I scour listings in *Time Out* and alight on one by a band called The Broken Noses. I even buy tickets, to give the whole thing an air of authenticity, plus two extra, in case he wants to come with a mate. I will pretend some other friends pulled out at the last minute. This lie costs me just under £50.

I need to have a good outfit, something different from my usual uniform of bootcut jeans, ballet pumps and vests. I decide to buy a pair of skinny jeans, despite worrying that they will make my legs look like sausages. But if I'm going to wear skinny jeans, I have to wear heels. My usual Topshop numbers won't cut it. I go all out and purchase a pair of bright red, five-inch platforms from Biba. Biba is cool, right? I get an artfully distressed T-shirt from All Saints, and bung in a directional blazer. I imagine that when he sees me, it will be like the scene at the end of *Grease*, if Sandy had started the film as a promiscuous booze-hound with an occasional taste for drugs.

When Chloe sees me, she laughs. This was not the reaction I was going for. 'You spent £150 on a pair of heels for tonight? For a date you haven't even been asked on? When you've only just managed to get rid of a payday loan? Jesus, I've heard it all now.' Whatever. The payday loan, settled with this month's extra cash, is gone, so surely I should be allowed a treat, a reward for my financial achievement? These shoes are an investment piece, I tell myself.

I'm too nervous to go directly to the pub I have every right to go to whenever I want, so I insist we go to another one first. By the time I have steeled enough courage to leave, thanks to three large glasses of wine and a shot of tequila, I can barely walk in my £150 heels. 'Are you really sure you want to do this?' says Chloe, as she holds me up. 'I mean, you've turned into a bit of groupie. And for a band that NOBODY HAS EVER HEARD OF, AND NOBODY EVER WILL HEAR OF. It wouldn't matter if you were a groupie for a world-famous band on the road, because at least then we would get free drugs and

Cristal. But this . . . this tramp hasn't even bought you a drink. You've had to buy his. You've let him camp at your house . . .'

'He's not camped, he's shared my bed.'

'Whatever. You've let him stay at your house, eat your food, use your hot water, and has he even once bought you a drink?'

I think about it. He hasn't.

'Honestly, Bryony. Even by your particularly risible standards, this is a shocking new low.'

But I can't hear her. I'm more determined now than ever. I pull her towards the pub. I'm going to prove her wrong. I imagine that when I walk through the door the pub will fall silent and Dylan as in Bob will jump over the bar and gather me up into his arms. And I will have the last laugh, and at our housewarming, Chloe will pull me aside and tell me she is sorry for ever doubting me . . .

'Slow down would you!' she is squealing, as the pub draws into our sights. 'We don't want to look desperate.' She shoots me a look. We are outside the pub. I take a deep breath, delicately put one £75 shoe in front of the other and . . . we make our entrance.

The pub is stuffy, hot, packed. The queue for the bar is four deep, and try as I might I can't see him over the heads of the punters.

'You join the queue,' I tell Chloe. 'I'm going to the loo to touch up my make-up.'

'Bryony,' she is starting to say, 'you have six layers of

foundation on and enough mascara to take off in flight.'
But I am a woman on a mission, a woman who needs to
touch up her lipstick.

When I come back, the crowds have thinned out. Chloe
is standing at the bar, talking to . . . him. HIM. I let out
an involuntary shudder as my stomach flips. This is it, I
tell myself. This is the moment I have been waiting for.
I start to move forward, but feel myself moving only
towards the floor . . .

The next thing I know, I'm lying on my fat arse, my
outfit covered in dust from the fall. I'm like Laurel and
Hardy rolled into one, without so many laughs. 'Jeez, are
you OK?' says Chloe, who has rushed to my aid. 'I knew
those shoes were bad news.' She hauls me up. I am trying
to brazen it out, to pretend it hasn't happened. I get my
bearings, pat down my arse, try to brush off the dust. I
see Indie Barman staring right at me.

'Well, if it isn't the girl with the most beautiful eyes
in Camden,' he shouts. He leans over the bar, takes my
hand. It's like he has never been away, never acted like
a dick. 'Can I get you an ale? I know how much you like
them . . .' Chloe looks at me, confused. I raise my eyebrows
in a motion that I hope says 'don't say a thing'. Indie
Barman plonks down a frothing pint of Doom Bar. So
apt. I try to drink it without gagging.

'So, listen, I'm knocking off now. Shall I join you?'

'Actually,' says Chloe, 'we're supposed to be going to
a gig.'

'You mean YOU'RE supposed to be going to a gig,' I correct her. 'I'm just meeting up with her for a drink because she's in the area. I'd love for you to join me.'

Chloe picks up her bag, puts on her coat. 'Well, I know when I'm not wanted,' she says, a fake grin across her face. 'Wouldn't want to miss this gig now, would I? See you at work tomorrow, Bry.' She goes to give me a kiss on the cheek and mouths something to me. I think it's 'you little shit', but right now, I don't care. She goes towards the door, and it's just me and him.

'So what have you been up to?' asks Indie Barman, as we ease ourselves into a booth. 'Oh, stalking you on Facebook, obsessing over whether or not I had farted in your face the last time you stayed over,' is what I don't say. 'You know. A bit of this, bit of that. I've been kind of manic at work,' I fib. 'It's soooo stressful at the moment.'

'Well I'm glad you came in.' He sips his wanky whisky mac. 'I thought I was never going to see you again!' I like this lie. It makes out that the ball was in my court, that he has just been sitting here all this time, serving people pints of beer, waiting for me to turn up. It also gets him out of explaining where the hell he has been.

We drink and flirt for a bit, and then the last bell is ringing. The last bell, I find, is the sound of hope or the sound of doom, and never anything in between. I know my mood for the next few hours, days and weeks will depend upon the result of its chimes. Will he stay, or will he go? Will he decide to carry on with me, or will he announce he has to get home – does he even have a home? – because he has to be up early tomorrow morning?

'So shall we get another beer somewhere?' he suggests. RESULT.

Back at mine, things go as smoothly as I had meticulously planned them to go. We sit on the sofa, drinking cans of beer, whispering so as not to wake up Steve or my sister. Emboldened by the alcohol, I ask him where he disappeared to for the last few weeks. 'I mean, it's fine, it's cool and all that, it's just that one minute you were here, the next you were gone.'

'I know, I know,' he says, acknowledging that he knows and I know that it's totally not cool. 'I got a new place to stay and had to spend ages moving all my kit in. I mean, you can just imagine how hefty the drums are, right?'

'Rebecca said you were working on the album,' I blurt. Play it cool, play it cool.

'Well, I was, sort of. But I should have been in touch with you. And for that I am sorry.' He moves in to kiss me, carries me to the bedroom. In a haze of nakedness, all is forgiven.

I fall asleep, feeling blissful. At 4 a.m., I am awoken by the sound of the window being wrenched open. I leap up, go to grab Dylan as in Bob for safety, and then I realise. I realise that we are not being burgled, some lunatic isn't trying to climb in. I realise that Indie Barman is trying to climb *out*.

'I'm sorry, babe.' He's straddling the window frame, holding the window up as the cold air blows in. 'It's not you, it's me. You're a great chick, but I'm too all over the place to give you what you want. You've still got the best eyes in Camden, though.' He blows me a kiss. And then he's gone.

I get on with my life. I am fine. I am better than this, than he is. I decide to wash him out of my hair. Except no matter how many times I do wash my hair, it won't stop itching. It drives me to distraction. A week after the window incident, I am standing on the tube platform after work, reading my copy of *Grazia*, and scratching my head furiously, wondering if I have a dandruff problem. I see something fall onto the pages of my magazine. I look closely at it.

And with a jolt, I realise that Indie Barman has given me nits.

10

I just called to say you gave me chlamydia

It takes me five weeks to remove the last head louse from my locks, to wash Indie Barman out of my hair entirely. This, for me, is a relatively quick period in which to move on. I still ache a bit from Sam, even though I haven't heard from him for eons and for all I know he has moved on from Edinburgh to Carlisle to Calcutta. Even Josh, with whom I had the briefest of friendships, left me smarting for ages. It wasn't, I suppose, that I had really liked him. It was that he had made me feel like a fool; he made me feel ashamed. I only really stopped feeling stupid about him when I went and did something stupid with someone else, namely Indie Barman. And now I don't think of Josh at all, and it's almost like he knows.

It's almost like he senses it.

The Wrong Knickers

Two months after my head-louse incident, my phone starts to ring. My phone starts to ring and it's Josh. I'm shocked that I still have his number saved somewhere in the dark recesses of my mobile. I thought I had deleted it, but as I'm learning, the iPhone never lets you delete anything, unless it's something you actually want. I stare at my phone, which is quacking like a duck. Why have I still got his number, I think. And then, why didn't I choose a normal ringtone?

As the quacking continues, I survey my options. There are only two, really. They are a) answer it, and b) don't answer it. If I do answer it, it could look like I've spent the last few years sitting next to it, waiting for him to ring as my sister pushes slices of bread under the door. Then again, he might not think anything of the sort; he might just think, 'She has answered the phone, as is quite usual in people who have portable communication devices that they carry around with them.'

But then . . . well, then I could not answer it. I could not answer it, and he would have to stew in his own sweat for a bit, just as he made me do after the wrong knickers incident. I could not answer it, and then not bother to call him back for several hours, make him a bit anxious, make him . . . no. We all know that's not going to happen. It's pointless, because in reality, he would just get on with his life for those few hours, while I would spend them obsessing over why it is that he has called, and how my voice might sound when I ring him back, and Jesus Christ, what is the point of that exactly?

So I answer it.

'Hello?' I say. My tone is questioning. It says I don't know who it is on the other end of the line. It says I'm busy. It says I have deleted your number, or, better still, I never even bothered to save it to my phone in the first place.

'Bryony!' he says cheerily.

He wants me back.

'It's Josh!'

He definitely wants me back.

'Oh hi,' I respond. 'How are you?'

'Ah, you know.'

He is so going to ask for me back.

'I've not been well actually,' he continues.

He loves me so much he has been depressed about my absence from his life.

'And that's why I'm calling.'

You see, I told you!

'The thing is, Bryony . . .'

Wait for it, wait for it.

'There's no easy way of saying this . . .'

God, I'm irresistible.

'You see, ah . . .'

Pause. Here it comes.

'I think I've got chlamydia. And I think I may have caught it from you.'

I start to laugh.

AHAHAHAHAHAHAHAHAHAHAHAHAHAHA. HA. HA HA. What else can you do? Cry? And to think that I actually thought he might be calling for a reprieve! This reminds me of the time an ex called me 'by mistake', as he mumbled, mortified, when I excitedly returned his call. It's just like that, only with added skanky diseases that can render you infertile.

'You think I gave it to you?' I repeat back to him. I mean, this is the best bit. This is the real killer element of the whole shebang. He's not calling just to tell me he has chlamydia. He is calling to lay the blame squarely at my feet. Or my vagina, even. Josh could never have caught chlamydia from any of the other women he has shagged in the years since I heard from him. Josh couldn't have caught it from the girl with the silky Agent Provocateur knickers. Josh obviously caught it from manky old me. I am entirely to blame for this turn of events.

'Yes,' he says, solemnly, as if he has turned into a Benedictine monk.

'Right.'

'So I thought you should know. Get it checked out. I'm really sorry that I've had to make this call, but I thought it was for the best I got in touch.'

He just called to say I had given him chlamydia. Nice.

I thank him for his – what? Decency? I say I will get tested and let him know the results. I ring off and I go back to my desk and I send a message to Chloe telling her that we need to go to the pub as soon as the clock strikes six. 'OKkkkkkkkk,' she replies. 'Why?'

'I've had a diagnosis of a terrible disease,' I type.

'WHATTT????!!!!'

'I'm joking. Sort of. Tell you later.'

I spend the next two hours of work Googling chlamydia, and pretending to anyone who passes my desk that I'm working on a possible health piece about it. I don't think a single one of them believes me, but nor do I care. I am distraught, distressed, deranged with worry. I picture my fallopian tubes on fire, my womb an empty, echoing chamber through which the biological equivalent of tumbleweeds roll. I learn that 70 to 80 per cent of women never get any symptoms of chlamydia, compared to just 50 per cent of men – why is life so cruel to us ladies?! – which means I could have had it for years. For a *decade*. I could have caught it when I was sixteen and lost my virginity for all I know. It could have been burning away at my reproductive organs for all of my adult life.

I see pictures that nobody should ever have to see, of cervixes red with disease, and penises crusty with discharge. 'It's for a piece!' I say, to the sixth person to ask what the hell I am doing. I learn that chlamydia is from the Greek, χλαμύδα meaning 'cloak', and I picture a hooded figure stalking through my ovaries. I read on Wikipedia that: 'Of those who have an asymptomatic infection that is not detected by their doctor, approximately half will develop pelvic inflammatory disease (PID), a generic term for infection of the uterus, fallopian tubes, and/or ovaries. PID can cause scarring inside the reproductive organs, which can later cause serious complications, including chronic pelvic pain, difficulty becoming pregnant, ectopic (tubal) pregnancy and other dangerous complications of pregnancy.'

By 6 p.m., I am infertile, a spinster. I have been found dead at the age of fifty-six in my tiny flat, where I have been lying for weeks unnoticed, my six cats eating my face for sustenance. My life will be relegated to a nib in the local paper. 'Bryony Gordon, 56, had been deceased for some time, though neighbours were alerted to her condition only when they detected a strange smell in the communal area of the tower block. "She was a quiet woman who didn't seem to have any friends or family," said one resident. "She kept herself to herself and often wheeled a shopping trolley of belongings around. She was quite eccentric, but no bother." It is thought that Gordon became a recluse after the love of her life left her when she gave him chlamydia . . .'

No, no. That creep is not being cast in the role of love of my life in the footnotes of my history.

'So what's up?' asks Chloe, as we settle down with a bottle of wine.

'Josh called,' I say. She looks completely uninterested. She couldn't give a toss about Josh. She is done with listening to me whinge about blokes, only for me to ignore the carefully considered advice she has given me. She has fallen in love with a man she met through some dating website, a bloke who lives in Stoke Newington and grows his own mung beans to eat. I think she might be having an early mid-life crisis.

'He just called to say I had given him chlamydia,' I say, solemnly.

Chloe laughs. It's obviously the normal response when someone tells you they have a sexually transmitted disease.

'He what?' she says, trying not to choke on her laughter.

'He just called to say I had given him chlamydia.'

More laughter.

'I'm serious, Chloe! I've given him chlamydia and I've probably had it for years and years, I've probably given it to everyone I've ever slept with, and I'm going to have to call them all and explain, and then, to add to it all, I'm going to find out I'm infertile and WHAT IF I ALSO HAVE AIDS?'

'You don't have AIDS,' Chloe says, calmly. 'And even if you did have HIV, it's a totally manageable disease now, no worse than living with asthma.'

'You think I've got AIDS, don't you?'

'Bryony, how can I know if you've got AIDS or not? I'm not a freaking doctor.'

'Oh God, I've got AIDS!'

'Look, you need to go and get tested and find out if you've even got chlamydia first,' says Chloe, blinding me with logic and reason. 'There's a place around the corner from work that you can just walk into. We can go tomorrow lunch and then you will know if you have anything wrong with you, and they can fix it. In the meantime, I think you probably need another glass of wine.'

We go outside for a whole packet of fags.

I've definitely got AIDS.

The clinic has yellow walls, a bit like the Bethnal Green bedsit I used to live in. I have a strange feeling that, like the bedsit, they didn't start that way and have turned a different colour through decay and disease. The floors are plastic, blue with speckles of grey in them, as all floors in public-health buildings are. Who decided this was a good look? Which design guru reckoned this was what you wanted to look at while you waited to have a spatula stuffed into your cervix or blood taken from your arm?

We sit down to wait the inevitably lengthy wait to be seen. Next to us are the usual suspects I always imagined populated sexual-health clinics: women with heavy eye make-up and spangly jewellery for whom these tests are just part of the job; men with biceps and shaved heads and too-tight T-shirts. But they are not the whole picture. They do not tell the whole story. Across the room is a Filipino nanny, trying to amuse someone else's small children with Peppa Pig on an iPad as she waits her turn; there are men and women in suits, fiddling nervously with BlackBerries and letting out sighs as they check their watches.

'Wouldn't it be embarrassing,' I say to Chloe, who is reading about Katie Holmes in *Grazia*, 'if someone from work was to walk in and see us?'

Chloe doesn't look up from the magazine. She just lets out a little laugh and flicks the pages to a story about Miley Cyrus. I stare at the clock and tap my heels against the plastic floor and it is like God – if I believed in Him – is in the room right here with us, having some fun as He waits to find out if He has the clap.

Through the door walks Jamie, a work experience who has just left uni and who looks a bit like Zac Efron, a fact I try hard not to think about too much, given that Zac Efron is almost a decade younger than I am and looks as if his voice wouldn't break if you tried to chop it with an axe.

'Chloe,' I whisper, elbowing her in the side. 'We need to move, now!'.

'Jesus,' she says, finally putting her copy aside. 'Watch where you stick that elbow, Bryony.'

'SHHHHHHHHHHHHH,' I hiss. 'Don't say my name! A colleague has walked in and we need to move behind that pillar over there NOW.' I look in the vague direction of Jamie. Jamie looks in the vague direction of us. It's too late. It's all over. I smile awkwardly . . .

'BRYONY GORDON,' bellows the sexual-health nurse across the room. 'BRYONY GORDON, PLEASE.'

The Wrong Knickers

Our cover is blown. If previously I might have been able to pass this off as Chloe's trip to the clap clinic (and wouldn't that make a nice title for a kid's book? 'Now, children, we are going to read a cautionary tale called *Chloe's Trip to the Clap Clinic*'), it is now very clearly my trip to the clap clinic. I scuttle into the nurse's room, followed by Chloe – more blue, more decaying yellow – and note with something approaching horror the equipment all around the room. Lube. Speculums that look like submarine funnels. Lamps to be able to peer better into things that shouldn't be peered into. Condoms, condoms, condoms.

'So,' says the nurse, 'what seems to be the trouble today?'

Chloe starts laughing again.

'I'm sorry about my friend,' I say, shaking my head. 'She's not all there. My ex called me yesterday to say that he had chlamydia. And that he thought I had given it to him.'

'A real charmer,' notes the nurse. And then she points me to the bed, covered in paper towels. I dread to think what conditions have been diagnosed in this room.

'I'll need you to take your knickers off,' she says, drawing a curtain on my mortification, 'and then you can cover yourself with this towel if you are for any reason embarrassed.' We both know this is just a pleasantry, given that she's about to see more of me than even Josh has, but I wrap the towel around me anyway, keen to keep some veneer of modesty, however – literally – paper thin it is.

And then I am horizontal, looking at a blinding light as a woman I have never met before roots around between my legs, covering me with KY Jelly.

I get flashbacks.

'This might be a little uncomfort—'

'ARGGHHHHHHHHHHH,' I scream, as she does whatever it is she has to do. From behind the curtain, I hear Chloe sniggering again.

When it's all over, I'm told to call back in a fortnight – a whole freaking fortnight! I get dressed and scurry out of the room and the building without looking at anyone, let alone Jamie. 'Now that's done,' says Chloe, 'we can go and get ourselves a sandwich from Pret.'

'I've just had a horribly invasive test. One of the interns thinks – knows! – that I'm a disease-carrying whore, basically dirtier than a cockroach scurrying around in shit. And all you can think about is PRET A BLOODY MANGER?'

'A girl needs to eat,' comments Chloe. 'And anyway, what I want to know is what was he in there for? There's every chance that he's just as dirty as you.'

'Let's just get some lunch and go back to the office,' I snap.

And when we are back there, I wonder what to do. Do I ignore the fact that I just bumped into an intern in a sexual-health clinic, or do I confront it? Do I spend the rest of his time at the *Telegraph* smiling innocuously at this man – this boy! – pretending that I have never seen him outside of the office? Or do I just send him a message acknowledging that we saw each other, informing him that I will never tell anyone, and let that be the end of it?

I send him an email. To the general work experience account. Am I mad?

It reads like this: 'Hey Jamie, thought I would just get in touch to say that mum's the word re earlier. Hope you're OK!'

Ten seconds later, he replies.

'Ha. I noticed you immediately, and not just because we work for the same company. You were by far the most beautiful girl in the room.'

I reel back from my computer screen. Is this the world's most back-handed compliment? Given that most of the other women in the room were weathered sex workers, should I be flattered?

He looks like Zac Efron.

I decide to take what little crumbs I can.

'Err, thanks. Shame the look was somewhat ruined by the sexual-health tests I was there for.'

'I think it's great when a woman looks after her sexual health. The sign of a healthy, happy person.'

If only he knew.

He looks like Zac Efron.

'Ha!' I write, because what else do you write to that?

'Fancy a drink this evening?' he replies.

And this is a dilemma, because he is a man I saw earlier in a clap clinic, and thus he could be riddled with something. Plus, he is almost ten years younger than I am. Legal, but almost ten years younger than I am. And also, who finds it a turn-on that someone has been for a sexual-health check-up? But . . .

He looks like Zac Efron, he looks like Zac Efron, he looks like Zac Efron.

He looks like Zac Efron.

And my only other plans are to go home and mope about the state of my fallopian tubes.

So, I agree to go for a drink with him.

I mean, he does look like Zac Efron.

I don't tell Chloe because she would see it for the ludicrous situation that it is, and she would laugh some more and then she would make a joke about how we would be able to tell our children that our eyes met across a crowded clap clinic. But that's enough of my imagination. As we know, I have chlamydia and thus will never be able to have children. I just keep quiet, put my head down and suggest we meet at a pub nowhere near work.

He agrees.

When I arrive at the allotted meeting point, he is sipping a pint of lager and playing with a lighter. He gets me a beer, removes his tie. Without it, he looks even more like Zac Efron. It would be almost disturbing, if the alcohol wasn't going straight to my head.

I want to know why he was in the sexual-health clinic, whether he's riddled like me or if he was just there for a friend, like Chloe. I wonder, given the circumstances, if it would be rude to ask, or if it would just be expected. We make small talk about work, about how his internship is going. Then he goes there. He beats me to it.

'So why were you there?' he asks. He doesn't even add an 'if you don't mind me asking', because clearly he doesn't mind that he's asking. He is cocky, of course he is. He looks like Zac Efron.

'My ex called and told me he had chlamydia,' I say, matter-of-factly. 'Fag?'

'Don't you want to know why I was there?' he asks, looking almost wounded by the fact I haven't asked.

'I don't know. Do I?' I'm brave from the alcohol. I can be cocky, too, even though I don't look anything like Zac Efron. 'I mean, will it put me off you?'

He smiles, leads me outside for a cigarette.

Over several fags, Jamie tells me that he, too, was there because he had received a call from an ex. 'Syphilis!' he explains. 'I mean, I didn't know it was still the nineteenth century. Anyway, the nurse said I was showing no symptoms of it, so that's a relief. And I'm trying to look on the bright side. I mean, as I sat there and looked around at all the human life in that room, I thought, "This would make a really funny piece".' You should write about it, Bryony. Blow the lid on the world of sexual-health clinics!'

'I think that might be a step too far even for me,' I

say, stubbing my fag out. 'But, hey, at least we've become friends thanks to it, eh?'

His reply comes in the form of a snog.

The relationship between Jamie and me never progresses further than that kiss outside the pub. Shortly after, he gets a proper job at another paper and leaves. Our friendship serves exactly the purpose it needed to serve – as balm for both of our souls. Or mine, at the very least. I think back to the time I performed snog nurse duties on Steve, and I realise that Jamie has done the same for me. My God, I must be getting old. Now all that is left to find out is whether or not I'm going to need the attention of a real nurse, and possibly even a doctor, too.

The fortnight between taking the tests and getting the results is the longest I have ever endured. I feel constantly sick. I can't eat. I'm convinced it's because I'm dying of AIDS. I call up the Terence Higgins Trust, and with the nice young man on the other end of the phone, I detail every single sexual encounter I have ever had.

It takes some time.

'Do you think it's likely I have HIV?' I ask him, when I've finished the epic account of my twenties so far. I feel sorry for the man on the other end of the phone – he must feel soiled. 'I think it's unlikely, unless any of the men you've slept with have also slept with men, or have spent time in Sub-Saharan Africa putting it about.' Oh

God, what if they have? It's entirely possible they have. 'Look, even if you do have HIV, it's totally treatable. I've had it for six years, and am right as rain.'

That's so typical of me. Banging on about how scared I am of getting HIV to someone who actually has it.

'I'm so sorry,' I say.

'It's fine,' he replies.

'No really, I can't believe how insensitive I've been.'

'Honestly, it's no problem.'

On the day my results are due, I can barely think straight for worry. I dial the number of the clinic six times, only to hang up each time in terror. If I *am* clear, I'm never going to behave badly again. If I *am* clear, I'm going to start volunteering for an orphanage. If I *am* clear, I'm going to become a nun, or at the very least, only sleep with men I really love who I know really love me too. That seems reasonable, right?

Finally, I let the number ring. A busy sounding man picks up. 'I'm calling about my results.' I'm almost crying into the phone. 'All right,' says the man, completely monotone. It's almost as if he's working for a bank's call centre. 'Can I take your name and date of birth.'

I stutter them out.

'Hold the line, please,' he says.

Classical music starts playing. I imagine what is happening in the sexual-health clinic. The man is consulting a higher authority about my results, asking what he should do. 'I've never seen results as bad as this,' he is telling his colleague. 'Shouldn't we call her in to tell her? Shouldn't we offer her therapy?'

The classical music stops. 'Miss Gordon?' says the man.

'Yes?' I say, panicked.

'You're completely clear. Have a good day!'

I am never going to behave badly again. I am going to start volunteering for an orphanage. From now on, I am only going to sleep with men I really love who I know really love me too.

I feel as if I have got my life back.

11

The beginning of the affair

Afew months short of my twenty-ninth birthday, shortly after the chlamydia debacle, I get just what I think I have always wanted – a husband. The only problem – and there is always a problem, isn't there? – is that he isn't mine. Michael is forty-four years old, the father of three children and the beloved of one wife, who is most certainly not me. I don't know how I became such a cliché. I have no idea how I ended up so morally bankrupt.

It's not like I go looking for a married man. It's not as if I've done a Chloe, and logged into www.sugardaddies. com, only to be turned down – as she was – because she was the grand old age of thirty-eight. (This was before she turned to Eharmony and met Mr Mung Bean.) It's not like I make a concerted effort to become the other woman, a mistress. To be a mistress at twenty-nine seems far too young, too early. I have this image of a mistress as a Samantha in *Sex and the City* type, glamorous, early forties – but then perhaps I have just grown weary from the last decade, old before my time. Old before my time, without any of the maturity that is supposed to come with it.

I have never liked the idea of affairs any more than the next person. When I was a child, I was convinced that the reason my parents were always late home was because they were having affairs. It wasn't because they had to work, or because they got stuck in traffic trying to make the mad dash home to put the kids to bed. It was because they were having it off with imaginary figures I had created in my fevered pre-pubescent imagination. I was terrified my family was going to be torn apart by these fantasy relationships. While other children had imaginary friends, I had imaginary step-parents. So I have always seen affairs as bad. They are wrong, they are not for me, until, that is, I find myself in the throes of one.

'Have you met Michael?' asks a colleague one night down the pub, introducing me to his friend. Michael is a honcho at some big digital company. He isn't handsome, not in the traditional sense – he doesn't have much hair, and what he does have is almost white – but he has a certain something about him, that certain something being the huge charisma non-handsome men have to develop in order to get ahead with women. He wears sharply tailored suits, and the kind of spectacles that you just can't get down at Dolland & Aitchison, the type bought from a boutique optician. Had you put him in front of me ten years ago and told me I would end up having an affair with him, I would have slapped you in the face and told you not to be so ridiculous.

'Ah, Bryony,' says Michael, extending his hand for mine. His grip is strong, confident, commanding. 'I've been reading you for a while. You're quite the character, aren't you?' He raises his eyebrows, narrows his eyes and extends his lips – which are quite full, now I come to think about it – into a flirtatious smile. Later, I will wonder if he does this to every woman he meets, if he goes about all introductions like some sort of sniper searching for his target, before focusing the barrel of his gun on someone stupid enough not to have ducked and hidden. But right now, I am too stupid to see that. I am a rabbit caught in the headlights, one who craves a bit of sophistication in her life after the mankiness of the STD clinic and the immature mess that was Indie Barman.

Michael spends the evening asking about me, touching my shoulder and arm as we discuss where I live, who with, what my hopes and dreams are for my career. I can see full well that he is wearing a wedding ring, but I am stupefied by the attention he is paying me, turned completely dense by the interest he is showing. When he leaves, he suggests we go for a drink some other time, to discuss ideas. 'That would be great,' I giggle girlishly, my heart thudding in my chest.

Over the following days, I spend my time Googling him. We exchange emails in which he pretends to be wowed by my hectic single-girl lifestyle. I like to think he is dazzled by my youth, my sense of fun, when in fact he is probably just in awe of my tits. Eventually, he suggests that drink. 'Dukes?' he messages, naming a discreet little bar nestled somewhere in St James's. 'Martinis?'

And the thing about Martinis at Dukes is that they are so good. They inspired Ian Fleming to make them James Bond's drink of choice, and each of them is now named after a character from the series in Fleming's memory. They are so good, so strong, that you are allowed just two. Unless, like Michael and me, you manage to persuade the bar staff to let you have just one more Tiger Tanaka, before moving on to wine and then again to beer. We are so sozzled that Michael spills his glass down his expertly ironed shirt. 'I think I'd better take it off,' he teases. We are so pissed that before we know it, we are snogging over the table in full view of a table of American tourists. We are so drunk that we don't care.

The next morning I wake up in my bed with a warm glow about me, a memory of Michael dropping me home in a cab and snogging my face off before telling me we must do it again. I get into the shower and sing. I make my sister and Steve coffee, and take it to them in their rooms. 'What on earth has happened to you?' asks my sister, clearly concerned by my sudden transformation from morning grump to morning glory. 'Oh nothing,' I trill. 'It's just a beautiful day!'

Outside, it's pissing it down.

I am early for work for possibly the first time in my career. I am a woman with a purpose, refreshing my inbox for a sign of Michael. I know this is bad, I know that I am probably a terrible person for even wanting this. I have told myself that I am not going to go through with this, that the last thing I need in my life is a married man. When he emails 'Coffee at 4 near your office? xx' I find myself typing 'Yes xx'.

We meet for our coffee in the lobby of a hotel that is a five-minute walk from my office. That seems close but it's not the kind of place you would ever expect to see a colleague – not unless he/she is having an affair, too – and so it seems safe, a haven. Michael is hidden in a corner, caressing a double espresso. 'I need it for the hangover,' he smiles, as he gets up to kiss me on both cheeks.

On the table is a brand new copy of Fleming's *You Only Live Twice*, in which the Tiger Tanaka of our Martinis appears. 'This is for you,' Michael says, handing it to me. The cover features a photo of Sean Connery in full black tie. I smile to myself. Michael is my Sean Connery, I decide. He is my James Bond.

No man has bought me a book before. If you can forget

for a moment the wife and three children – and I have managed to brush them from my mind completely – it seems incredibly romantic. I open the book, thumb the fresh pages. And then I come across the inscription on the title page. 'I blame Mr Tanaka,' it says. 'M xxx.'

I gaze at his writing for what seems like an age. It is beautiful, neat, surely placed on the page by an expensive fountain pen. I've never snogged a man who uses a fountain pen, I think. It suddenly becomes clear to me that what I have needed in my life all this time is a man who uses a fountain pen.

'So last night was kind of amazing,' he says as I sit down. 'I haven't stopped thinking about it ever since.' I smile shyly. What I should really do, right now, is ask him about his wife, about his darling little children, about what the hell he was thinking, leaning across the table and snogging me after plying me with superstrong Martinis. But that suggests I am entirely innocent and we both know that I am not and I knew full well, from the ring on his finger, that he was a taken man. This is the moment to stop it all, to tell him that the kissing was a drunken mistake and if he wants to do it in future, he needs not to have a wife, or at the very least to be estranged from her. It's the moment to claw back some self-respect, to get up and leave with my dignity intact. But I'm ashamed to say that I'm having too much fun to do any of that. Instead, I just giggle. I am behaving like a pathetic school-girl with a crush on her physics teacher.

The Wrong Knickers

'So I was thinking,' he says, leaning across the table, taking my hands in his, the wedding ring glinting at me, as if asking if I'm really, truly, sure. 'Shall we have an affair?'

And just like that, it is done.

In life, there are people who do the dumping, and people who get dumped. I have always fallen into the latter category, and that's if I ever manage to get into a relationship in the first place. And so if you are wondering, right now, what exactly the attraction is of this two-timing rat with very little hair, I can tell you it is this: Michael can't dump me, because we're not really going out. He is hardly my boyfriend. I can't turn up at a party with him, or introduce him to my mum. He's not going to take me to the cinema any time soon, and there is little chance of us planning to spend summer holidays together.

When I look at Michael, I feel sophisticated by proxy. I feel I have come a long way from the feckless and witless men of my past, from snowboarding Sam with his single bed and his love of pot. The truth, of course, is the complete opposite. If anything, I have gone back not just steps, but whole miles. He is fulfilling my older man fantasy, while I like to think I am fulfilling his younger woman one, feeling sexy and hot in the process. Michael is a bit of class, despite the fact that anyone else would see his behaviour as anything but. He has a bit of money and stability, even though that stability belongs to someone else and there is a real possibility I will fuck it up. And when I look back on my chequered love life, I will realise that while Michael and Sam and all the other men appear to have little in common, there is one huge bonding factor, and that is their unavailability. None of them are really there for me, be it physically or geographically.

But right now I am so blinded by great sex, and deluded by the giddiness of it all, the naughtiness, that none of this matters to me. We throw ourselves into the affair with gusto, or at least I do. You know when you read about affairs in literature, it's all diamonds and clandestine weekends in Paris and gorgeous penthouse flats to keep the mistress quiet?

Well, it isn't like that with Michael and me. Again, I convince myself that this is because he is different, not like other men who shag around. But in reality it's probably because I'm so eager to please him, so keen to see him that I say yes to every possible meet up he suggests, even if it means cancelling on other people. He never really has to make an effort. I hand myself to him on a plate, and it's a soggy paper one that has been fished out of the bin at that.

He never spends the night, and he rarely comes round in the evening, fearful of bumping into Steve or my sister and awkwardly having to introduce himself to them, thus making everything real. Instead, we sneak back to mine in our lunch breaks for a quick shag before we have to be back in our respective offices. He never buys me dinner, doesn't once send me flowers – if you're supposed to send flowers to your significant other because you have cheated on her, I suppose he doesn't have to – and he takes five hours, sometimes six, to reply to my texts. If he was a boyfriend, a normal person would dump him. But he is not a boyfriend, and I have long since moved out of the realms of normality.

I become happy to live off crumbs. Actually, not even that. I become happy to live off the crumbs of crumbs. I feel joyously alive when he texts me a thank you after a lunchtime shag – 'You are simply DELICIOUS xxxx' – as if I'm lobster bisque and not a human being. When I don't hear from him for a day, I feel miserable, alone. When he texts me unprompted, I'm on top of the world. I become addicted to him. He is like heroin, only cheaper.

When, one day, he gets in touch to suggest that I join him in Manchester for a conference he has to attend, I can hardly believe my luck. I am going to spend A WHOLE NIGHT WITH HIM. I don't mind that he doesn't even pay for my train fare, expecting me to spend £90 to have sex with him while he gets to do it all on expenses. I just picture anonymous walks through Manchester town centre, hand in hand, dinners in restaurants, breakfast together in bed.

He calls to talk through plans for the weekend. 'I have a dinner on the Friday night so what I'll do is leave you a key on reception and see you in the room when I've finished.' I don't protest. I just tell myself it will be a chance to get drunk on the mini bar while I bounce up and down on the superking bed in a fluffy towelling robe. I go to Agent Provocateur and blow almost £200 on a corset and stockings and suspenders. Finally, I am going to be wearing the *right* knickers. I take the afternoon off work to get there in good time. I don't care that I'm using up my holiday allowance – it's not as if I ever really take it all anyway.

That's a lie. I have been to Los Angeles three, four, five times, to stay with a friend who works there, but I always come back feeling faintly depressed about the fact that my tits don't stay up on their own, and the sun doesn't shine all day long on my home. Plus, the last time I went, the plane ended up making an emergency diversion to Salt Lake City, where we spent a whole day sitting on the runway, with me becoming increasingly concerned that I was going to have to spend the rest of my life in this goddamn city, the teetotal fifth wife of a mormon. The only holidays I go on now are with my mum, short breaks to places like Normandy and Barcelona, but I don't like to talk about them on account of the fact it makes us both sound like tragic old harpies. So yes, I rarely take my holiday allowance, and if I do I'm always forced to take it all at the end of the financial year – three weeks spent stewing in my flat, vaguely meaning to go to the British Museum or some such. So who really cares if I use up half a day to go and shag a married man, who gets to do it all on company time so he can use his full allocation taking his lovely little family to their villa in Spain or gîte in France, or whatever it is normal people have?

I arrive in Manchester with a knot in my stomach and a corset that looks like it belongs in a bondage club, not my luggage. I go to the taxi rank and ask the driver to take me to the hotel, which turns out to be round the corner. 'Easier to walk,' he says, closing his window on me. Armed with the vaguest of directions and the knowledge that it should take only three or four minutes to get there, I set off for the hotel with my corset in tow.

Within moments, it starts to rain. Of course it does. It's Manchester. I have no umbrella on me, have never been practical enough even to own one, and am wearing suede boots with five-inch heels, just in case I bump into Michael at the station, him having magically decided to surprise me. A three-minute walk in these heels is more like fifteen minutes, while a three-minute walk with my local knowledge is more like half an hour. I loop round and round in circles, the rain on my coat making me smell like a damp teddy bear, one step, two step, be careful not to fall there on the shiny wet cobbles.

When I finally find the hotel, it's dark and I'm cold and my suitcase has wobbled off its wheels. The place is large, corporate, the kind done up to look like a Barratt interpretation of an Ian Schrager hotel in Miami. I totter to the reception and stare at the fish tank behind as I wait for a member of staff to notice me. 'Can I help you, madame,' says a man with a heavy French accent. It rolls of his tongue in such a way you can tell he thinks I belong in a brothel, not a respected world-wide hotel chain. I give him my best rictus grin.

'Yes, you can,' I say, fixing him with an icy glare. 'I'm booked in for the night. I believe that Michael Alleyne has left me a key.'

'Ahh, yes,' says the little French shit, suddenly warming up. 'May I welcome you to our hotel, Mrs Alleyne. If you will just wait a moment, I will get a colleague to show you to your room.'

And in a moment of clarity, a moment of danger, a moment of wanting to wipe the smile of this little tosser's face, I say it. 'Actually, I'm not Mrs Alleyne. I'm his lover. You probably get that quite a lot in places like this, middle-aged businessmen sneaking in their trollops for a bit of fun on the company credit card. So if you could please get someone to show me to the room, Mr Alleyne and I can get on with it.'

He looks at me, gobsmacked. Neither of us can believe what I have just said.

'Just a moment, madame,' he says, his lip curling into a perfect S of distaste.

Perhaps if I was Mrs Alleyne, the Frenchman would have got someone to take me to my room. Perhaps if I was Mrs Alleyne, I would have had someone carry my bags, instead of having to lug them up myself. I arrive at the room sweaty and out of breath, my hair on end and the soles of my feet burning in pain.

The room is not as palatial as I had imagined it, more functional and business like than I would like, the trouser press only hammering home the possibility that I might be nothing more than a passing convenience to Michael Alleyne. There isn't a big bath for us to share, and the bed is not really any bigger than the one we have sex in at my flat. There are no his-and-hers towelling robes. Why would there be? This isn't the kind of hotel you take someone special to. It's a place in which business is done, transactions are carried out. I try to shake away the feeling that I do, indeed, belong in a brothel.

I text Michael to let him know I have arrived. An hour later, he replies. 'Great, should be back by 10!' That gives me almost three hours to kill. On a Friday night, when all my peers are out at pubs having fun, I am in a soulless hotel room waiting to have soulless sex I will mistake for being full of passion. I have a shower, rub moisturiser all over, and pace up and down the room in my underwear wondering what to do. I order up a bottle of wine, drink it quicker than I should, leaning out the window to smoke fags to pass the time. At 9 p.m., I switch on the telly and start to get ready as *Have I Got News For You* plays in the background. This is exactly how a twenty-nine-year-old should be spending her Friday night, right?

I spend fifteen minutes trying to squeeze into my corset, and briefly consider phoning down to reception to get somebody to help. Having eventually crawled into it, like sausage meat into its casing, I put on the stockings and suspenders. I stand in front of the bathroom mirror, convinced I look like something out of a Victoria's Secret ad campaign, when the reality is probably more Victoria Wood. The stockings keep falling down and I can barely breathe in the corset. Ten o'clock comes and goes without a peep from Michael. At 10.25 p.m. I text him, asking when he thinks he might be back, and at 10.53 p.m. he replies, saying he is just finishing up and will be back soon. When I hear the keycard in the lock, I jump to attention, positioning myself on the bed in what I think is a seductive manner. 'Well, well, well,' he says. 'Aren't I a lucky boy? Let me just stick on *Newsnight* for a bit – there's always hell to pay in the office if I miss one.'

And so it is that we end up having sex to the dulcet tones of Jeremy Paxman berating an MP over the financial crisis. When it's over, Michael falls into a fitful sleep, each toss and turn feeling like a rebuke. When he wakes up in the morning, he doesn't try to have sex with me again – he's too tired – instead, he gets up, jumps in the shower and announces he has a breakfast meeting. On a Saturday. When he's gone, I smoke a fag on the bed, not even bothering to open the windows, pack up my stuff and head for the station. As the train chugs back to London, I work out that I have spent almost £300 on a shag with someone who had one eye on my tits, the other on *Newsnight*. And still I don't realise just what a mess I have become.

I am the worst person in the world to have an affair with, owing to the fact I am incapable of keeping my mouth shut. While at first I loved the idea of having a secret romance, I soon discovered that it was no fun when you had to keep it to yourself, and so on drunken nights out I blurt it all out, in the morning waking with terrible anxiety about having blurted it all out. I write lists of the people I've told, and then I try to work out the likelihood of each of those people telling anybody else. I endlessly beat myself up for having a huge blabbermouth. In my head, it's not him who is in the wrong – it's me.

I don't tell Sally and Andy, because I know they would disown me immediately. They would see my actions as an affront to every married person on the planet. Steve and my sister do not approve. Of course they don't. They think it's a bit gross, and they don't really want to spend evenings after the pub watching YouTube videos of him at a conference. They find it totally sad when I drunkenly implore them to 'listen, would you, just listen, his voice is like SILK!'

Honestly, I don't get why they are so hostile to him.

At work, Steve has befriended the new boy, a toff called Harry who wears a signet ring and always looks at me like I'm a lunatic. He is the banking correspondent – zzz – and although he's handsome in a posh, clean way,

I imagine he wears loafers with red socks at the weekend. They are always together – anyone would think that Steve was having an affair with Harry – and I find this new friendship far more bewildering than my relationship with Michael. Harry never really says anything. He's always in our living room, laughing at Steve's jokes, quietly judging me for being a fuckwit.

'Harry can't believe you're having it off with Michael,' announces Steve one day, while we are sitting in front of the TV watching *Coronation Street*.

'You told HARRY?' I squeal. 'Oh, why am I even surprised? Of course you were going to tell your BOYFRIEND.'

'Bryony, you've told everyone. I didn't have to tell Harry. It was practically part of his induction day. "Oh, here's the canteen and there's the loo and that's Bryony, she's having an affair with some dude who thinks he's Steve Jobs." '

'Another reason for him to disapprove of me,' I sigh.

'He doesn't disapprove of you.'

'He does. He's always sitting there, silently tutting about my behaviour. I mean, has he ever done anything risky in his whole entire life? Is his idea of a good time wearing a Guinness hat and getting tanked up while watching the rugby?'

'Bryony, that's not fair,' says Steve, anger tinging his voice. 'You've never even tried to have a conversation with him. If anything, YOU'RE the judgemental one. Just because he doesn't blurt everything out like you do, doesn't mean he's boring.'

I get up, storm to my room, slam the door, get locked in. I have a little scream. 'ARGGGGGGGH. I HATE MY LIFE.'

I make absolutely no attempt to change it, though. I carry on as normal. I try not to think about his wife, but he seems to be more successful at this venture than I am. In my mind she is a nagging, sagging cow with a baggy vagina, but when I look her up, I discover she is actually a glossy businesswoman with lovely hair and a sharp line in designer suits. I become obsessed with her. I think about her almost as much as I do him. I play out scenes in my mind: handing the children back to her after their weekend with daddy and his new girlfriend, our relationship eventually turning from frosty to warm as she finds a new man and declares that she is actually grateful to me, because she was never truly happy in her marriage, and always suspected that she and Michael would be better with other people. And before we know it, we are hanging out together, going to spas, taking trips to the hairdresser, and we are all one big happy family, the end.

But although I often imagine playing at being stepmum, becoming the very ogre I feared as a child, I never once bring up the subject of his family with him for fear of rocking the boat. The subject stopped being the elephant in the bedroom a long time ago. Now, it's a whole fucking savannah of the creatures. I tell myself that it's not my problem – he's the one with the family, after all, not me – but it's beginning to eat away at me without me even realising. I hate myself for what I'm doing, and I don't even know it.

As my thirtieth birthday approaches, I tentatively decide to suggest we go to a hotel to celebrate. We are in my room at the time, in the throes of foreplay, when I let him know I have a big life event approaching. 'The big three oh,' he says, and I worry that he is going to think me too old, cast me aside and replace me with a younger model. 'I hope you're going to have a party.'

'Well, actually,' I say, 'I thought maybe you and me could celebrate together. You know, maybe get a hotel?' I am straddling him. The position gives me a full view of the pity that spreads across his face. 'Oh, Bryony,' he sighs. 'I don't think that's a good idea. I don't think you should spend such a big occasion with me. I'm not worth your energy.' I feel like my face might crumple in on itself. 'You know this is just sex, Bryony, don't you?'

I jump off him, tell him to leave. I realise in an instant that this relationship is not even a relationship, that he entered it with nothing more than a raging hard on. He has never cared for me, never had any respect for me. But I think it's about time I get some for myself.

12

I somehow make it to thirty

My thirtieth birthday is six days away, and I still have nothing planned. I have nothing planned because I am incapable of planning anything other than nothing. For the last two weeks, all I have been able to do is weep. I weep at my desk, very quietly, so it sounds to my colleagues like a peculiar video someone might perhaps be watching on YouTube for 'research' purposes, rather than an actual person having a mini-breakdown. I weep about Michael, because I am an ocean-going idiot. He seems completely unbothered by my first-ever attempt at dumping somebody, possibly because he knew he couldn't actually be dumped, that his lovely wife would always be there for him at the end of the working day. If anything, he left my flat that lunch with an air of relief about him, as if I had done him a favour in shooing him out the door. How typical that I can't even dump some-body properly.

Anyway, the odd person notices my tears – like the man who sits next to me, for instance – but he pretends not to, taking the sound of my sniffles to be just one of those things that girls like me do, like a particularly crap party trick. I weep in the loos (not even inside the cubi-cles, like a normal person, but next to the sinks) and I weep in the corridor everyone frequents to make hushed phonecalls to husbands and lovers or the bank. I, mean-while, weep down my phone to friends about the husbands I do not have and the lovers I do not want and the bank that won't get off my back because oh-yeah-I-went-through-my-overdraft-again-so-shoot-me. I am not embarrassed about weeping in public. Quite the opposite. I feel no shame in it. I see it as honest and open; as hot, salty proof of how dramatic and crazy and yet ultimately pointless my life has become. I don't care what my bosses think – they probably just think it's good column material.

One day, as I'm weeping these hot, salty tears next to the snack machine, Harry comes up to me. This is JUST what I need, some sanctimonious tossbag getting hard evidence of what a fuck-up I am. I shake my head as he approaches, wipe my eyes with my sleeve and prepare to walk away. 'Wait up, Bry,' he says.

'Bryony,' I spit.

'Sorry. Bryony. Don't run away. Are you OK?'

271

'I'm fine,' I huff. 'Please just leave me alone.'

'OK,' he says, seeming irritated. 'I wasn't actually following you around, though. I was coming to get a can of Coke.' He smiles the fakest of smiles. I storm off towards the ladies loos.

The only person who understands me is Chloe, whose bubble of love has popped, the boyfriend disappearing into thin air, only getting in touch two months later to tell her he was getting married to someone else, and could she please send back his *Breaking Bad* box sets care of his mother, who, incidentally, she should contact in future if she wanted any further information.

'Like WHAT?' she says one night, slamming a drink down on a table covered in fag ash. 'THE DETAILS OF THE JOHN LEWIS WEDDING LIST? As if I'm going to send back his fucking *Breaking Bad* box sets. I am not wasting the price of a postage stamp on him, let alone trekking to a post office to get a package weighed and send it recorded delivery. I am not sending him the DVDs so he can watch the end of season three all snuggly on the sofa with HER. Fuck him. Fuck *Breaking Bad*. I'm going to sell those fucking DVDs for a supply of my own crystal meth so I can get out of it and forget about him, the little piece of shit.'

So Chloe and I have been crying on each other's snot-covered shoulders, but even her patience with me is wearing a little thin.

'Don't talk to me about post offices,' I say, welling up.

'You what?' says Chloe, shaking her head.

'I said, don't talk to me about post offices.'

'I wasn't talking to you about post offices. I was talking to you about my ex-boyfriend potentially turning me into a crystal-meth addict.'

'Do you know, Chloe, I haven't been into a post office since I was a child. I have only ever been into a post office with my mother,' I wail, warming to my theme. 'If I was a PROPER GROWN-UP, I would forever be in the post office, to send THANK-YOU LETTERS and BUY STAMPS and CASH IN THE CHILD BENEFIT FOR MY LITTLE CHERUBS. I would be COLLECTING IMPORTANT GROWN-UP PACKAGES. But nobody sends me packages. NOBODY! Chloe, I'm about to turn thirty and I STILL HAVE NO REASON TO GO TO A POST OFFICE.'

Chloe looks at me in total disbelief. She puts her head in her hands. 'Bryony, why do you have to make absolutely everything about you?'

So Chloe and I fall out, which means I'm approaching my thirtieth birthday with no boyfriend, no best friend and no reason to go to a post office, unless I offer to take the DVDs there for Chloe and post them back to her ex. Even Sally has dropped off the radar, owing, I think, to the scan of an unborn foetus she posted on Facebook the other week. I liked it, and started to type out a text message congratulating her, but then something distracted me and I never finished it. I feel so sorry for myself that even I can see how pathetic I must seem, a fact that, ironically, only serves to make me feel even more self-pity. Over the past year, I have received invitations to extravagant thirtieth birthday parties on boats and in marquees and country houses, drinking wine only from the vintage of the year the host was born, as their parents and husbands and boyfriends make gushing speeches about them. But it's becoming increasingly clear that nobody will ever make a speech about me, unless a policeman makes one to a class of secondary school teachers to warn of the dangers of alcohol, fags and narcotics. I don't want to celebrate my thirtieth, there is nothing *to* celebrate, other than the dawning of another decade of total and utter fuckwittery, one that's going to be worse even than the one that has just passed. My thirties are going to go down as a hideous period in which mine dry up, the end of hope entirely, the gateway to the rest of my pointless, lonely, childless life. 'I think your thirties are when you are going to come into your own,' says my mother, hopefully. But I know she is wasting her time, as does she, surely.

When Steve hears me crying in my room for the eighth day running, he suggests that maybe I go to the doctor. 'Perhaps they will be able to give you something to make you feel better,' he tries to comfort, patting me gently on the back.

'You mean you think I need PROFESSIONAL HELP,' I wail.

'No,' he says, clearly meaning YES, 'just that we can all do with a bit of support from time to time. There's no shame in reaching out.'

'Reaching out?' I say, stunned. 'What are you? An American management consultant?'

Still, he has a point, however badly made. But there's just one problem – I don't have a doctor. I am almost thirty years old and I don't have a doctor or a reason to go to the post office or a boyfriend or a best friend. The last GP surgery I was registered at was the one of my childhood, and the only doctors I have had reason to see in between have been sexual-health ones, which in itself feels like a reason to go and see one.

'Hello, what can I help you with?' I imagine they will say, when I turn up.

'Well, the thing is, I haven't had a doctor for over ten years, and I'm beginning to worry about it. What if I'm not the kind of person who has a doctor? What if I'm incapable of having doctors? What if I'm doomed to a life of only seeing other people's doctors, locum doctors? OH GOD, A NORMAL PERSON WOULD HAVE A DOCTOR.'

'Don't worry, Miss Gordon. We can see you really need a doctor, and will do all we can to get you one.'

At work there is a doctor who comes in twice a week to tend to the aches and pains of the employees. He looks exactly like a GP should – a bit like a learned badger in spectacles. I went to see him once, two years ago, when

The Wrong Knickers

I became worried about the constant pain in my lower back every time I woke up in the morning. 'At first I thought it was just the bed I was sleeping in, but – and this is all confidential, right?'

He nods.

'But the thing is, doctor, I have slept in a LOT of beds since, if you know what I mean . . .' The look on his face says he does, but that he doesn't want to. 'And still, the same dull ache in my lower back. So I was thinking, maybe it isn't lower back pain. Maybe I have kidney disease from drinking too much, which could also mean I have liver disease.'

'Well, Miss Gordon, it seems like you don't need to see me at all since you're so good at self-diagnosing. But what I would say is, and remember this is all confidential, right? What I would say is, how much are you drinking every day? Are you drinking when you wake up in the morning?'

'God no! I always feel WAY too lousy in the morning even to contemplate ever drinking again. Or at least until that evening.'

'OK. Do you drink every day?'

'Of course,' I say with a shrug. He shuffles his papers around on his desk.

'Have you ever drunk until you blackout?'

'Have I ever,' I say. 'I do it almost all the time. Doesn't every twenty-eight-year-old who works in media in a city and doesn't have any dependants? I mean, no offence, but get real, doc.'

He takes some blood from me to test my liver function, 'just as a precaution' he is careful to say. I squeal when he puts the needle in, and make a big fuss over the fact that I will probably bruise. It's clear he sees me for the person I am – someone who has never felt real pain, other than when she had appendicitis aged eight, someone who has never had any real troubles, a middle-class drama queen who has it so cushy she has to invent medical problems just to feel alive. A week later I return to his room for the results, and am pleased to discover that they show me to be in rude health. 'That doesn't mean you can carry on drinking as much as you do,' says the doctor, sternly. 'Au contraire, doctor, au contraire,' I reply. 'I think this is a great reason for a drink!'

And now I need to see him because I think I'm having a breakdown, possibly because I drink too much, but he doesn't need to know that. Imaginary liver problems, a breakdown caused by being totally self-obsessed – I imagine that all he's going to do is send me away with a prescription for a large dose of perspective. I sit down opposite him and he asks how he can be of assistance, and I burst into tears.

'I just feel so . . .' I weep a bit more, unable suddenly to grasp even basic vocabulary. 'HELPLESS.'

'Oh dear.' He passes me a box of tissues. 'Why is that?'

'I dunno,' I snivel. I do know. It's because I have spent the last decade drinking too much and sleeping with unsuitable men and all I have to show for it is some distressingly yellow eyeballs. 'I just can't stop crying. I'm about to turn thirty and it's like it's set something off in me. It's like I've stored all this stuff up inside of me hoping that it will just go away, and suddenly I've realised that I'm not getting any younger and things aren't going to get any better unless I make a decision to change my life. But I don't feel able to. I don't even know how to. I've let myself slide so deep into a pile of shit – and the worst thing is it's my own shit, it's shit of my own making, you know – that I can't see the wood for the trees. Or the toilet bowl for the shit. I can't see the toilet bowl that's my LIFE,' I continue, feeling pleased with this analogy, 'for the shit, if you will.'

'Ahhhm,' is all he says.

'And here I am, almost thirty years old, and I have precisely nothing that I thought I would have by this point in my life. Nothing that I'm supposed to have, that society says I should have by the time I reach thirty years of age. I don't have a house, I can't drive a car, I have no significant other. I don't even have an insignificant other. I still can't get to the end of the financial month without having to borrow fifty quid off my mother, and talking of my mother, I think she is just really, really heartbroken because I am never going to give her grandchildren, not at this rate anyway, and I think she blames herself for that when of course it's nobody's fault but my own. I have a career, but I worry endlessly that I won't do tomorrow because some bank is going to default – I'm almost thirty years old, and I don't even know what that means, or if it even makes sense – and bring the economy crashing back to the ground again, meaning I get made redundant. You know, every freaking day I wake up convinced I'm going to get the sack, not because I've misbehaved – though, Jesus, I could really do with sorting out my ability to stick to a deadline, given that this problem has been going on since I was, like, at SCHOOL and couldn't hand my homework in on time – but because a bunch of wankers who have everything I should have – a fuck-off big home, a car, a family – have been reckless and PISSED ALL OF OUR FUTURES UP THEIR EXQUISITELY PAINTED WALLS.'

I can't believe I have just said all of this to someone I don't even know.

'Well, I think it's a good thing that you can see all of this,' says the doctor, writing out a prescription. 'It shows you have a good amount of self-knowledge if, as you claim, little else. I think what you probably need is a boost, something to get you through the next few months and help you get back on your feet. So I'm going to prescribe you a mild anti-depressant that should at least stop you feeling tearful all the time. Hopefully, it will enable you to see the toilet bowl of your life for the shit, as you so wonderfully put it.'

I stare at the prescription and it dawns on me that not only am I about to turn thirty with no boyfriend or best friend or need to go to the post office, but I am also now on anti-depressants. As the young people say, FML.

'Oh, and Bryony,' says the doctor, as I get up to leave. 'You should know that it's totally normal to feel this way. You should meet my daughter. Thirty-one and by her own admission, a complete fuck-up.' He smiles benignly at me, and we both start to laugh. After all of the tears, it feels really good.

The leaflet that comes in the packet of sertraline explains that it is 'one of a group of medicines called Selective Serotonin Re-uptake Inhibitors (SSRIs); these medicines are used to treat depression and or anxiety disorders.' There is a list of possible side effects to watch out for. Very common ones include insomnia, sleepiness (caused by insomnia, I imagine), headache, diarrhoea, feeling sick, dry mouth, fatigue, ejaculation failure. On the last count I, at least, do not have to worry. But reading on, I learn that taking sertraline can cause vaginal haemorrhage (what the . . .?), female sexual dysfunction, excessive vaginal bleeding, dry vaginal area, genital discharge, breast discharge, and *bedwetting*. That's all I need – to turn thirty and have to take up buying adult nappies. There are yet more worrying side effects – abdominal pain, vomiting, constipation, upset stomach, gas, hair loss, high blood pressure, hallucination, convulsion, amnesia, speech disorder, ear pain, eye swelling, burping, coma, difficulty moving, CANCER, heart attack, glaucoma, abnormal skin odour. I am getting palpitations and grinding my teeth – both, incidentally, possible side effects – just reading the damn leaflet. 'Wow,' says my sister, scanning the lengthy document. 'It says here that taking anti-depressants can actually make you suicidal. Not to mention paranoid and aggressive. On the plus side, between one and ten out of a hundred patients who take sertraline become anorexic, meaning you might finally get that eating disorder you've always hoped for.'

'You're so funny,' I say sarcastically. I grab the leaflet off her and shoot her a withering look. 'It's nice to know that in my time of need, you can still find the time to be a complete and utter arsehole.'

'Hey,' she says, sitting down on the bed next to me and rubbing my back. 'It's going to be OK, I promise. This, too, will pass. And while we wait for it to go, I think we should have a party for your thirtieth. I know you say you don't want one, but I also know you well enough to work out that deep down you probably wouldn't mind a bit of a shindig. It doesn't have to be a big thing, but we should at least get a load of people down the pub. I've emailed Chloe . . .'

'You've emailed CHLOE?'

'Yep, and she thinks it's a good idea too.'

'I thought we weren't talking.'

'She says she's over it and she hopes you are too. She's rounded up a load of people, as has Steve. We've booked an area in the pub up the road for Saturday night.'

I smile, give her a hug.

'Will you make a speech?'

'Don't push your luck, kiddo.'

For my thirtieth birthday I receive six bottles of champagne, a knit-your-own boyfriend, a candle I will never use because I have a fear of burning things down, some Topshop vouchers, and a wrap of cocaine. I haven't done drugs since the incident at Glastonbury – not non-prescription ones, anyway – but I decide that since it *is* my thirtieth birthday, it can't do any harm to treat myself.

That's the first mistake I make on the night of my birthday party.

The second comes as the pub closes, and I decide it's a good idea to invite everyone – bar staff included – back to our flat to carry on the evening. Harry is here with Steve, his silent sidekick, and though the look on his face says he disapproves of everything, that doesn't stop him from tagging on to my party. We buy crates of beer and all the wine in the pub that hasn't been drunk, and leave, a drunken, high congo line, waking up the good residents of Camden as we wend our way back to mine.

We play Beyoncé at what we believe to be a reasonable decibel level. But the problem with working out decibel levels when you're drunk is that you're usually some way out. The neighbours come banging on the door two, three, four times over the course of the night (actually, by now it's the next morning), one even threatening to kill us if we don't turn the music down immediately. 'You should be ASHAMED of yourself,' says the woman, who looks delightful in a pink floral nightie and a pair of slippers.

'Calm down, dear,' says one of the bar staff. 'It's a thirtieth birthday party. It's not like they do this all the time.'

She looks daggers at him. 'But they DO!'

I get off with the manager of the pub. I'm so drunk I have to be reminded several times what his name is. I notice that I'm not the only one who allows myself an inappropriate snog. In the corner, Steve is all over Chloe, as my sister points and laughs at them. 'Poor Harry,' I say, keen not to miss a sarcastic dig at him. 'Your boyfriend has abandoned you for another woman.'

'Do you think,' he says, opening a can of beer, 'that now you're thirty you might decide to grow up?'

'Not where you're concerned, posh boy.'

I don't go to bed because I couldn't if I tried – I'm wired to the eyeballs on sertraline and cocaine. I try to clean up around comatose bodies, and note that someone has written on the bathroom mirror in my Mac lipstick. 'HAPPY 30TH FUCKER!' it reads. I spend an hour trying to scrub it off, but the damage is done, the words stuck there forever more, a reminder of my fuckwittery every time I look in the mirror.

I cry and I cry and I cry some more. I spend the first week of being thirty feeling drained, hollow, on a booze and drugs comedown. It's not an auspicious start to my thirties, but it is, I think, an entirely expected one.

I don't, as my mother predicted, come into my own in my thirties – unless by coming into my own she meant turning into even more of a booze-addled mess than before. It's as if the wheels spin off entirely, in the process knocking down any hope there ever was of me straightening myself out and becoming a successful human being. I drink copiously, snog indiscriminately and spend recklessly. I decide that if I'm not going to have a family and do the whole happily ever after bullshit, I may as well do the whole living fast, dying young thing instead. I get back in touch with Michael, who after a period of relief at my absence now claims to miss me terribly, welcoming me back with open arms.

I tell myself I'm having a relationship on my terms – one that allows me to have sex and affection without the whole getting tied down thing. Inside, I have darkened; I feel dead behind the eyes. I'm going to stop looking for a boyfriend, stop beating myself up for wanting a boyfriend. I'm going to live as I choose to live, free from the constraints that society has imposed on me.

On Valentine's Day, Michael asks if I will have a drink with him. I hate Valentine's Day, have never spent it with anyone and am not about to start now, but Michael seems oddly insistent that we meet. 'We really need to talk,' he says, in a hushed phonecall one evening, and for one last time, I allow myself to hope. I wonder if Michael is about to throw a curveball into my plans for spinsterhood, if he is going to announce that he can't live without me, that he needs me more than he ever really knew.

We meet at a bar in Trafalgar Square, one that tourists frequent, so again we are free from the prying eyes of anyone who might know us. This should be my first clue that the evening is not going to pan out as I might hope, but I tell myself he's just used to picking these kind of places, so it has become second nature to him. When I arrive, he's already there, draining the dregs of a large glass of red wine. He kisses me on the cheek nervously, asks me what I want to drink. He seems nervous, aloof, not at all himself.

'So, did you have a good weekend?' This is a new one. This I haven't heard before. In all the time we have been together – or sort of together but mostly apart – he has not once asked me about my weekend. He isn't interested in me as me. He's only interested in me as his seductive sex strumpet.

'My weekend?' I repeat back to him. 'I can't even remember now. Are you OK?'

'Not really.' He stares at his wine. He hasn't looked me in the eye once. 'Bryony, I need to tell you something before anyone else has the chance to.' My stomach tightens – the only time it's tight nowadays is when someone is about to deliver me bad news – and a wave of anxiety washes over me. Has his wife found out? Is she currently on the way to my flat with a collection of kitchen knives and a bottle of bleach to throw all over me? He stutters quietly. I can't hear what he's mumbling over the din of crappy pop.

'What is it, Michael? You're freaking me out.'

'Bryony,' he says, finally looking at me. 'My wife is pregnant. I can't carry this on. It's not fair on her or the kids. I feel as if this is a second chance for me and her, an opportunity to start over again. I'm really so...'

'You got me here on VALENTINE'S DAY to end things, and not only to end things but to tell me you have IMPREGNATED ANOTHER WOMAN?'

'Jesus, is it Valentine's Day?' he says, scrambling around for his wallet to pay the bill. 'Shit. Thank you for reminding me.'

I run out of the door of the bar. I run and I run and I run until I can flag down a cab. He is a complete tosser, and I am a complete bitch, shagging a man who all along had a pregnant wife! Breathless, I phone Chloe, who I know is having an anti-Valentine's Day party somewhere in Soho (despite their snog on my birthday, Chloe and Steve decide to keep things on purely platonic terms).

'Chloe!' I wail. 'I need to see you!' She tells me where she is, and I send the taxi in the right direction.

That night, I drink shot after shot and get drunker than I have in a long while – which, for me, is really saying something. At some point, and my memory is hazy here, Chloe puts me in a cab home, but when we get there I realise I have no money and have left my card behind the bar of the pub. Nor can I seem to find my keys. I ring on the doorbell frantically, suddenly feeling sober again. Steve eventually answers after what seems like an eternity, the meter on the cab going up and up all the while. I try to explain what has happened.

'Bryony, what have you done to yourself?' he says, putting his shoes on. 'Go inside and sit with Harry. We've been having some beers watching the football. He can look after you while I go and get some cash to pay for your cab.'

And when I get into the living room, I start to weep. I let out big, racking sobs that shudder through my whole body. I sound as if I'm in physical pain, and perhaps I am. 'Michael,' I just about hiccup. 'His wife, pregnant.' Harry makes his way over from the sofa and puts his arms around me. I cry into his pin-striped shirt. 'It's OK, Bryony. I'll look after you,' he soothes, as my tears smudge mascara onto his clothes. He smells nice, feels warm. I realise that ever since we moved to Camden, he, Steve and my sister have been the only steady things in my whole life. 'You know what? You are wonderful, you really are. Any man would be lucky to have you. And it's about time you realised it.' I collapse on the floor, bringing him with me.

Sometimes, you have to fall to the bottom in order to make your way back to the top again.

13

Something happens when I least expect it

It started, as ever, with a kiss.

It always starts with a kiss.

It never starts with five pints of lager, three shots of tequila, and your bottom being groped in a dingy bar, does it? And that isn't, actually, how it starts this time. It's actually two bottles of white wine, a shot of Sambuca and a hand on the lower back. The hand on the lower back is a magical manoeuvre, don't you think, one carried out by a classier level of bloke, a manoeuvre that suggests to you this won't just be a one-night stand. But this time, I don't start thinking about how we will recount this story at our imaginary wedding, or to our theoretical grandchildren. I am done with daydreaming, done with getting carried away with myself. Getting carried away with myself has done me no good. It has left me with the wrong knickers. It has got other women pregnant and given me head lice.

So it started with a kiss, in Clapham, of all places. Clapham, that land of toffs and yummy mummies whose days revolve around baby yoga! That place I always said I would never be seen dead in, and yet here I am, in a basement flat around the corner from Clapham Common tube, after a night braying like a mule with the best of them in a pub in the heart of the area. And it isn't that bad, not as bad as I had imagined it to be. In fact, it's sort of kind of nice, kind of leafy. And the bloke I'm with isn't that bad either. He's kind (kind!) and funny and, dare I say it, normal, which, after Michael, is all new to me.

It's a warm August evening, and so it seems a shame to spend our night at the pub, especially when I learn his flat has a garden. So off we go, the few hundred metres to the flat he shares with two other blokes. They are sitting in the living room, drinking beer and playing cards and watching *Predator* – and not for the first time, judging by their ability to recite off by heart every line that Arnold Schwarzenegger delivers. He introduces me to them, explains that we are going to have a few drinks outside, and they wave and say hi and then return to their action fest.

The flat is homely, not flash, and nor, surprisingly, is it a total tip. These are three thirty-something men who clearly have a healthy respect for cleanliness and cooking.

'We're too old to be living it up all the time,' says my date, opening a fridge full of wine and vegetables and hunks of meat, 'though obviously, we like to think we've still got it.' He pours me a glass of Sauvignon Blanc and himself a Merlot, and leads me out into the garden.

I don't remember if there are stars in the sky; probably there weren't. All I really remember is the anxiety-inducing screech of foxes mating, their cries echoing around the neighbourhood. 'I told you Clapham was posh,' I say. 'You even have wildlife. In Camden, the local animals are sadly mostly human.' He smiles, we make polite conversation for a bit. I feel comfortable enough in his company to light my umpteenth fag, even though he doesn't smoke. 'I'm too much of a wuss,' he told me earlier. 'But I like the smell on everyone else. It's like being cool by proxy.'

We listen a bit more to the foxes, and then it's make or break. Either he kisses me soon or the night passes off entirely chastely, ending with me ordering a cab and us probably never meeting up again. If I have learnt one thing during my disastrous dating career so far, it is that all dates have a tipping point, where they either go off or go on, and I can feel ours reaching it now. 'You're a gem, Bryony Gordon,' he says, interrupting the foxes, not to mention my train of thought. And then he kisses me. It's a warm, delicious kiss that tastes of beer and *him*. And unlike all of the other ones, it doesn't need changing.

In fact, it doesn't even occur to me that it's anything other than normal.

I start being friendlier to Harry after the night of the collapse. I join him and Steve on nights out. We discover a mutual love of sci-fi movies and one night we sit up drinking beer and watching *Alien* long after Steve has gone to bed. I notice that he's actually quite handsome. He has this awesome quiff, lovely bright blue eyes and a nice bit of stubble. He's tall without being overbearing, solid but not too muscly. One evening, I notice that he doesn't wear deodorant. I know I must feel something towards him, because I realise I really like his smell.

At work, we start messaging each other, me popping down chat windows whenever Steve hoves into view. I start to look forward to popping to Pret with him, and having coffees in the canteen. He makes me laugh with his Donald Duck impression; when I see him across the office, I catch myself smiling.

All the books and the films and the magazines – they all told me that there would be a thunderbolt. Things would slow down, an orchestra would start playing around us and suddenly everything would seem right. But it doesn't happen that way, does it? My God, it's such a cliché, but after all that moaning, I think I might just have found someone when I was least expecting it.

It takes a long time for him to go from seeming mind-numbingly ordinary to soul-pleasingly extraordinary. In fact, that process is still going on some time after our kiss in his garden to the soundtrack of foxes shagging. He's just so normal, so OK in himself, so content and free of shit, that for a while I find him utterly mystifying, a peculiar creature who should be kept at arm's length while I try to work him out. 'I don't think there's anything to work out,' is what Steve says to me, when he finds out we have been snogging. 'With Harry, you get what you see.'

'But there must be SOMETHING wrong with him,' I reason, because aren't all men just a little bit shitty? 'Surely he has issues with his family. Or he's still secretly obsessed with his ex-girlfriend. Or he wets the bed. I'm worried he's a bit BORING.'

'You mean, there needs to be something wrong with him for you to like him? He needs to be a flighty scumbag with nits or a wife? I can see why you're not that keen, Bryony. I mean, he's single, has no dependants and the only baggage he carries is the iPad case he takes to work. Now I come to think about it, you're right. I can see that he's an absolutely terrible prospect.'

The reason it goes so slowly is because I've forgotten what it is to have a normal relationship. I'm so used to fireworks and drama that I don't actually realise that Harry isn't booby-trapped. The simple fact is he likes me. I had always thought he was silently judging me, wondering why the hell anyone would put up with my behaviour, but after Valentine's Day, I realise the opposite is true. He has never judged me, never thought ill of me. He has only ever wondered why I was wasting my time with Michael. The time at my birthday party, the moment by the snack machine – I was so defensive, I failed to see that he only wanted the best for me. Maybe part of the reason he hung around with Steve was because he liked being with me.

I try to fuck it up, really I do. It's not as if I can just allow a good man into my life and enjoy it. No, no, no. I'm convinced something is going to go wrong. I'm going to send him an abusive text in my sleep. I'm going to get really drunk and become so blind with booze that I will try to get off with one of his flatmates. He may not wet his bed, but I become convinced that I will.

We go out for dinner one night, which is full of potential pitfalls in itself. I can't remember the last time I went out for dinner, and I'm pretty sure the last time a man took me for one was that time Sam dumped me in Nando's. I'm going to spill food down my top, or belch between courses. 'I don't really do dinner,' I tell him, when we sit down at the tapas restaurant.

'You don't?' he says, eyebrows raised.

'No,' I shake my head. 'I usually prefer just to drink.'

'Well, we can do that, too,' he smiles.

A few wines in, I start to ask him about his family.

'My dad was in the army,' he reveals. 'I grew up on bases all over Germany.' I take a large gulp of wine in an attempt to drown the feeling that we are so very different.

'That must have been . . .' I search for the word, '. . . interesting.'

'It wasn't really.' He eats his chorizo. 'But when we moved to Dublin because my dad became the defence attaché, we did have an armed guard. That was kind of cool.'

I am too cowardly to ask him what a defence attaché is exactly.

'And what about your mum?' I pour more wine. 'What does she do?' He looks at his food, shakes his head. 'She's not around any more.'

'I'm sorry,' I say. 'My parents are divorced, too.'

'No,' he says, putting his knife and fork down. 'I mean, she died a few years ago.'

'What of?' I blurt out, rudely.

'She had breast cancer,' he says simply.

'I'm so so sorry.' I'm panicking. Could I be any more insensitive?

'It's OK.' He's eating some more chorizo.

'If it's any consolation,' I actually say, 'my grandparents are dead.'

Yes, yes, I could be more insensitive.

'Bryony, you don't have to comfort me,' he says, touching my hand. 'Although your ineffectual attempts to do so are kind of sweet.'

A few weeks later, I try to fuck it up properly. He tells

me he can't see me on Friday night because he has an early start to get to a family gathering, and I go into full panic mode. That Friday, I go to the pub with Chloe and over umpteen glasses of wine, I decide that he is going off me.

'He could really just be going to see his family,' reasons Chloe.

'Or he could have met SOMEONE ELSE,' I say, slamming my glass down on the table. 'Oh God, he's met someone else. He's trying to let me down politely because he knows I'm vulnerable from Michael. He doesn't want me to feel rejected AGAIN, so he's weaseling out of it by faking a family engagement. I mean, if he really liked me, he'd still spend Friday night with me, even if he did have to get up early. If he really liked me, he'd TAKE ME TO THE FAMILY GATHERING WITH HIM.'

'Jesus, Bryony, would you listen to yourself?' Chloe is shaking her head in her hands. 'It's quite possible that he's terrified of you – watching you now, I am, too. But it's also entirely feasible that he knows if he saw you tonight, you'd only end up getting drunk together, and then he'd be in a bad way when he went to see his dad.'

'Oh man, his dad. His dad is going to hate me, I'm sure of it. He's going to think I'm a flighty strumpet. He's going to think I'm vapid and shallow and pathetic.'

'Bryony, WOULD YOU CHILL THE FUCK OUT?'

When the pub closes, I tell Chloe I am heading home. But I have lied to her. In my booze-addled mind, I have cooked up a plan. I am going to jump in a cab and go to Harry's, and surprise him with a seductive grin. He's going to love it. And if he doesn't love it, then that's because he is actually having it off with another woman. And surely it's better I find out this way, right?

Right?

I hail a cab and tell him to go to Clapham. Drunk, I reveal to the driver what I'm doing. 'I mean, if he really likes me, right, he won't mind, right, and if it's meant to be, he'll probably quite like it,' I witter, 'and anyway, we're almost there now so . . .'

'Are you sure you want to do this, darling?'

'I have never BEEN SO SURE OF ANYTHING IN MY LIFE,' I say, handing him twenty quid and telling him – quite generously, I think – to keep the change.

Later I will remember that the fare was £19.80.

I stand in front of his flat and straighten my hair, before checking my make-up in a compact mirror. I notice the lights are off, and tell myself he wasn't lying; or he was, and he and his new bird have gone to bed early for a night of passionate love-making. Better to find out now, Bryony, better to find out now. I walk up the steps and take a deep breath. I ring the doorbell and brace myself. Nothing happens. I ring again. Nothing. But I haven't come all this way to stand outside a flat, so I take out my phone, and I ring him. It's done. That is that.

'Bryony?' says a sleepy voice.

'Hi, I'm outside your flat!'

'You're what?'

'I'm outside your flat! I wanted to surprise you!' I see the lights go on. He must be coming out. 'I know you said you had an early start, but I thought I bet he'd still really love a late finish with me!'

'But Bryony, I'm looking out the window and there's nobody outside the flat. Are you sure you're here?'

Inside, I can hear a kerfuffle as people say things like 'Who the fuck would it be this late?' and 'Has so and so forgotten his fucking keys?'

'What number are you at?' asks Harry.

'Thirty-nine,' I say, walking backwards down the steps onto the pavement, slowly realising what I have done.

'But I live at thirty-seven you idiot.'

I run. I do not look back.

Once inside, I compose myself with another glass of wine. I can see that Harry is alone, and, judging by the suitcase packed in his room, that he isn't lying to me. I make an ill-conceived attempt to seduce him, but pass out pissed in his bed in the process. When I wake up the next morning, I am covered in my own drool. Harry, I note, is wearing earplugs.

'You were snoring for England,' he tells me as he drives me home. 'I particularly liked your rant about polar bears and how we shouldn't help them because if they came across us in a dark alley, they sure as hell wouldn't help us.'

'Polar bears?'

'And it was a high point when I poured you a glass of wine and you immediately knocked it to the floor, smashing it into a thousand pieces in the process. I have a plaster on my foot to show for it.'

'I'm sorry,' I say, suddenly feeling ashamed. 'I was worried you had lost interest in me and had made something up to get out of seeing me.'

'Bryony,' he says, reaching for my hand as he navigates the road. 'Not everything has to have some dramatic subtext. If I lose interest in you – and how could I, given how endlessly entertaining you make things? – I will let you know, I promise.'

So yes, I try to fuck it up, and yet he doesn't really let me. He doesn't really care. He isn't phased by my manicness. He has seen it all before while he was hanging out with Steve. It's the only way he has ever known me to be, I suppose. It's refreshing, to be able to be me. It's nice to feel that my behaviour is somehow lovable, that I am a good person and not simply a court jester whose only purpose is to be mocked. With Harry, I don't have to pretend to be anyone else, because he has only ever been interested in me.

Over a period of months, we become friends, lovers and, without even saying it, boyfriend and girlfriend. We start hanging out with Sally and Andy, who have just welcomed a bouncing baby boy into their world. 'He's nice,' says Sally, watching as Harry holds her son. 'Good with kids, too. You know, now you've sort of got it all

– the career and the man – bugger me, I was jealous of you before, but now I'm about to explode with envy.' All the time, I was too busy hankering after Sally's life ever to notice that she was hankering after *mine*.

'Do you think we could clone Harry for me?' asks Chloe one day, when I apologise for the classic dropping off radar manoeuvre. 'You know, I don't mind you spending all your time in Clapham.'

'You don't?'

'I'd even brave the northern line and come there for a drink if you asked,' she says. 'Do I need to get a visa?'

'I'm sure I can sort you one out,' I smile.

'You know why it's OK that you're hanging out with braying hooray Henrys? Because you actually look quite calm. After all these years of being totally manic, you're sort of . . . chilled. I even noticed you eating properly at lunch the other day, and if I'm not mistaken, when we were in Topshop last week you actually refused to buy a pair of heels on account of them being too "dear". So Harry must be doing something right.'

I sigh. 'I never thought it would be like this. I thought my heart would flip every time I looked at a boyfriend, but this . . . this is different. I just like *being* with him. Chilling with him. I look forward to eating couscous with him, and we have even just started watching *The Killing* together. I mean, a BOX SET, Chloe. I'm watching a box set. He's just so sweet and funny and kind. Do you have any idea how underrated kind is, Chloe? Everyone says they want someone tall, dark and handsome who can do the DIY and shag them senseless before cooking them a slap-up meal, cleaning up afterwards and then suggesting a trip to the opera. But whatever. All I want is kind! And I've got it, and I couldn't be happier!'

'Bryony,' says Chloe. 'You're sounding a bit manic again.'

I tsk her. 'Is it totally tragic that it has taken a *man* to make me calm? I mean, I haven't even realised that I've been calm. It's just crept up on me, like a . . . like a serial killer who's been stalking me for ages, waiting for the right time to pounce. And now it's like, wow, this is so EASY. There are no waiting games with text messages, no complications . . .'

'Other than the ones you've tried to create,' interjects Chloe.

'Well yeah. I'm not going to change completely.'

In truth, it isn't as if I stop being a mess just because I have a boyfriend. I am not magically cured of my ills, I do not suddenly stop making mistakes. I still find it hard to pay bills on time, I still can't cook and I have yet to develop a hobby. But with him I can be a mess and it's OK. He gives me the confidence to just be.

I think of all the other men who have made me want to be someone different. I think of Sam, who made me want to be the kind of girl who surfed and smoked dope and whom he wouldn't want to leave the country for. I think of Josh, who made me want to be the kind of person who wore silky Agent Provocateur knickers. I think of the Australian kickboxer, who made me want to be thinner, fitter, sober. I think of Dylan as in Bob, who made me want to be an indie kid. I think of Michael, who made me want to be his wife.

And I take responsibility for all of these things. I realise that I was the only person who made me want to be these things.

And I am so thankful to them for being who they were. I am so thankful to them for not wanting me. Because in doing so, they have led me to someone who does.

I have been in a hospital bed for six hours now, hooked up to a drip, bleeding heavily. It is Friday night, and on the other side of the thin curtain I can hear the screams of drunks and drug addicts. I haven't had a drink for six weeks now. A cigarette hasn't passed my lips for just as long. And yet despite my mended ways, I don't think I have ever felt so ill in my life.

Harry is sitting on a chair next to my bed. For the past few hours he has been pacing up and down the small cubicle, trying his best not to show that he is scared for me. But I can see it in his eyes. I am white as the sheet I lie under, drifting in and out of consciousness. They have taken my blood, carried out numerous internal examinations. I don't know for sure what is wrong with me, but I have a good idea.

The Wrong Knickers

The doctor slides through the curtain, then pulls it so she knows the area is as private as it can be. She can't be much older than me, or Harry; it is entirely possible that she is younger. If before, she had tried to be professional and methodical, now she is trying her best to look kind or soothing. I know before she has even said anything that something has gone really wrong.

'So, we're going to send you home, Bryony,' she says, a benign look on her face. 'We can't say for sure, but we think you might be having a miscarriage. I want you to go home and rest. I've got you the first appointment I can at the early pregnancy unit. They'll be able to tell you more on Monday morning.'

I crumple.

A few months after Harry and I had become 'official', we decided to mark it properly by moving in together. I left Camden for Clapham – I was always there anyway, and I liked watching Arnie movies with Harry's flatmates – while Steve bought a flat and my sister moved in with an old school friend.

Harry and I had been together for less than a year when we had our first proper argument. We had gone to a leaving do together, and I had got completely wasted. This wasn't new to Harry – he saw it almost every week – but what was different was me vomiting all over the bedroom floor, suddenly, strangely, unable to hold my drink. 'This needs to stop,' he had told me, as he tried to soak up the mess I had left on the carpet. 'Having a few drinks is one thing, but getting so blasted that we have to spend two hours cleaning up your sick is quite another.'

'I told you,' I screamed, wiping vomit from my face with my hand. 'I must have had my drink spiked or something.'

'Bryony, we were at a party with people we know. Do you honestly think anyone there would have reason to spike your drink?'

'Mr Perfect,' I start to taunt. 'That's you. I'm Harry, I don't get pissed, I don't smoke, I don't take drugs, I just sit and judge anyone who does. God, I wish for once you'd just FUCK UP like everyone else.'

He doesn't rise to it. Mr Perfect never does.

We go to sleep not talking to one another. In the morning I have my usual coffee and cigarette, but instead of them making feel better, as they usually do, they make me throw up again. I feel odd, not myself. I take some Nurofen and hope the feeling will go away. It doesn't. That afternoon, it starts to dawn on me what might be wrong. My period is three days late.

I will the afternoon away, count down the hours until I can get home and tell Harry what I think might be wrong. I want to take a pregnancy test, have my suspicions proved wrong and get on with my life. We have been together less than a year. This really wasn't how it was supposed to happen. This wasn't supposed to happen at *all*.

The Wrong Knickers

I go to Boots and buy the cheapest test I can get my hands on. We go home on the tube together in silence. When we get in I go straight to the bathroom and decide to get it over and done with. We can confirm that I'm just being silly, have a drink, make up, go to bed happy. I piss on the piece of plastic as Harry waits outside the bathroom door, and then I get ready to wait the requisite three minutes.

Except it doesn't even take that long.

Within thirty seconds, the test has done its work. I start to wail. Harry runs through the door and bundles me into his arms. He looks at the test. One line, two lines, and our lives have changed for ever.

The early pregnancy unit is not a happy place. It's a small room just off the maternity ward, which seems somehow inappropriate. We are not the only people here this Monday morning. Across the tiny room sit another couple, pale, sad. I wonder if they have had a weekend like ours, of tears and silent cuddles and the most overwhelming sense of loss for something that, just six weeks ago, we didn't even know we wanted.

And now, as I sit in this room, I think my heart might die for this child inside me. If it has gone, if it is lost, I do not know how I will carry on. All this time, not thinking I would ever be a mother, not sure I was even meant to be one, and now I can imagine nothing else. When we found out I was pregnant, we read everything we could. We knew that we couldn't count on anything until twelve weeks, and even then we would have to be careful. But that didn't stop us becoming attached, that didn't stop us imagining the being inside me, whether it would be a boy or a girl and oh God, did it even matter? There was never any question that we wouldn't go through with it – 'none at all', Harry had beamed, shortly after we found out – and yet here we were, nature making the choice for us.

The receptionist calls my name, and we slowly make our way into the room where we will find out what has happened. If I don't hurry there, I can put off finding out, I can still have some hope that this ball of cells inside me might grow to be something bigger. In the room there is a bed and a computer and a kind-looking woman who asks me to remove my knickers and lie down. I almost laugh at the ridiculousness of it all.

She is going to do an internal scan to see if she can find a heartbeat, she explains. It shouldn't be too uncomfortable, she adds. I lie back and take a deep breath. Close my eyes. Harry holds my hand as the stranger starts to root around inside me. I stare at Harry hoping that she will be quick.

And then we hear it.

The heartbeat.

'Congratulations,' says the woman, pointing with the hand that isn't in my cervix to a screen. On it, I can just about make out something that looks a bit like a bean bag. 'You are just over nine weeks pregnant with what appears to be a perfectly healthy baby. Would you like a picture of the scan?'

'Yes!' says Harry.

Holding hands, we look at the grainy picture of our unborn child. We can see the umbilical cord that attaches it to my womb. I start to cry as hard as I ever have. I don't stop for an hour, possibly two. They are tears of utter joy and relief. When I stop crying, I start to laugh.

'We are going to have a baby,' I giggle. 'We are going to have a baby!' I nuzzle into my boyfriend's chest. My boyfriend, my baby. I laugh and laugh and laugh and laugh. After everything, this is how it really starts.

Acknowledgements

The majority of names in this book have been changed to protect the guilty, but there are plenty of people I want to identify so I can thank them for all the help they have given me while I was writing this memoir. My agent Janelle Andrew deserves so much gratitude I do not know where to start – without her this book would not exist. I would also like to thank her colleague at Peter Fraser Dunlop, Annabel Merullo, who first contacted me about writing something many years ago. Thank you for sticking with me.

At Headline, I would like to thank Sarah Emsley for believing I could get the book done, despite the fact I came to her with the proposal when I was eight and a half months pregnant. Her faith, and that of Georgina Moore, meant I somehow managed to write it by the

The Wrong Knickers

time the baby was nine months old. A mention to Sarah's trusty assistant Holly Harris, too. I'd also *really* like to thank Joe at the Apple Store on Regent Street, who fixed my collapsed laptop a week before deadline. I don't know your surname or if you will ever see this, but Joe – you were a lifesaver.

From the *Telegraph*, I would like to thank Elizabeth Hunt, Fiona Hardcastle, Tony Gallagher, Becky Pugh, Maureen O'Donnell, Chris Deerin, Sally Chatterton and Rob Colvile. I was often late for work and almost always hungover, and yet for some reason none of you sacked me. What's more, you actually allowed me to turn my manic twenties into a career. For that, you are all ace. Special credit should go to Anna Murphy and Tim Auld, at Stella magazine, for commissioning *How the Other Half Lives* and being endlessly patient with deadlines.

For being great drinking buddies and making my twenties so much fun (and also for jogging my booze-addled memory about things that I could put in the book): Meredith Davies, Ian Melding, Catherine Elsworth, Paul Antrobus, Greg Cheverall, Lucy Cockcroft, Richard Alleyne, Duncan Gardham, Sam Leith, Neil Tweedie, Olivia Lamb, Louise Wilkinson, the Hoggs, Kate Fassett, Mireia Manguel, Anna Ekelund, Louise Pepper, Matt Moore, Jon Swaine, Rupert Neate, James Quinn, Ed Cumming, and anyone else I've forgotten because I was drunk for most of the decade. Jane Cullen and Laura Wilkins, for reading the book and giving me their sound advice. For their endless sage advice and glasses of wine: Polly Vernon and Lindsay Frankel.

My mother, for being the kindest woman I know, and my father, for being the funniest man I know. I hope that this book doesn't horrify them *too* much. My brother Rufus and my sister Naomi, for putting up with me. And finally, I would like to thank Harry and Edie. Because without either of you, I would never have had the energy and optimism to write this book. You are not my happy ending. You are my happy beginning.

In the 14 years that she has worked for the *Telegraph*, Bryony Gordon has become one of the paper's best loved writers. Her weekly column in the *Sunday Telegraph*'s *Stella* magazine, 'How the Other Half Lives', has won her an army of fans who over the last four and half years have followed her journey from single girl about town to – finally! – settled mum. Bryony is now 33 and lives in South London with her baby daughter Edie and her husband, a financial journalist. The last sentence is one she never thought she would see written down on paper.